CARIBBEAN
EDGE

EDGE \'ej\ *n* [ME *egge*, fr. OE *ecg*; akin to L *acer* sharp, Gk *akmē* point]
1 a : the cutting side of a blade   **b :** the sharpness of a blade   **c :** penetrating power : KEENNESS   **2 a :** the line where an object or area begins or ends; *also* : the narrow adjacent part : BORDER   **b :** a point near the beginning or the end   **c :** a favorable margin
—*Webster's Seventh New Collegiate Dictionary*

CARIBBEAN EDGE

EDGE

*The Coming of Modern Times
to Isolated People and Wildlife*

BERNARD NIETSCHMANN

THE BOBBS-MERRILL COMPANY, INC.
Indianapolis / New York

The author and publisher are grateful for permission to reprint material from the following works:

Robert Bustard, *Sea Turtles: Their Natural History and Conservation*, Taplinger Publishing Company, 1972.

Archie Carr, "Great Reptiles, Great Enigmas," *Audubon*, © March 1972.

Archie Carr, *The Reptiles* (second edition), LIFE Nature Library, Time-Life Books, 1977.

Archie Carr, *So Excellent a Fishe: A Natural History of Sea Turtles*, The Natural History Press, 1967.

Archie Carr, *The Windward Road: Adventures of a Naturalist on Remote Caribbean Shores*, copyright © 1956 by Alfred A. Knopf, Inc.

Rachel Carson, *The Sea Around Us*, Oxford University Press, 1950.

Edward Long, *The History of Jamaica, . . . and Account of the Mosquito Shore*, T. Lowndes, 1774.

Peter Matthiessen, "To the Miskito Bank," *The New Yorker*, October 28, 1967. Copyright © 1967 by The New Yorker Magazine, Inc.

NASA, *Apollo Mission Commentary*, National Aeronautics and Space Administration, Washington, D.C.

Bernard Nietschmann, "Drift Coconuts," *Natural History* Magazine, November 1976. Copyright © 1976 by The American Museum of Natural History.

Bernard Nietschmann, "Ecological Change, Inflation, and Migration in the Far Western Caribbean." Reprinted from the *Geographical Review*, Vol. 69, 1979, with permission of the American Geographical Society.

Bernard Nietschmann, "The Nicaraguan Skin Connection," *Natural History* Magazine, January 1977. Copyright © 1977 by The American Museum of Natural History.

Bernard Nietschmann, "When the Turtle Collapses, the World Ends," *Natural History* Magazine, June–July 1974. Copyright © 1974 by The American Museum of Natural History.

Published by The Bobbs-Merrill Company, Inc.
Indianapolis   New York
Designed by Rita Muncie
Manufactured in the United States of America
First printing

Library of Congress Cataloging in Publication Data

Nietschmann, Bernard.
  Caribbean edge.

  Includes index.
  1. Miskito Indians. 2. Nietschmann, Bernard.
I. Title.
F1529.M9N545   980'.004'98   78-11211
ISBN 0-672-52556-9

For Judi and Barney Sirpi
and others who have traveled the edge

Acknowledgments

This book had many contributors and counselors. Some were the reason for the journeys, some went along, and some were there when we arrived. My wife Judi and son Barney went on all the trips, participated in the research and experiences, and learned with me, while teaching me many things too. The Miskito taught us about old ways and new times, sea turtles and forest animals, society and friendship. We went to sea in their boats and they in ours, and we shared many adventures and episodes. Baldwin Garth, Flannery Knight, Pungi Perez and Cleveland Blandford were a few of the many Miskito who patiently tutored us in the skills and knowledge of the forests and the sea. They are in all respects co-authors of this book, for it contains what they taught and also what they themselves wrote. In Bluefields, Sunshine and Nena Downs graciously provided sage advice and channeled mail and supplies that helped us stay in the field for long uninterrupted periods. In Managua, Jaime and Velia Incer guided us through bureaucratic and logistical problems and greatly expanded the scope of our research. And at Tortuguero, Archie and Margie Carr introduced me to the study of sea turtles and the Caribbean, and they have helped in many other ways since then.

Many people in Ann Arbor, Madison, Washington, D.C., Los Angeles and Berkeley have continually provided help and encouragement over the years. Students in my classes at the University of Michigan were the first to urge me to write this book. Bill Denevan, Barry Bishop, Brian Weiss, Charles Bennett and James Parsons inspired me to finish it. Cheryl Zello was the Rumpelstiltskin who magically transformed ragged and stapled pages into a manuscript, and Ellen Brandstadter added her typographic spinning-wheel to help finish before the deadline morning came. Mike Bruner did the maps.

Several foundations and institutions supported the research and travels that form the context of this book: the Foreign Area Fellowship Program; the Social Science Research Council; the

Rackham School of Graduate Studies, University of Michigan; the National Geographic Society; and the Banco Central de Nicaragua. A fellowship from the John Simon Guggenheim Memorial Foundation and a leave from the University of Michigan enabled me to write it.

Barbara Norville, my editor, nemesis and friend, held the thin blue line against frontal assaults by the author and rearguard action from the publisher and still kept her faith in the book.

To those mentioned above and to others encountered along the way, my thanks and appreciation.

Contents

Preface

There is a place east of the lakes and mountains and west of the open South Caribbean where humid forests and warm marine waters meet on a broken coastline, scalloped by long, thin lagoons, frayed by river bars and narrow beaches, and fronted by a maze of cays and reefs and shallows rarely seen to such an extent anywhere else. This place belongs neither to the land nor to the sea, but to both. Big swells run the reach of the Caribbean to pound and tear at beaches fed by silt-thickened river outwash. Coral reefs that have emerged from the sea are colonized by drift and waif biota and then denuded by tropical storms and hurricanes. Strandline vegetation pushes out from under beach-edge forests seeking the sun, but it is trimmed back by the lash of sea wind and salt spray. And longshore currents cut and build beaches and distribute debris flushed from inland by the heavy rains.

Once isolated by the eastern forests and the western sea, strand-dwelling and sea-dependent indigenous peoples have long lived here. But like the place itself, they are now in a state of flux; they belong neither to the past nor to the present.

Follow one·of the rivers down from the mountains until the hemming lowland forests confine visibility and make the muddy river seem too lifeless and too hot to be endured. Keep going until you can feel the first breeze pushing in from the nearing river mouth and smell the freshness beyond. Get out when you can and search for a trail that cuts through the river-wall tangle and leads to the beach-scrub thickets and coconut palms and the sea. Face into the trade wind and lose the drag of the land and the heat of the river; feel the breeze fill your shirt and dampen its front. Look out and imagine the sea to windward filled with sails running toward the main from the offshore reefs and shallows. Think of the herds of sea turtles that migrate past here on their way south from Miskito Bank to Turtle Bogue. Walk along the beach and look for things carried from the world beyond and washed ashore by the sea. Look too for other trails that lead to interior mangrove and palm swamps, creeks and lagoons, and the rain forest.

xi

Here on the far rim of the Caribbean, between forests and coral reefs and among the Miskito people, is where we lived and studied. The longer we stayed on this tropical coast, the more certain we became that what we saw and learned was influenced by the physical, cultural and economic history hidden on the edge that separates the land from the sea, indigenous peoples from outsiders, the past from the coming of modern times.

This is an account of events, places, people and animals that we encountered during several trips and years to the far edge of the Caribbean, the Miskito Coast of eastern Nicaragua. It's about involvement between another culture and our own, either of which can be discerned only from the presence of the other. Parts of the account are about the Miskito Indians as we saw them and they us. Other parts are about indigenous contact with the outside world, conflicts between old and new economic systems, the passing of sea turtles and other animals, and the knowledge we gained from coping with and enjoying little-known and isolated places and people.

I've written other descriptions of our research, but they only dimly reflect what really happened and what we really learned. At the time, few of the events that make up this book seemed to pertain to the research at hand. Yet each was sufficiently stirring that I took notes on what happened, with no other objective than to record the incidents that were so personally rewarding and revealing that they caused us to reconsider much that we had thought. Some deflected the course of our lives. Over the years, the experiences and memories accumulated, but were shared only with one another or with small groups of people, until I was made to realize that, taken together, they hinted at things not found in most books about the Caribbean or about research on other cultures.

Academics are accustomed to treat ecological and cultural data in a highly abstract manner several steps removed from the vividness and intimacy experienced during the research. There is nothing wrong with this at all, and the result is usually a more reasoned, dispassionate report. We all do this; it is trained into us and later reinforced. But sometimes much is left out—often the essence and spirit.

Many things don't get written about for a variety of reasons, some justifiably so because of the triviality of the subject or the perspective, others because they were simply overlooked through inattention or from too narrowly focused interests, still others because their stories were too deeply lodged in another cultural matrix and defied all but surface description. And some things are seldom mentioned because they are too effacing, are cut too close to the raw edge of deeply moving human conditions, or are so absurd that their revelation would jeopardize academic credence. Yet peculiar and wondrous incidents often do occur. And whether they live only in one's thoughts or are made public, they frequently provide the prismatic lenses that collect and refract images and interpretations from the double-faced mirror that separates one culture from another.

We were out on Man O' War Cay, a tiny speck of coral and wind-sheared sea grape and cocoplum thicket and stunted buttonwood fifteen miles east of Río Grande Bar, staying with some Miskito turtlemen at their drift lumber camp. They were teaching us the ways of sea turtles and something of the knowledge and skill it took to catch them. It was a rewarding and restful time; the days were filled with sailing to the turtle grounds and around the coral shoals, skin diving off the reef face or into the small blue hole at the edge of the cay, or simply sitting to windward on the sea-built coral rock rampart looking out into the empty Caribbean. At night we talked of turtles and turtle people, of times past and new ones approaching, of Nicaragua and the United States. Often we packed into the small shelter to play Left-in-the-Bush, a local card game where the last person with cards remaining is the loser and figuratively has to spend as many days in the forest as he has cards. It was a real "seaman's game," they told us, and the threat of being left on the mainland kept it lively and spirited. Those were delightful days, remote from the main, away from the day-to-day pressures of village life, with cool trade winds, clean white sand, clear reef waters and good companions.

One morning when the sea was particularly rough, we heard the drone of an approaching outboard motor above the stiff wind. Finally, we could make out a small canoe bucking against the white-frosted swells as it fought its way toward us. Whoever was coming out to the cay was on an important mission, significant enough to brave weather and sea conditions that had kept us pinned to the island since the day before.

It was Clarence (a Miskito from Little Sandy Bay) and a man from the Bar. They cut the motor and drifted in the rest of the way to the small leeward beach where we waited.

"Mr. Barney, I bring a letter from one of your country-men in the U.S. of A.," Clarence announced with a high degree of ceremony as he produced a single envelope from his homemade natural-rubber bag.

I was astounded that they had come all that way in such heavy weather to carry a letter to me. Everyone crowded around, impatient to find out what the message was and to learn "what

▼

happened strange on the outside." I opened it. It was a brief, typed note and a drawing on paper once crisp but now creased, stained and damp from its long journey from Bluefields to Río Grande Bar and to Man O' War Cay. The letter was from the editor who was working on a manuscript of mine. He wanted to dress up the beginning of each chapter with a drawing of a turtle: "Is this a sea turtle—and a green turtle at that? If not, please let me know quickly; if so, please let me know quickly." A copy of their artist's effort to stylize a sea turtle was enclosed. I was displeased with the turtle. It looked more like a forty-nine-cent one-ounce painted dimestore freshwater turtle than a powerful and graceful 250-pound green turtle. Looking at that drawing in the middle of one of the world's major sea turtle areas and among some of the most skilled turtlemen to be found anywhere seemed slightly ironic and surreal. But there it was, nonetheless.

By now the turtlemen were becoming anxious. They all wanted to know what the letter said, especially Clarence, because he was the one who had taken it upon himself in Río Grande to borrow the canoe and motor for the trip. They began to ask questions as I continued to stare blankly at the letter and drawing.

"What's the news?"

"What's strange up that side?"

"Is there a dead? Did your people send for you?"

I showed them the drawing. Everyone took a long, considering look at it and then gave it back.

"What is this?"

"That's supposed to be a turtle. What do you think about it?"

They examined it further, every once in a while glancing up at me with questioning expressions.

Flannery asked me if this was the "quality" of turtle in the States. No, I told him, it was really a drawing of a Nicaraguan green turtle.

"Then they have it wrong. Maybe your countrymen don't study down the situation here properly. We never buck up this quality of turtle in the sea. Sometimes the real turtle get in tow with a hawksbill and consort. We see those different-looking turtles before, but they still look like turtle. I mean to say, that United States turtle favor hicatee more than the real turtle," Flannery concluded, referring to a large freshwater turtle found in the creeks and river edges on the mainland.

Everyone agreed. It was a strange-looking turtle, almost a hicatee, certainly not a sea turtle, and not at all fitting for the book they had helped me with the year before. Together we modified the drawing, adding and crossing out edges and changing dimensions. The poor thing grew and shrank. First it was too "meager," and then too fat.

The paper was wearing thin from erasures. And once we came dangerously close to violating the integrity of all turtles in general. It was a turtle by committee, and the finished product no longer resembled the imported rendition, but neither was it my idea of what it should look like. But we had all had a hand in its creation and had passed the fail-safe point; any further tampering would have infringed on our shared collaboration. The drawing was as it was, not as it ought to be. The turtlemen probably thought the same thing but from a different viewpoint. It was all a matter of perspective. Coming from a background where many of my academic colleagues persisted in their explanations of why native women break rocks with wet clothes, who was I to say when a turtle isn't a turtle?

Clarence refused our invitation to stay until the weather cleared; he considered the reply too important to be delayed; he cranked up the motor, and they headed for the main. At least the going would be easier with a following sea and wind.

We watched the receding canoe until it disappeared in the distant wave troughs. Then Flannery turned to me and said, "That turtle going to the States now. But turtles are a mystery. Don't worry yourself if they don't understand."

The turtle drawing was a small thing in itself, but the context in which it was created was significant and instructive, and symbolized much of what this book is about.

THE WESTERN CARIBBEAN

1. The House at Cotton Tree

Field research can be a profound human experience. Yet the accounts of many studies are written as if the investigation had taken place in a vacuum—as if the researcher suddenly had been teletransported to the site and, by means of clairvoyance or immaculate conceptual perception, had faultlessly initiated and completed the research project in one blinding flash of academic ingenuity.

Let me tell you, it usually doesn't work this way, especially in foreign settings. Even though they are exorcised from articles and books, there are awkward, stumbling, agonizing, often humorous personal encounters and problems that give each research experience a special character and texture. When I was in graduate school reading papers on ecological research done in the tropics, I often wondered why anyone ever ventured to foreign places if all investigations were as dry in the process as they were in the product. Well, they are not, and that's what keeps many of us going back.

When I returned to the east coast of Nicaragua in 1971 to continue a research project begun in 1968, one of the first persons I saw at the small airport outside Bluefields was Mr. Seymore (Robinson is his last name, but in this part of the world the surname is usually dropped for informality and the Mr. retained for politeness). He was still the eternal optimist, scanning the passengers for some important but long overdue Godot who was to be the key figure in one of his strike-it-rich business scenarios. Seeing him again brought back one of my most extraordinary and tragicomic experiences. After we had exchanged personal and family news, I could not help but ask him about the house at Cotton Tree. He assured me that it was still there, pretty as ever, but wanting a coat of fresh paint. As we talked I thought of my first trip to the area and of Mr. Seymore and the house at Cotton Tree.

In 1968 I went to Nicaragua to study the impact of commercial hunting and fishing on the local fauna and on the subsistence economy of the Miskito Indians. Because we had little idea of what we might encounter in the designated research site on the east coast, I left my wife and son in Managua and went on to Bluefields to reconnoiter the situation and to rent the house that would be our main study base.

There are two ways to travel to Bluefields from Managua. You can go by air on a one-hour flight, or you can spend all day going overland and by river. I chose the latter in order to see as much as possible. It was September, and the rains had started again. The 180-mile trip by microbus over the Rama Road was made up of constant bouncing and sloshing through ruts, mud and water. During the entire journey the number-two driver hung out the window yelling "Rama, Rama, Rama" in a melodic staccato, hoping to pick up more travelers to add to his increasingly claustrophobic load of passengers. By noon we had reached the end of the road and the town of Rama, which was something of a letdown after seven hours of "Rama, Rama, Rama."

The Río Escondido was just below flood stage, and its muddy, debris-strewn waters lapped at the improvised cobweb wharves. Tied to one of the wharves was a strange, almost amphibianlike craft which was to be our means of transport for the remaining eighty miles to the coast. The *Bluefields Express* was a patchwork vessel pieced together from a surplus PT boat, with an MTA bus body welded to its deck. She carried her passengers with a functional dignity that transcended her amalgamated structure.

Like a platypus, the town of Bluefields is a bizarre sum of disparate elements that defy description. The cascade of my first night's impressions was a cross-cultural overdose: loggers, ranchers, pioneer farmers, missionaries and shrimp boat crews crowded the main street. Blasts of Jim Reeves's country and western music spilled from the open doorways of cantinas—"Miami Beach," "Tamarindo Number 2," "OK Corral," "Torpedo Alley," "Bay of Pigs"—drowning out multilingual street conversations in Spanish, Creole English and occasional Chinese and Miskito. Trucks and cars tacked up and down the streets, avoiding pot holes and people as they navigated the few short roads that terminated at the edge of either the lagoon or the surrounding rain forest. Cerveza Victoria and Ron Tropical signs hung from second-floor balconies on British colonial wooden buildings that sagged and leaned from damp rot.

I was directed to Sunshine Downs's "Majestic Saloon" for good food, said to be the best in Bluefields. It was true. Big, fresh sea shrimp, cooked Creole style, with plenty of onions, vinegar, lime, garlic, and black pepper, and a local *salsa picante*. Honest bread with a hard crust and a solid feel to it, and all the Chontales ranch butter you wanted. And a huge pitcher of soursop *fresco*—perhaps the best drink in the tropics.

While eating, I watched the sidewalk parade through the open space beneath the saloon doors: bare feet of all sizes and shapes; rubber "Tico" boots, some split and wire-stitched; men's pointed high-heeled black leather *gallo* shoes; rubber thongs, a few mixed pairs, one set tied on with yellow nylon rope; and one pair of Sears canvas wedgies, the kind with the little flowers and the toe hole cut out of the front.

After visiting the Supermercado William Woo (one shopping cart from who knows where) to buy nails to hang my mosquito net, I took a room at the Hollywood Hotel and fell asleep wondering how—in that cultural maze—I was going to find a house to rent.

The next morning it was hard to distinguish the knocking at my door from the drum roll of rain beating on the corrugated metal roof overhead. When I answered, I found an older man standing on the veranda outside my room. He was dressed in a wool suit, a hat and, amazingly, a starched white shirt.

"Not to molest you this fine mornin', but I come to engage you in our dealin' with the skins," he said in delightful Creole English.

I was sure he had the wrong morning and suspected he must have the wrong man as well. He mistook my hesitation for a sign of acceptance and went on.

"My name is Seymore Robinson, pleased to meet your acquaintance, and I made to understand that you is here to see me."

I explained that I was not in Bluefields on business and was not looking for him, although I was happy to meet him.

Looking somewhat dejected, he said, "These last days things a little hardish so I is keeping bright eyes for my business contact."

After telling me that he owned a small store, and also bought and sold many things on the side, he inquired what had brought me to Bluefields. I told him that I was looking for a house to rent and started to explain about my research project.

Interrupting, Mr. Seymore said, "Then this is your lucky day. You is here on business and you come to the right man. I have me own personal house yonder in Cotton Tree, which is available at the moment. This be the proper place for you, and, God willin', we'll take a little stroll and see it."

While we waited for the rain to let up, Mr. Seymore explained that Cotton Tree was an adjacent neighborhood named for a prominent large tree on the bluff over the lagoon. He extolled the virtues of his house. "It catch a fine sea breeze that keep the fly from humbugging you."

When the rain stopped, we walked to Cotton Tree, passing

Cotton Tree Point, Bluefields, Nicaragua, ca. 1910. Moravian Mission postcard.

several desirable-looking houses, all built on stilts, with wooden sides and metal or thatch roofs. But no, Mr. Seymore informed me that these were only ordinary houses and to pay no mind to them. I had to agree with him when he stopped in front of a bright, Shell Station–yellow house with a shiny new corrugated metal roof. Mr. Seymore pointed to a tree-house ladder, to the front porch eight feet above the ground, and up we went.

"I'm gon'a fix this to your satisfaction, Mr. Bernard. This be a first-class place for you."

He unlocked the door and pushed it open, letting the early-morning Caribbean sun illuminate the inside. "I surely hope we does reach an agreement, God willin'," he added as he opened the wooden shutters.

It took a moment for my eyes to become adjusted to the suddenly brightened interior. At first, all I could see was a floor completely covered by dark bumps. I squinted to get a better view. There could be no doubt about it. In the house where we might live—the place that would serve as a field base while we studied the impact of commercial exploitation on local fauna—were crocodile skins from wall to wall, neatly rolled like so many loaves of bread, row upon row, one after another.

Stunned, I could only muster a weak, stuttering question—"How many hides do you have here, Mr. Seymore?"—as if the exact number would somehow defuse my shock.

Mr. Seymore smiled as he rocked up on his toes, the extra height

Seymore Robinson, skin dealer. The ocelot skins were purchased during one week and eventually exported to West Germany. Bluefields, 1969.

giving emphasis to his words. "Mr. Bernard, I got me one thousand nine hundred in this here room and another four or five hundred in the next room. Mostly they is crocodilly, but some be alligator that favor the crocodilly. Right now the place have a high scent, but don't let these animals worry you none, Mr. Bernard. I'm gon'a fumigate this place and paint it up, pretty, pretty."

Hardly paying any attention to what Mr. Seymore was saying, I stared at the brownish black and light yellow mass of bundles. Twenty-four hundred skins. Think of it. Two thousand four hundred crocodiles and caimans. This place was the Forest Lawn of the reptile world.

Mr. Seymore led me through the skins, pointing to small bare spots on the floor where we could place our feet.

"Are these skins fresh?" I asked.

"Why, no, man. These skins be prepared. They been salted three, four times. They be all right. I'll fix the place up to your likin'." With a sweeping gesture he encouraged me to imagine the Bluefields House Beautiful, as if a coat of paint could cover a cemetery.

"Don't do anything until my wife sees the house. I wouldn't want you to go to any extra trouble."

Now more interested in the skins than the house, I asked how he had obtained them.

"They come from my little sellin' and buyin' business that I have on the side. I does buy all kinda skins and things: water dog, tiger, tigercat, peludo, 'awksbill, calipee and such-like thing.''

Mr. Seymore then went on to explain that he had been buying skins for many years, purchasing them from hunters, loggers, ranchers and farmers from as far away as the Costa Rican border. These people had to come to Bluefields for supplies, and when they did, they brought the skins to Mr. Seymore or another buyer.

"But all is gettin' scarce now. Most of these skins here are smallish. Only one, one, be big. So I got to wait to get the right price. That is the speculatin' part of the skin dealin'. I is waiting on a man who is to come to Bluefields, check out these skins, and buy them.''

We then launched into a lengthy discussion on the decline of various species, the increase in the market prices, the destination of the skins, and the chances of survival of these animals and of Mr. Seymore's business.

"If I don't buy, then the people gon'a sell to de next man. The market gettin' a little tightish count of the laws in the States. But I sellin' now to Europe and Japan. They is the ones buyin'.''

I thanked Mr. Seymore for his help and the information, said good-bye, and retraced my steps through the carpet of skins. Even though the rain had stopped and the sun was now warm and powerful, it was a cold and gray day for me.

During the months that followed, Mr. Seymore and I became friends. Strange. While he was trying to export skins, hides, hawksbill shell and other such items, I was writing reports to the Nicaraguan government, trying to press for new and stronger conservation laws. The differences in our viewpoints were enormous, but we remained friends, and he taught me a great deal about his business and about the varieties of wildlife in the area. He showed me his records, detailing the types and numbers of wild animal products that he had purchased and exported to distant markets. He knew how I would use this information, yet he offered it to me. "You got to know these things, Mr. Bernard, for your work.''

No, my family and I never rented that pretty yellow house that was a graveyard on the inside. But after studying faunal decline for several years, we felt that we had lived there.

Some time after that first morning with Mr. Seymore, I asked him if he had sold the skins.

"I never get the chance to sell them," he replied. "Worm and bug bore hole in them, and I had to dash the whole shipment away in the lagoon. The big buyer never come.''

2. To the Cape

A tropical storm, the worst kind, came out of the southeast. The wind was howling, drowning out the hum of the outboard motor and ripping and lashing the crests of the fifteen- to twenty-foot seas. Each wave was a maverick—rising, pitching and breaking from a different angle. The wind-whipped spray pelted my face. I had kept my sunglasses on as protection from the stinging wind and salt water, but by now they were smudged with oil, gasoline and salt streaks. Nevertheless, without them I wouldn't be able to face into the wind and steer the canoe. Fogged vision and the wind-atomized sea surface made everything murky and misted. Although difficult to see, the danger we were in could be felt and heard. Despite constant bailing, the water was still up to my knees in the stern of the canoe. Even in calm water we had no more than five or six inches of freeboard, and now the water was blown and wave-thrown into the open canoe; often a fragment of a wave face would collapse and fall over me and the motor in a liquid green shroud. Alternately skimming and wallowing between the huge storm-blasted jade seas, our tiny craft staggered into the storm that we had first thought only a squall. We were at least fifteen miles from the coastline somewhere around Gorda Point. But after almost five hours of increasingly rough weather and almost no visibility, it was difficult to tell exactly where we were.

Baldwin, wrapped in a poncho, was in the bow giving me hand signals for the incoming seas. He held up two fingers to tell me that we had at least two hours more before we could make Puerto Cabezas and then pointed to the gas tanks. Our last six-gallon tank was almost empty, and we both knew we'd never make it without refilling from our gasoline reserve. Already the engine was starting to sputter as the last of the gasoline was sucked from the tilted orange tank. The situation was critical. If we kept the motor running, the water and dirt at the bottom of the tank—ever present in the gasoline available on the coast—would go into the carburetor and plugs and kill the engine, resulting in fifteen minutes of work

7

even under the best of conditions. We had to refill a tank from one of the plastic reserve bottles. But the storm and the motion of the canoe were so violent that pouring gas from one container to another seemed impossible. Baldwin signaled that I should throttle down the motor and keep the canoe headed in the general direction from which most of the seas were coming. He then started to untie the tarp covering the gasoline supply.

Storms like this one weren't supposed to occur in April. But as I was learning, few things are predictable on the coast. I was beginning to agree with the Miskito of Tasbapauni: it was a fool thing to do—I recall one person's saying suicidal—a thousand-mile voyage in a twenty-one-foot-long canoe with a near-novice at the helm. Not only was I a novice; I was referred to frequently as a *kuku awra* (drift coconut), a homeless foreigner who had drifted into their village from the outside world. Worse yet, I wanted to make an outrageous trip. Against the advice of his family and the entire community, Baldwin had decided to go with me. The small group that saw us off from the village said good-bye to Baldwin with a pronounced finality. It would have been easier for me to stay in the village, do my research, and have the Miskito paddle and sail me around to where I needed to go. Instead I had chosen to get my own canoe and to learn some of the sea skills that up to then I had studied only vicariously. Besides, I wanted to follow Squier, even if it was 120 years later.

The nineteenth-century traveler Squier was one of the reasons I'd originally come to the Miskito Coast, and he was the primary inspiration for this trip. Baldwin had read Squier's book too and supported my plan to retrace his route. I think he based his decision to accompany me on the book, his belief that he could teach me enough about the sea and river bars to survive, and the fact that April was supposed to be a calm-weather month.

Baldwin untied one of the gas bottles and dragged it back to the tank. Meanwhile, I was bailing furiously with the cutoff plastic Clorox bottle that served as both funnel and bailer. Trying to keep one hand on the motor to steer, I took off the cap and stretched to hold the bailer over the mouth of the tank. We were pitching and yawing so tremendously that it was hard for me to keep the bottle in place. Holding the ten-gallon gas container in his arms, Baldwin stood with his feet on the gunwales, balancing himself across the canoe's narrow three-foot beam. Standing as high as he was, every movement of the canoe was magnified.

"Watch those seas, Mr. Barney. No need to get salt water in the tank with the gas. It will humbug the motor." Baldwin spoke as if he were calmly filling the tank on a glass-surfaced lagoon instead of in the middle of a Force-8 tropical storm.

His legs plunged up and down like unreal bionic shocks, absorbing and damping the bucking canoe motion. All the while, the gas gurgled into the tank. I had once spent several years surfing in California, so balancing on a moving sea was not exactly novel. But Baldwin's feat was beyond both my experience and my comprehension. I believe he could have rolled a surfboard like a kayak and still finished the wave.

With the gas topped off and the gear stowed, covered and lashed once more, we were ready to hit it again. But it was then that Baldwin displayed his greatest weakness—coffee.

"How about a cup of java?" he asked. A good deal of his English vocabulary had been learned from the U.S. Marines who had been stationed at Río Grande Bar in the early 1930s and to whom he had smuggled Scotch whiskey as a young boy. I believe I got more salt water in my cup of coffee than the amount of gasoline Baldwin had spilled. Running at three-quarters throttle, the little 18-hp Evinrude outboard should give us two and a half hours on the six-gallon tank. Enough to make Puerto Cabezas if our luck held.

When I first began hearing about the Miskito Coast and thinking about going there someday, I went to the library to find something to read about the area. I came home with Squier's *Waikna: Adventures on the Mosquito Shore* and read most of it the first night. It was informative and interesting. One section made me decide to go to the tropics and to eastern Nicaragua.

> "Go to the tropics boy, the glorious tropics, where the sun is supreme, and never shares his dominion with blue-nosed, leaden-colored, rheumy-eyed frost-gods; go there, and catch the matchless tints of the skies, the living emerald of the forests, and the light-giving azure of the waters; go where the birds are rainbow-hued, and the very fish are golden; where—"
>
> But I had heard enough. . . .
>
> "Hold; I'll go to the glorious tropics!" [pp.17–18]

Regarded as the leading authority on Central America in the nineteenth century, Ephraim George Squier wrote more than a hundred publications on Nicaragua and Central America, as well as on Peru and the United States. His book *Waikna: Adventures on the Mosquito Shore*, written under the pseudonym Samuel Bard and published in 1855, was his only novel. Squier traveled widely and had training in civil engineering as well as experience in studying archaeology, ethnology and history. In 1849 he was sent by President Zachary Taylor to Nicaragua as the U.S. chargé d' affaires in Central America. At this time the United States was attempting to discredit British influence in Nicaragua and Central America in order to prevent them from constructing an interoceanic canal route across Nicaragua at the Río San Juan. English control of the Miskito Coast was necessary for their foothold in the western Caribbean and in order to ensure the political stability of that area for a potential canal. The Miskito had long been allies of the English and permitted them access to the coast for settlement and resource procurement. As one historian wrote in 1774, "These Indians gratify the English most willingly with tracts of land for establishing settlements, and make themselves extremely serviceable by the commodities they procure for barter, and by their adroitness in fishing and hunting."

English influence on the Miskito Coast had expanded from early seventeenth-century buccaneering activities—focused on Spanish gold and silver shipments from Porto Bello on the Panamanian isthmus to Havana, Cuba—to include trade, commerce and settlement. Trade relations with the Miskito and other native peoples were profitable, and the English wanted to ensure their continuation against possible interference from other interests, especially the Spanish. In 1697 the English established the first of what came to be a series of Miskito kings in order to validate their claims to the coast. Kings in name only, these figurehead representatives of an egalitarian society gave England and her traders and settlers almost exclusive commercial rights to the Miskito Coast. The area became a political protectorate of England, and the Miskito became their allies in trade and commerce and against the Spanish. The Miskito held the English in high esteem. William Dampier, the great travel writer of the seventeenth century, noted in his book *A New Voyage Round the World* (1697) that the Miskito "are in general very civil and kind to the *English*. . . . but they do not love the *French*, and the *Spaniards* they hate mortally."

The primary aim of Squier's *Waikna* was to malign English control of the coast and their influence over the Miskito. In short, by means of a book written so that it would be widely read, Squier hoped to put the English in an untenable position, thereby adding to the pressure on them to abandon the coast. Because of the political intent of the book, Squier often portrayed the Miskito in derogatory terms.

Squier's book was widely read in the United States and served in some measure to marshal the already strong support to pressure England into divesting herself of her commercial and political influence on the Miskito Coast. In 1859 and 1860 England signed treaties with Honduras and Nicaragua granting them control over territories formerly held as protectorates. Nicaragua created a "reservation" from the newly acquired land, but the English continued to be involved in commerce and resource extraction until 1894, when the area was formally incorporated as the Department of Zelaya, a move that almost doubled Nicaragua's area and added the Miskito and other Costeños to her citizenry.

More than 250 years of friendly relations between the Miskito and the English left a strong cultural legacy. English is widely spoken as a second language; the Anglican Church is popular; weights and distances are measured in pounds, ounces, miles, feet and fathoms; Nicaraguan twenty-five-centavo coins are called shillings; many Miskito men and women have old English names; and pictures of the Queen are to be seen in many Miskito houses.

The storyline of *Waikna: Adventures on the Mosquito Shore* focuses on a trip made by an American and two Indians in a small sailing canoe from Bluefields to Cape Gracias a Dios and up the Río Coco into Honduras. This route traversed the principal Miskito settlements and provided sufficient backdrop for Squier's arguments against the English and their Miskito cohorts.

There is some question as to whether Squier actually made the entire trip or whether he based some of his account on descriptions from contemporary books and on interviews with individuals who had lived on the coast. One thing is clear, however: whatever the basis for this largely autobiographical novel, Squier's descriptions of the physical environment, villages and indigenous cultures were amazingly accurate.

In early 1969, after several months in Tasbapauni, studying Miskito hunting and fishing and related knowledge and skills, I was becoming increasingly fidgety. I was tired of writing things down in a notebook—things I hadn't done, places I hadn't seen, and facts I really didn't understand. It wasn't as if the data weren't good; they were; that is, they conformed to my preexisting theories. The trouble was that most of the information was secondhand, told to me in the comfort of the village by people who relayed the content but not the structure or the meaning of the information. My research methodology consisted of being a slipstream scribe; in the academic literature it is usually called "participant observation."

To overcome my self-imposed cloistered perspective and embarrassingly limited understanding of Miskito environmental knowledge, I decided to accompany Miskito hunters to the upriver forests for white-lipped peccary and to go with the turtlemen to the distant offshore turtling grounds and coral cays. Unfortunately, my requests to go along were unanimously turned down by the

Miskito. There was never a direct refusal, but there were many excuses: "You wouldn't like our traveling food," "The canoe is too small for a passenger," "You'll get seasick." Several times I pushed the situation to the point where a couple of individuals gave in and said they would take me, only to discover the next morning that they had left at two A.M. instead of three or had decided not to go after all. The message was clear: I was considered an untested liability, acceptable in the village but potentially burdensome at sea or in the rain forest. I gave up after one Miskito told me a local variation on the World War I three-lights-on-a-single-match story. "In the bush we walk one behind the other; first the best trail man, then the best shot, then the youngest, and then the rest of the hunters. There are plenty of bad snake in the bush and on the trails. They say that the first man wakes the snake, the second makes it coil, and it strikes the third man. You are the youngest, Mr. Barney."

In order to travel with the Miskito and prove myself, I would first have to acquire some of their skills and knowledge. It was similar to not being able to get your first job because of no prior work experience. I decided to get my own canoe and to find someone to teach me Miskito forest and sea skills. This led me to Baldwin Garth and then to our plans to follow the route to the Cape that Squier had described in his book.

I had first met Baldwin Garth under a large breadfruit tree. There in the cool shade he worked almost every afternoon building sailing canoes. I made it a practice to stop by as often as I could to talk with him and watch as he turned rough planks, chunks of wood, and long, thick logs into the best sailing canoes in the region. His were the fastest and most seaworthy available, and consequently he had a long list of orders from turtlemen. All about his work area the ground was covered with a thick, multihued carpet of wood shavings which resembled October leaves on a mid-latitude forest floor. Working with an economy of movement and tools, he did wondrous things with wood.

He was tall for a Miskito, six feet, very slim and well muscled. He said he was "home grown," born in Tasbapauni in 1909. It was difficult for me to believe that he was fifty-nine; he looked and moved more like a well-conditioned man in his early forties. His strength and stamina were even more remarkable and, as I was to learn quickly, far superior to mine. As a young man he had traveled up and down the coast of eastern Nicaragua, working for various American-owned banana and lumber companies. He had been a lumber scout, a camp game-hunter, and a pilot for the tugboats that pulled the banana barges through the treacherous river bars to the ships anchored offshore. After the collapse of the banana and lumbering industries in the 1940s, he returned to the village. His great delight was hunting, and he was considered the best tracker and shot in Tasbapauni. He earned small amounts of money building canoes, at which he said he was "self-taught," and by pulling teeth, using an old rusted set of dental pliers acquired from a missionary many years back. He probably had more experience working with English-speaking foreigners than anyone else in the village and considered himself a spokesman for the Miskito. If asked a question about Miskito customs or beliefs, Baldwin usually prefaced his reply with "We Indian say . . ." and then told a short parable that both compounded the question and confused the listener.

There in his work area beneath the hard green leaves, we talked. The old tree was covered with epiphytes, orchids, bromeliads; the quart-bottle-size breadfruit were young and needed a couple of months more before they would be ready.

Our conversations ranged from life in Tasbapauni to life in the United States. He spoke good English, so communication was much more direct and detailed than if we had relied on my fledgling command of Miskito. Gradually, unobtrusively, he began to use more Miskito words and phrases to increase my language ability. As we talked, I tried to help him with whatever he was doing at the time, finding that I still retained some familiarity with woodworking, thanks largely to a pre-Sputnik Los Angeles secondary education which included shop courses.

As I was later to find out, Baldwin knew about my lack of success in trying to accompany hunters and turtlemen on their expeditions. I don't know when it happened, but at some point during those first languid weeks under the breadfruit tree, Baldwin must have decided that besides being merely courteous and helpful he would begin to take an active role in teaching me. I became an apprentice to him in canoe building and his student in Miskito language and culture. Under his tutelage I began a new education, one that was to include physical and mental challenges that went far beyond my suburban middle-class and orthodox educational background.

One day while reminiscing about the coast's recent history and his own life as a boy, Baldwin mentioned that he had gone as far as the *Third Royal Reader* during the few years he was able to go to school. He asked if I had anything to read that he could borrow so that he could "keep bright eyes" and not have to "condemn" his schooling. I loaned him my copy of Squier.

Several weeks later, when we were trying to repair a leaky old canoe with a caulking compound made from a mixture of paint and sifted ashes from a burned termite nest, I asked Baldwin if he thought the owner would sell the canoe to me, as he obviously needed a new one. "This rotten stick is not for you," he said. "A heavy sea will mash it into kindling wood. We need a pretty sea canoe like the one Squier had."

"What do you mean, 'we,' Mr. Baldwin?"

"You and me. We're going to build a little canoe—I know where there is a first-class mahogany tree—and make that Squier trip you're always talking about. That is, if you're not afraid of the sea and learn what I teach you."

After discussing it for several days, we decided to try to leave in April. It was then the end of January, so we would have one month for building the canoe and one month for getting accustomed to it and for Baldwin to teach me as much as he could.

The mahogany tree that Baldwin had in mind was far back in the rain forest. He had seen it one day while chasing a drove of white-lipped peccary and had mentally marked its location. Mahogany is in high demand for canoes, but few good trees can be found anymore because of the long years of foreign logging operations. Several different woods are used for canoes, but mahogany is the best, as it is the strongest and outlasts all others.

It took us three days to bring the log back to the village. After cutting the tree down with axes, we cut out twenty-four feet of the main trunk and then "tabled it down," squaring off the sides and ends with axes. Baldwin then drew a crude canoe outline on the log with a fire-charred stick, and we set about digging out the interior with axe, adze and hatchet.

To enlarge the opening, we made several small fires of a special wood that burned slow and hot and greatly reduced our cutting effort. After the log was dug out, we used adzes to "fish scale" it and rough cut and shape it *parejo* ("even") until it resembled a long pig trough. With the aid of log rollers, we slid, pushed and sloshed it through a quarter-mile of shin-deep mud and decomposing leaves to the creek's edge. Then came a twelve-hour back-breaking paddle to tow it down the creek and across the lagoon to the village.

Now came the part that required tremendous skill for we were making not a simple dugout canoe but a Miskito sailing canoe—a thing of art, grace and beauty, bearing little resemblance to the shaggy trough now set up on braces under the breadfruit tree. To aid with the final trimming of the hull, Baldwin got Alvin to help. A huge hulk of a man, Alvin was Muhammad Ali in size, could easily carry two 100-pound sacks of rice at once, and didn't smoke or drink; once he got the hang of telling time from observing my preoccupation with my watch, he could tell me the time to within five minutes at any time of the day without any timepiece at all. Because he was so good at it, I told him that if he ever wanted to give up working on canoes, I could get him a soft job in the States where all he had to do would be to sit in a little room, answer a telephone, and say, "The time now is . . . "

Baldwin and Alvin did most of the final shaping of the canoe hull. They would transform the rounded, unstable U-shaped dugout into a sculptured, symmetrically balanced, gently contoured sailing canoe. Although the canoe is traditionally designed for sailing, we had decided to use an outboard motor on it to give us the speed and power necessary to maneuver in and out of the many river bars we planned to cross. Therefore, it was necessary to modify the usual canoe measurements to allow for added motor weight and new transom shape.

In order to trim the hull to the desired symmetrically tapering contour, a series of four holes were drilled with brace and bit every three feet along a cross section of the hull. Using these as gauges, a canoe builder can shape the craft proportionately so that the bottom is evenly tapered with smoothly thinning sides from four inches thick near the bow to two inches in the stern. These gauge holes will later be plugged with pieces of wet cedar, a hard-to-find wood that never dries out and expands slightly in salt water and seals.

The next step was to widen and gently flare the sides of the canoe. The hull was filled with water, and a number of stout sticks were cut and wedged between the inside edges of the canoe. Every day for approximately a week each stick was tamped farther down to place additional outward pressure on the sides which had been weakened and softened by the weight of the water. Gradually the canoe stretched until it had a V-shaped cross section. Cross braces were tacked into place to hold the shape until ribs could be fitted to the interior sides.

While the canoe was filled with water, Baldwin noticed a long wet line on the outside of the hull where the water was leaking through a six-foot hairline crack. Baldwin wanted to cut out the crack and replace the section with a carefully fitted piece of wet cedar. This was the common solution to repairing hull cracks, but cutting, tapering, beveling, and fitting the new piece would take at least two days, and as I saw it we would end up with two cracks instead of one. I suggested we use fiberglass instead.

"Fiberglass? Fiberglass? What's that?" Baldwin asked.

"You put a liquidlike paint on a piece of cloth made out of glass, and it gets hard and will seal a crack like this one."

Building a sailing canoe, Tasbapauni. Baldwin fits a new piece of "wet cedar" to replace the cutout soft mahogany heartwood in the bow while Alvin trims a piece of mahogany to build up the hull's sides. (This is the canoe we used on our trip to the Cape.)

Baldwin looked skeptical. Alvin asked me if I knew what time it was. I got them to agree to wait until I returned from Bluefields with some fiberglass. I had to go there anyway to order the motor. We'd try the glass, and if it didn't work, they could cut out the crack.

With the help of El Diablo, the manager of the Booth shrimp company at El Bluff (so called because he wore a large gold devil medallion around his neck), I placed a radiophone order to Galveston for an 18-hp Evinrude outboard with a long drive shaft for deep-water work; I also bought three quarts of polyester resin, hardener, and three yards of twenty-ounce glass cloth from the Booth stores.

The Miskito freaked out over fiberglass. Word had leaked out that I was going to repair a crack with glass cloth, and a crowd of twenty or thirty men collected around the canoe on Fiberglass Day. Up until then we had been able to keep secret the ownership and destination of the canoe. No longer. Baldwin was vociferously defending our work-study alliance, which everyone else called a suicide pact. They badgered him to pull out before he lost his life at sea in a glass canoe and my death brought back the U.S. Marines to investigate. One of the older men said it would be worth it if they could be sure the marines would come. Baldwin's grandchild was wrapped around his leg, crying, begging him not to die. Alvin asked if anyone wanted to know what time it was. Turmoil.

I mixed up a batch of the sweet-smelling resin, wondering how much hardener to add because of the high humidity. I brushed the resin over the eight-foot-long ten-inch-wide patch. We waited. All were quiet, watching the patch, occasionally touching it and then smelling their fingers. "It's hardening," I said, and rapped the patch with my knuckle. Pandemonium. With shouts of "first class" and "number one glue," everyone ran home and returned quickly with things needing repair. Alvin used the resin to patch his shirt, Pana glued a leather sole back onto a shoe; turtlemen dug into the resin can with sticks and then plugged holes and cracks in their canoes. I'd put too much hardener in, so most of the mixture dried before it was of much use. But people were thankful for the entertainment as much as for the glue.

Yet they all still thought we would be lost at sea.

Another two weeks were spent finishing the canoe. With the aid of a metal rod template bent to match the inside contour of the hull, mangrove trunk buttress roots were individually selected for ribs, which would give strength and rigidity to the canoe. Although difficult to work with, mangrove ribs are much stronger than those cut from cedar planks, as the grain runs with the curve. The canoe's sides were built up with long three-inch-wide mahogany strips and capped with an abrasion-resistant wood. Each of the planking strips was painstakingly beveled and fitted with saw and hand plane to ensure a watertight seal. A two-inch-thick mahogany transom was nailed and bolted to the stern. An assortment of different woods, each specially selected for its particular properties, was used for the bow stem, keel, mast thwart, and rigging brackets. A lateen-rigged sail was made from a variety of cotton flour- and sugar-sacks.

The next month was spent in a flurry of constant activity. After arriving from Texas by shrimp boat, the motor had to be broken in and minor adjustments made to adapt it to the severe weather conditions to be encountered. A stronger shear pin was fitted to the propeller shaft; the thermostat was removed; the gears were packed with heavier grease; and the engine was tuned for a lower oil-to-gas ratio—things that Bluefields mechanics swore by and that outboard engine manufacturers tore their hair over.

Baldwin and I made several trips in the canoe across Pearl Lagoon and up the Kuringwas and Wawashan Rivers. I taught him how to run the motor and make minor repairs, and he began teaching me how to sail a Miskito canoe and how to navigate. A six-foot-long wide-bladed mahogany paddle is used to steer canoes; the Miskito do not use rudders or deep keels on their canoes because of their open-beach, rough-surf launchings and landings. Steering a small sailing canoe with a paddle instead of a rudder increases the feeling of intimacy with nature. Tiny movements of canoe and waves which otherwise would be diminished by a rudder system of hinges and pins are transmitted by the paddle as if it were a sensitive monitoring rod dipped into an underwater world of motion. A steering paddle is also an aggravating nuisance because it forces you to stay in one position in a cramped place without the luxury of movement.

Baldwin insisted that we do a lot of sailing at night so that he could teach me to sail more by feel than by sight and to navigate by using stars, winds and waves. To a Miskito sailor the night sky is a vast and complex map that reflects the positions and pathways of myriad land and water features. With no charts and hardly any compasses, the Miskito use a variety of natural cues to guide them as they sail in the big lagoon and at sea or make long treks in the rain forest. Much of this navigational system is not predicated on Western sight-oriented equivalents, and thus the patterns of smells, feelings, tastes and textures that Baldwin—and later many others—began to teach me were both challenging and perplexing.

Toward the end of March we began to assemble the gear and supplies for the trip. Most of the stuff we had or could make in Tasbapauni, but we had to go to Bluefields, seventy miles to the south by inland water routes, for gasoline and some tinned emergency foods. Baldwin's front room became a storehouse for our trip materials. Each new item carried to his house provided visible evidence to the entire village that we were going in spite of the collective advice of the community. Baldwin oversaw the selection of equipment for the canoe and provisions for the trip, while each of us put together his own personal gear. A final checklist for the trip included a wide variety of items.

CANOE AND MOTOR

    mast, three paddles, mainsail and jib

    sailmakers needle and thread, for repairs

    a number of short, smooth sticks for repairing a broken mast

    a two-inch-diameter long pole used for the sail boom and to pole the canoe through shallow water

    various lines of different sizes, lengths and materials (nylon, cotton, and bark rope)

    two bailers: one a Miskito calabash, the other made from a plastic bleach bottle

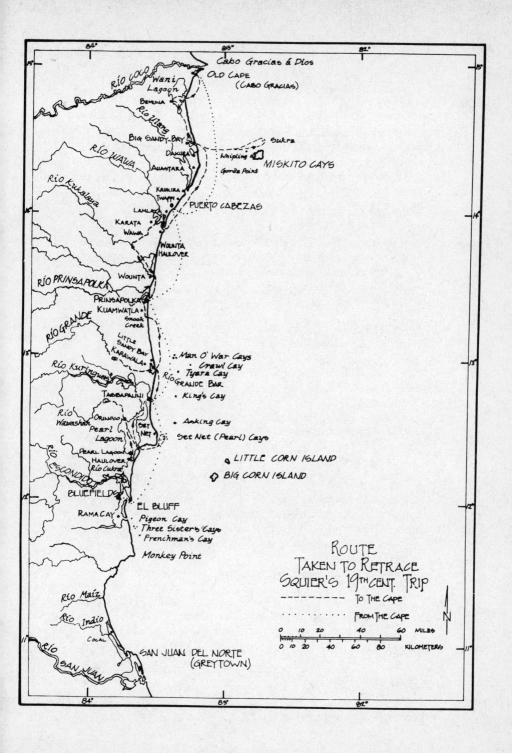

Cabo Gracias á Dios
OLD CAPE
(CABO GRACIAS)

84°   83°   82°

RÍO COCO
Wani Lagoon
BEMUNA
Río Kling
BIG SANDY BAY
DAKURA
AUASTARA
RÍO WAWA
Río Kukaleya
KRUKIRA
TWAPPI
LAMLAYA
KARATA
WAWA
WOUNTA HAULOVER
WOUNTA
RÍO PRINSAPOLKA
PRINSAPOLKA
KUAMWATLA
Snook Creek
RÍO GRANDE
LITTLE SANDY BAY
KARAWALA
Río Kuringuas
TASBAPAUNI
Río Wawashan
ORINOCO
Pearl Lagoon
SET NET
PEARL LAGOON
HAULOVER
Río Cukra
BLUEFIELDS
RÍO ESCONDIDO
RAMA CAY
EL BLUFF
Pigeon Cay
Three Sisters Cays
Frenchman's Cay
Monkey Point
Río Maíz
Río Indio
COCAL
SAN JUAN DEL NORTE
(GREYTOWN)
RÍO SAN JUAN

Sukra
Whipling
Gorda Point
MISKITO CAYS
PUERTO CABEZAS

Man O' War Cays
Crawl Cay
Tyara Cay
RÍO GRANDE BAR
King's Cay

Asking Cay
Set Net (Pearl) Cays

LITTLE CORN ISLAND
BIG CORN ISLAND

ROUTE
TAKEN TO RETRACE
SQUIER'S 19TH CENT. TRIP
–––––––– TO THE CAPE
············· FROM THE CAPE

0 10 20   40   60 MILES
0 10 20   40   60   80   KILOMETERS

N

a six-pound anchor and chain

18-hp Evinrude outboard motor, long shaft

a waterproof box containing tools, spare sparkplugs, ignition breaker, points, tubes of grease, and a felt gasoline filter

one spare propeller

20 one-quart cans of engine oil for mixing with gasoline

two six-gallon gasoline tanks

plastic containers for gasoline, one 20-gallon, one 10-gallon

42 gallons of gasoline

tarps, two plastic and one large canvas, used to cover and protect supplies from water and sun and as an emergency tent

two large burlap bags filled with sand, used for ballast

COOKING—CAMPING

rice, beans, flour, baking powder, sugar, coffee, salt—sealed and covered with Miskito-made tarps of natural rubber-coated cloth

15 gallons of water stored in three large orange plastic fishing net floats

three pounds of dried shrimp

three pounds of fresh-baked bread, sealed in plastic bags inside an old cracker tin

12 cans of tinned fish, six each of tuna fish and sardines

fish line and various hooks and trolling lures

a fish harpoon and a six-foot cast net

two sets of tin plates, cups and eating utensils

machete, "Collins," five-riveted handle, the type said to be the strongest

hunting knife and flashlight

two light wool blankets

two mosquito nets, string and a dozen nails

a small first-aid kit

several boxes of wooden matches in a watertight can

PERSONAL ITEMS

swim suit, sunglasses, cotton hat, light nylon jacket

Squier book and Miskito dictionary

notebook, two pens, one pencil

1:50,000 maps of coast

one extra pair of pants, tennis shoes, underwear

camera equipment: 35 mm Nikonos waterproof camera, 20 rolls of black and white and color transparency film, L-86 waterproof Sekonic exposure meter, extra O-rings and grease, silica gel for desiccation, and small watertight cans for film storage

Of the above equipment the most important turned out to be the bleach-bottle bailer, clean spare sparkplugs, fish line and harpoon, sunglasses, machete and Squier's book.

By the end of March everything was ready: the canoe painted, the motor broken in, supplies assembled; I had learned the rudiments of sailing, and I knew about but did not yet understand the environmental aids used by the Miskito in navigation.

What remained was to work out a route plan, to familiarize ourselves with the coastal maps, and to acquire any information we could from villagers who had visited the upper coast.

We planned to follow as closely as possible the route described by Squier in 1849, some 120 years earlier. We would start in Bluefields and trace the system of interconnecting rivers, creeks and lagoons that supposedly ran parallel to the sea and provided inland water travel most of the way to Cape Gracias a Dios. To our knowledge no one had done this since Squier's journey, and in fact some of the old route through the mangrove swamps and low-lying marshes was no longer known.

Between the larger lagoons and rivers the maps showed a maze of creeks, marshlands and mangrove. As such, the maps could provide only the grossest outline of the coastal region and would be of little use in helping us to find our way. We would have to rely instead on information obtained from each village as we ventured northward and on Squier's general descriptions and his affirmation that such a route did indeed exist.

> . . . the whole Mosquito shore is lined with lagoons, only separated from the sea by narrow strips of land, and so connected with each other as to afford an interior navigation, for canoes, from Bluefields to Gracias. [p. 77]

No doubt it was the extensive shallow swamps that had kept anyone from rediscovering the entire travel route of the supposed inland water system. Plus the fact that only small canoes could pass over some of the shallower shoals and swamps. Since Squier's time most of the coastal traffic has gone by sea, using the rivers only to travel far inland to upstream settlements and using only a small fragment of the old water route between Bluefields Lagoon and Pearl Lagoon.

We planned to go as far north as possible following the inland route to the Cape and to make our return journey by sea to Tasbapauni.

The night before we left for Bluefields to pick up gasoline and to start the Squier trip, Baldwin and I went around the village to visit some of the older Miskito who might be able to offer information to clear up some of the blank places on our route map. In spite of the good dry-season weather and expected smooth, fair sea conditions, everyone we talked with tried once more to discourage us from going. It wasn't so much the distance we were to travel—300 miles to the Cape and another 200 miles or so up the various rivers—but the coastal river bars that worried them. If only the old men were younger and stronger and the young men older and wiser, they said, any one of them would accompany us in order to save us from capsizing in the river bars we would have to cross.

Theo Waggam, one of the older men who had done much traveling years before, spoke of the many ships and boats and lives that had been lost on the river bars. "You watch out for Río Grande Bar and Prinsapolka Bar; they're the bad ones. Plenty of boats have gone down there, piloted by better seamen than Baldwin. They saved some and some saved themselves, but the sharks and the sea killed the rest. Sharks pack up in those bars, feeding on the fish, and the river current will push anyone still floating in the water far out to sea. Those bars are the graveyard for us seamen."

Theo and Baldwin talked of the men lost at sea from Tasbapauni and other places. River bars and hurricanes appeared to be the main factors responsible, but Theo felt that "damn foolishness" and "no sea sense" were the real causes for the deaths. "Remember the last hurricane that passed by here? The boys on the cays fishing turtle didn't want to leave off for the main on account of them catching all those fat turtle, but everything on the sea and sky saying hurricane coming. Then it was too late to leave, and they had to lash themselves to the coconut trees. Rain come, wind blowing, and all the cays were awash with the sea. Tasbapauni lose three of her own that day. Foolish. They were following the turtle instead of the weather."

It was late when we left Theo's, a new moon dark night with warm air hanging dead calm over the village. The daytime trade wind off the sea had whispered down, and it was too soon for the early morning land breeze. I followed Baldwin as he instinctively picked his way around the invisible ruts, holes and open wells that pocked the bumpy, grass-covered village grounds.

"Don't worry about those things," Baldwin said, as much to himself as to me, as he walked ahead. "We'll be fine. April is a sweet weather month—sea calm, like oil on water, and the blue sea color come right up to the beach. Fair breeze and pretty sea. Oh, we're going to have a fine trip, just like Squier. All that talk about sharks, hurricanes and bars—that was just to show that he was once a seaman too. I know the sea, and I know the bars. We're going to sail with the fair wind, and that pretty little motor is going to hum us through the bars."

It was hard getting to sleep that night. The next morning we would leave for Bluefields and then begin the trip to the Cape. The smell of the trip filled the room: gasoline, fresh-baked bread, new cedar and mahogany paddles. The problem of the river bars would have to wait. The immediate predicament was how to cram all this stuff into the canoe.

Three days later we left Bluefields with forty-two gallons of gas on board and a few cans of food stored in the hatch for emergencies. We'd come down the inside from Tasbapauni; now we would retrace part of that route on our way north to Pearl Lagoon and the Set Net Cays before crossing the canoe from the lagoon to the sea at the Tasbapauni haulover.

The waterfront was packed that morning. Several long river canoes had come down the Río Escondido filled with hundreds of green-skinned oranges, most of which were immediately sold to the crowds of shrimp company workers waiting for the diesel boat to ferry them across the lagoon to the Booth company at El Bluff.

Oranges are a common fruit, and I'd seen hundreds peeled, all with one thing in common: no one ever accidentally cut through the peel spiral or nicked through the white. Every orange eater always peeled perfectly. It was one of the little-known culture traits of the east coast.

We picked our way slowly through the old cement pilings that littered the shallow waterfront waters, reminders of better days and better wharves for Bluefields. Now all that the pilings supported were small schools of puffer fish that swam lazily in the oil-slicked and debris-spotted brackish water. The taste and smell of diesel fumes receded as we sped out into the lagoon. We could no longer see Judi and Barney waving good-bye from the sagging Esso wharf. From a distance the old English town of Bluefields looked positively picturesque: rows of white frame houses with red corrugated metal roofs; clumps of breadfruit, mango, coconut and star apple trees; the rain forest–covered Aberdeen Hill coming into view.

We passed the last tide-carried orange peel as we neared the stakes that marked the channel to the Río Escondido. Puffer fish pulled at it from below so that it bobbed up and down; the long single-curl peel was the last we'd see of Bluefields for some time.

We were on our way at last. Ahead lay the Miskito Coast and the challenge of tracing a past journey and finding new things. Behind us now were my long checklists and the frustrations of trying to find specific items in general stores. Forewarnings from Tasbapauni and Bluefields folk evaporated in the April sun. Baldwin radiated enjoyment from being on the water again, and the canoe felt solid and lively. It was a very fine morning.

> It was a bright morning, and our little sail, filled with the fresh sea-breeze, carried us gayly through the water. . . . The white herons flapped lazily around us, and flocks of screaming curlews whirled

rapidly over our heads. I could scarcely comprehend the novel reality of my position. The Robinson Crusoe-ish feeling of my youth came back in all of its freshness; I had my own boat, and for companions a descendant of an aboriginal prince, the possessor of a mysterious talisman, devotedly attached to me, half-friend, half-protector, and a second strange Indian, from some unknown interior. . . . I gave myself up to the delicious novelty, and that sense of absolute independence which only a complete separation from the moving world can inspire, and passed the entire day in a trance of dreamy delight. I subsequently passed many similar days, but this stands out in the long perspective, as one of unalloyed happiness. [pp. 77–78]

After leaving Bluefields, Squier had gone a short way up the Río Escondido, which is one of the largest rivers on the coast and drains a huge watershed area that annually receives 150 to 200 inches of rain. Now at the start of the April-to-June dry season the river level was down, and the deep waters had lost their muddy red-brown color. We ran past Schooner Cay, a low teardrop-shaped island set in the steel gray jungle river waters. A machine shop and repair station for United Fruit Company during the banana boom of the 1930s, the small island is now used by the Pescanica Shrimp Company. The Río Escondido's banana plantations and banana barges are gone, replaced by the invading rain forest and rust-streaked black and white shrimp boats that line the island's long wharf.

Twisted water-worn stumps lodged in the mud and silt shoals mark the entrance to Fruta de Pan River and the interconnecting series of rivers and creeks that lead to Pearl Lagoon. Low-lying rain forest and palm swamps are cut by meandering river bends that require thirty or forty miles of travel to cross ten miles of straight-line distance. Big Lagoon. White herons standing on mud shoals. Twelve-pound freshwater turtles sunning on stranded, tide-marked, naked stumps and logs. Cukra River. Dense forest walls laced with lianas present a movie-set false façade that hides the relatively clear, open forest floor beyond.

The dry-season sun rises in the late morning sky. Shoulders and thighs warm in the hot rays. Left ear numbed from the high-pitched drone of the motor. Left hand slipping and cramped from too tight a hold on the twist-grip throttle steering arm.

Silico Creek. The most beautiful water course in Nicaragua. A narrow, water-floored tunnel that twists through the dark forest. Sun shafts from the overlapping tree-crown roof streak the green gloom. The slow-moving canoe's wake laps against *kowi* tree-root buttresses that line the creek's edges. Fallen silico palm fronds and yellowing evergreen leaves float on the glassy water ahead. I cut the motor and we paddle the remaining three miles through the creek. Mechanized sound is out of place.

Before 1928 canoes traveling between Bluefields and Pearl Lagoon had to be dragged over a mile-long haulover, a low stretch of land that separated the end of Silico Creek from the southern edge of the lagoon. Now the Moncada Canal gives straight-line water transit. Dredged out in the late 1920s, the once-wide canal is now a narrow, shallow channel choked by red mangrove. Interlaced stilt-roots trap silt and mud and anchor young plant seedlings started from foot-long seeds dropped at the outer edge of the parent mangrove.

We stopped and made camp on the lagoon side of the old haulover, where Squier and the two Indians had stayed the first night.

In order to be able to renew our voyage early the next morning, our few effects and stores were carried across the portage, over which our united strength was sufficient to drag the dory, without difficulty. . . . The transit was effected in less than an hour, and then we proceeded to make our camp for the night, on the beach. Our little sail, supported over the canoe by poles, answered the purpose of a tent. And as for food, without going fifty yards from our fire, I shot a half dozen curlews, which, when broiled, are certainly a passable bird. Meanwhile, the Poyer boy, carefully wading in the lagoon, with a light spear, had struck several fish, of varieties known as *snook* and *grouper*; and Antonio had collected a bag full of oysters, of which there appeared to be vast banks, covered only by a foot or two of water. They were not pearl oysters, as might be inferred from the name of the lagoon, but similar to those found on our own shores, except smaller, and growing in clusters of ten or a dozen each. . . .
. . . the Indians busied themselves with the fish and birds. I watched their proceedings with no little interest, and as their mode of baking fish has never been set forth in the cookery books, I give it for the benefit of the gastronomic world in general. . . . A hole having been dug in the sand, it was filled with dry branches, which were set on fire. In a few minutes the fire subsided in a bed of glowing coals. The largest of the fish, a *grouper*, weighing perhaps five pounds, had been cleaned and stuffed with pieces of the smaller fish, a few oysters, some sliced plantains, and some slips of the bark of the pimento or pepper-tree. Duly sprinkled with salt, it was carefully wrapped in the broad, green leaves of the plantain, and the coals raked open, put in the centre of the glowing embers, with which it was rapidly covered. Half an hour afterward, by which time I began to believe it had been reduced to ashes, the bed was raked open again and the fish taken out. The outer leaves of the wrapper were burned, but the inner folds were entire, and when they were unrolled, like the cerements of a mummy, they revealed the fish, "cooked to a charm," and preserving all the rich juices absorbed in the flesh, which would have been

carried off by the heat, in the ordinary modes of cooking. I afterward adopted the same process with nearly every variety of large game, and found it, like patent medicines, of "universal application." [pp. 79–80]

Instead of fire-pit-roasted grouper, we dined that first night on shrimp caught by Baldwin with his cast net, which yielded two pounds in eight throws, and rice and fresh johnnycake purchased in Bluefields that morning. Over the sighs of the dying trade winds and the popping of our campfire, we could hear the snapping and crackling of a large school of shrimp only a few yards away in the lagoon. During the dry season, when the freshwater river floods abate and the tidal salt water pushes into the coastal lagoons, several species of marine fish and shrimp migrate into the increasingly brackish waters to breed and feed. In June the heavy rains start again and the engorged rivers pour into the lagoons, flushing out marine waters and species. During this short period the shrimp boats drag their nets night and day off the river bars.

"Why do your countrymen buy the shrimp and lobster?" Baldwin was one of the few Miskito who would occasionally eat either, and he was doing so now only because we had to adapt to each other every way we could during the long trip ahead. "We Indian call the shrimp *wahsi sirpi* and the lobster *wahsi tara*, little and big sea insects. The turtle fishermen don't bother with the lobster unless they're marooned on the cays and run out of real food. Maybe your people live so far from the sea that they have to have a bite of those salt water insects just to know they're still living."

> Before the dawn of day, the ever-watchful Antonio had prepared the indispensable cup of coffee, which is the tropical specific against the malignant night-damps; and the first rays of the sun shot over the trees only to fall on our sail, bellying with the fresh and invigorating sea-breeze. We laid our course for the mouth of a river called Wawashaan (*hwas* or *wass*, in the dialect of the interior, signifying water), which enters the lagoon, about twenty miles to the northward of the *Haulover*. [p. 82]

Pearl Lagoon is the largest coastal lagoon in eastern Nicaragua. Fifty miles long by ten to twenty wide, it is a vast slate gray sheet of water opening to the sea only at Pearl Lagoon Bar. We were in the middle of it, crossing at the widest stretch, and we were out of sight of land. Distant Cerro Wawashan was obscured by clouds and no longer served as a homing marker. To be ten miles inland and still not be able to see land is a strange feeling. It was hard to tell where the horizon was; the grays of the lagoon and of the overcast sky were so close that it was as if we were traveling across an inside arc of a huge dome.

Orinoco. Near the mouth of the Río Wawashan, a long split-wood wharf juts out over the shallow lagoon, indicating the location of the village, itself partially hidden by a dense canopy of breadfruit and mango trees. Orinoco is a Black Carib village, a cultural outpost in the midst of the Miskito, the next closest Black Carib settlement being some 350 miles to the north in Honduras.

The Orinoco Black Carib are descendants of a mixture of black slaves and Carib Indians who resisted French and English settlement on the island of St. Vincent in the Lesser Antilles so fiercely that the English forcibly deported 4000 to the isolated Bay Islands off Honduras in 1797. Over the next century they migrated to the mainland coast and established settlements from Stann Creek, Belize, in the north to Iriona, Honduras, in the south. Besides being excellent fishermen, the Black Carib were noted axemen and provided an important labor supply for the mahogany works in Belize and Honduras. In 1885 the George D. Emery Mahogany Company hired several Black Caribs from Truxillo to work in the expanding lumber camps up the Río Wawashan in Nicaragua. Many of them decided to stay; they sent for their families and founded a settlement called San Vicente; later, under the leadership of John Sambola, they moved and renamed the village Orinoco. Even after more than seventy years of cultural isolation, many of the Black Carib ways still remain.

The Creole-Miskito river village that Squier visited has been long abandoned, so we decided to spend the night in Orinoco.

"We have to be very careful here. This place is pure obeahman-obeahwoman, and bush rum they call *kasusa*. This is the home of the devil himself," Baldwin said as we approached the landing.

We were just tying the canoe to the leeward side of the wharf when the church bell started ringing. Baldwin visibly relaxed. "That's a good sign," he said.

"The Father come. The Father come." Three young boys were skip-running toward us, bouncing over the randomly spaced limbs, boards and slats that made up the wharf top. They snatched up some of the bags that we were unloading and started back for the village. "When are you going to hold service?" one of them asked over his shoulder as he sped off.

"Later," replied Baldwin.

"What's going on here? Where are they going with our bags, and what's this about a service?"

"The people look out and see a white man with a beard coming with an outboard motor. They think you are a Catholic priest. That's the way the *padres* travel around here. We'll be all right here tonight—the obeah people don't molest priests."

"Look, I can't impersonate a priest just to ward off the evil eye and black magic." Baldwin began to look anxious again. "Besides, I couldn't fake a mass or a service. I never even made it to being an altar boy."

"You don't have to fake anything. Don't worry about that. Just smile a lot, and when you talk to someone, put your hand on his arm. That's the main secret to the priest business. We'll do it my way and get to sleep in the church tonight. Nobody is going to humbug a priest."

I smiled, looked Baldwin in the eye, and held him by the shoulder. "That's not the right thing to do; it's not right."

"That's it. You got it. Just say 'my son' every so often." Baldwin had a larcenous gleam in his eye. "Follow me, Father Barney. Orinoco is a pretty little place."

Well, we had to adapt to each other on the trip. If Baldwin could eat shrimp for me, I could smile and say "my son" for him.

Our gear was stacked on one of the mahogany pews in the back of the church. There was still plenty of time left in the day, so we asked if anyone wanted to accompany us on a run up the river. Florentine Sambola, one of the sons of the late founder of Orinoco, came with us.

We set out to find the settlement site mentioned by Squier. I also wanted to see the Wawashan area which had been so beautifully described by Archie Carr fifteen years before in his book *High Jungles and Low*. The abundant silk-cotton trees were in bloom, and the river air was awash in their fragrant perfume. Mile after mile we traveled upriver past the flowered landscape.

> The large trees . . . were of the variety known as the *ceiba,* or silk-cotton tree. They were now in their bloom, and crowned with a profusion of flowers of rich and variegated colors, but chiefly a bright carnation. It was a novel spectacle to see a gigantic tree, five or six feet in diameter, and eighty or ninety feet high, sending out long and massive limbs, yet bearing flowers like a rose-bush—a sort of man-milliner! Viewed from beneath, the flowers were scarcely visible, but their fragrance was overpowering, and the ground was carpeted with their gay leaves and delicate petals. But seen from a distance, the ceiba-tree in bloom is one of the most splendid productions of Nature—a gigantic bouquet, which requires a whole forest to supply the contrasting green! The flowers are rapidly succeeded by a multitude of pods, which grow to the size and shape of a goose-egg. When ripe, they burst open, revealing the interior filled with a very soft, light cotton or silky fiber, attached as floats to diminutive seeds, which are thus wafted far and wide by the winds. This process is repeated three times a year. [pp. 184–185]

We pulled up under one of the largest *ceiba* trees that lined the river bank. We ate the rest of the johnnycake, drank some cold coffee, and talked.

"We use these cotton trees to make canoes," Florentine said. "A big one can give a canoe forty or fifty feet long and six feet wide. We used to make them to carry banana to the company. Now that's gone, so we hardly bother with them anymore."

Baldwin leaned over and began whispering to Florentine. They spoke quietly for several minutes. Finally Baldwin nodded and said to me, "You got to be careful around these cotton tree. Some of them harbor *lasa*. You've got to know which tree have *lasa* and which don't. The Carib know plenty about this, almost as much as we Miskito."

I had read about various *lasa* in books and had heard some of the older Miskito mention them in Tasbapauni. A silk-cotton tree *lasa*, or *sisin lasa* in Miskito, is a magical spirit, the "owner" of the tree. It sometimes takes the form of a small three-foot-high man who can be either evil or good, depending on the nature of the encounter and exchange. Many peoples in various parts of the Caribbean and eastern Central America believe in the silk-cotton tree spirit and refer to it by a variety of names.

Later that afternoon when we were alone, Baldwin told me more about the *sisin lasa* and about his conversation with Florentine. "A *sisin lasa* can help or he can hurt. Depends. Supposed to be one back of Orinoco in a big cotton tree. You can deal with this *lasa*. If a man wants to get rich, he will go to a cotton tree late at night on a new moon. The *sisin lasa* can change his luck so that he'll soon get plenty of money. But the trick to the thing is that the man has to give the *lasa* something in exchange. What he gives is the name of someone in the town. That man will become unlucky, lose his things, maybe even his life. Some people want to dream about the *lasa* and get rich. They put a piece of the bark under their pillow at night to dream. Some wake up light in the head, act crazy like. The *sisin lasa* business is a serious thing."

Baldwin was adamant about the existence of the spirits, although he claimed that they had been more numerous and more powerful in the "back time," but like everything else, old-time lasas were mostly gone.

I never saw a *sisin lasa*, but then I never went to a cotton tree late at night either. It appeared to be a pretty bizarre belief. I interpreted it functionally by ascribing an economic rationale: a probable post-contact phenomenon which could "explain" the acquisition or loss of wealth in a previously egalitarian society.

The Miskito, as well as many other native peoples, believed that one's personal name contained power. If someone knew it and said it aloud, it could cause the individual harm. Therefore, in traditional societies people were usually referred to and addressed indirectly, either by nickname or as the son or daughter of so-and-so. When missionaries began converting the Miskito, quite accidentally they acquired tremendous power over each individual by writing down personal names and using them in services.

All that remained of what may have been Wasswatla, the Río Wawashan settlement that Squier wrote about, was an overgrown thicket only recognizable as an old village by the tall *supa* palms ("peach palm" or *pejibaye* in Spanish) that jutted from the green tangle.

"Not even the old-time people remember this place," Florentine said. "All that's left is the *supa*, but they're so old that they don't bear properly."

Florentine cut a long, thin sapling and tied his machete to one end. Using this extension, he cut down one of the yellow-orange bunches of palm fruits. The palm trunk is ringed with two- to three-inch-long needle-sharp spines. "You can't climb *supa*; no, papa, this thing juke you," Florentine remarked with reverence. "One time a drove of *wari* turn on old Emelio, and he forced to *salvar* himself up a *supa*. Those prickle cut him something terrible. He picked prickle out of his hide for months."

I couldn't imagine a worse option: either confront a drove of angry and vicious white-lipped peccary, often numbering over 100, each weighing sixty to seventy pounds with three-inch tusks; or climb a needle-studded palm.

We arrived back in Orinoco at sundown. It was dark by the time we tied up and began walking toward the church. The stick-walled houses leaked short beams of amber light from kerosene lanterns and cooking fires. We had made arrangements for food to be prepared, and Florentine guided us to Miss Nana's house and left us at the door. Before we went in, I told Baldwin not to refer to me as a priest.

"What if someone should die tonight?" I asked. "How could I give the last rites? Just forget the obeah and my being a priest, O.K.?"

"We Indian say that if a hunter is in the bush at night and sees red eyeshine from some animal ahead, he might believe he's looking at *tigre* instead of deer. Even though that's deer, he acts like it's tiger. Nothing will change his thinking, except if he knows that the real tiger eyeshine is lower to the ground than deer. That's the way to know tiger from deer in the dark."

I tried to figure that one out, but Baldwin had already gone inside and was washing up to eat.

Miss Nana had prepared a fine meal with many Black Carib dishes. There was a stack of *areba*, a tortillalike bread made from bitter manioc; *foo-foo* balls made from boiled and mashed green plantains and served in a spicy Creole soup; and a bowl of boiled pieces of *dasheen* (like taro), young manioc and breadfruit, covered with a chopped fish, shredded coconut and hot pepper sauce. Everything looked delicious.

As we began to eat, I kept smelling a very powerful odor. "Baldwin, we've got to get a bath in the morning and get these clothes washed. We're beginning to smell."

"Oh, that high scent is the stinking toe," Baldwin replied matter-of-factly and kept on eating.

I thought to myself, it must be those rubber boots he's wearing. I mean, that smell was unreal.

"You scrape the stinking toe and mix it with milk. It's first class. Try it." Baldwin certainly had a way with words, but I didn't feel like discussing some home remedy to cure foot problems while we were eating.

"O.K. O.K. Please pass the pitcher." Anything to change the subject.

I gagged, coughed and choked on one taste of the drink I'd just poured.

"What is in this *fresco*, Mr. Baldwin?"

"That is what we've been talking about. That's the stinking toe. They make *fresco* from it. It smells ripe, but it's a fine-tasting drink."

Gag.

Baldwin called to Miss Nana, who was in the kitchen, and asked her to bring a stinking toe for me to see. She handed him a foot-long seed pod that looked very similar to a St. John's tree seed.

"April is the season for stinking toe. Inside this seed is a sweet something that looks like grease and has a high scent."

My appetite suddenly returned.

After we had finished eating, I wanted to take a walk around the village; but Baldwin wanted to go immediately to the church, supposedly to sleep, but really to take refuge from what he called "the obeah people." As we were leaving Miss Nana's, a drum started beating nearby.

"Hear that, Mr. Barney? That's the obeah drum, and I don't like to be anywhere near that."

"Let's walk by and peek in the house and see what's going on. Then we can go to bed."

"That's only trouble you're talking about."

"Just a quick look. Come on."

The sound was coming from a small room attached to one side of a Carib house. A ten-watt kerosene lantern provided the only light. Several men and women were sitting at small tables, bottles and glasses at each; against one wall was a counter with bottles of Santa Cecilia and Flor de Caña rum. A cantina. An old Carib was seated at one of the tables, absentmindedly tapping his fingers on a huge, barrel-sized drum that stood beside him.

"Let's see what's happening. We can order something to drink." I went inside. The drum stopped. The talking stopped.

Baldwin came in. "Good evening, people." He went over to some of the men and sat down. He apparently knew most of them. I sat at an unoccupied table and waited while they talked. I wanted to get a drink. Sitting at a bare table in a bar without a drink seemed antisocial even if I was sitting alone.

After what felt like an hour but was probably only fifteen minutes, Baldwin came over and joined me. "We've come at a bad time, and they're worried about a priest being in here and in Orinoco tomorrow. That drum is the *walagayo* drum, and the man holding it is old Braulio, the head obeah man himself."

I glanced over Baldwin's shoulder. The man called Braulio wore a tattered brown fedora and a turquoise shirt open at the chest; he was smoking a ragged homemade cigar.

"Gentlemen?" A glassy-eyed young man suddenly materialized at our table and stood swaying.

"You have *kasusa?*" Baldwin asked. The man nodded affirmatively and returned shortly with glasses, two bottles of tepid Fanta Uva (a grape-flavored soft drink), and an old Flor de Caña pint bottle filled with what Baldwin called the "real kasus."

Someone had put an old Jim Reeves song on a battery-powered record player. The drum had disappeared. Country and western instead of the obeah man's drum. It looked as though they were cleaning up their act for us.

"What did you find out? Why shouldn't we be in Orinoco tomorrow?"

"They think you're a priest, and the *walagayo* is a Carib thing that the Catholic Church discourages; some say they outlaw it. When someone get serious sick, their family comes to the obeah man and asks him to do a *walagayo*. It lasts three days and two nights and is supposed to cure the sickness. The family has to butcher a cow and hog, have plenty of fish and *areba* and *kasusa*. Everybody comes and drinks, eats, dances and smokes that tobacco for the whole time. They're just warming up for the start tomorrow. But then we showed up, and they're afraid to do it in front of a priest. It seems like the old man is very sick, and they don't want to put off the *walagayo* until we leave."

Now we've done it, I thought; we've really blown it this time. Instead of just playing along with an apparently harmless subterfuge, we were disrupting a serious ceremony. I said so to Baldwin. We devised Plan B and ordered a bottle of *kasusa* to be sent over to Braulio's table.

In a short time we had moved our chairs over and joined them. Braulio sat frozen; the only thing that moved was his drinking arm. The cigar was dead center in his mouth, and his unblinking eyes stared at me through the smoke curtain. Also at the table were Enisia, an old woman who wore a cloth tied around her head with a French Foreign Legion piece hanging down in back, with stringy little gray curls poking out of the band, and who had teeth like crossed swords; "the Englishman," who wore ancient horn-rimmed glasses and was said to have "English blood"; and a young Creole girl from Corn Island who was not introduced but was referred to as "this loose girl." We told them about Squier and our trip and why we were making it. Everyone appeared interested but Braulio, who said nothing and kept staring at me.

At about the third or fourth bottle, Braulio unexpectedly sprang up from the table, knocking over his stool, and shouted, "The Lord be praised! We is saved. We is saved. Jesus sent us a nice man." This made me feel a little uneasy. I tried to get him to sit down and stop shouting.

"Look, all we're doing is following the same route that Mr. Squier took many years ago. I'm not a priest, and I'm not with the church." No effect. Nothing. Braulio and the rest may have thought that Squier was a messiah or something and I was one of his followers.

Braulio called for his drum. "Dance, Miss Enisia, dance the *walagayo*." He began to pound the drumhead. Everybody started to sing, almost chant, "*Walagayo, walagayo* mama, *walagayo, walagayo* ma-ma," over and over as Miss Enisia danced. Braulio said he couldn't dance because he didn't have any good moves left. But Enisia had good moves, and, once going, she kept dancing between puffs on a cigar and snorts of the *kasusa*.

One of the young men who had been sitting at another table muttering got up and started to mimic Enisia's dancing, yelling "*Walagayo* mama" too. Braulio glared at him. "Be quiet, boy; she is doing about our people," he said with enough menace in his voice to still a riot. Turning back to us, he commented to no one in particular, "These younger race have no respect. It's not like Honduras."

We drank and sang a long while after that. The entire experience became a blur. It's probably better that I can't recall what we talked about. Braulio guided us back to the church. I don't remember walking, so there's a good chance they carried or dragged me. I was alternately waking up and passing out, so that my perception was a series of freeze frames. The last frame contained Braulio looking down on me laid out on a church pew and saying, "This church is looking up."

The next morning Baldwin was in much better shape than I was, so he went out to reconnoiter. I was still lying on the pew, staring down a cockroach on top of our food box, when he returned.

"They're all gathering for the *walagayo*. They killed a cow and are cutting it up right now—" A loud squeal close by interrupted him. "That'll be the hog. The way Braulio has it, you told him to go ahead with everything. He says the church is working with the people now, so everything worked out fine."

"Everything will work out, Mr. Baldwin, if we stay clear of the real priest after his next visit to Orinoco."

We packed and got ready to leave, but Braulio came by and insisted that we at least stop by the *walagayo*. I think he wanted some witnesses to our attendance in case of possible repercussions.

We loaded the canoe and then went back to say good-bye. The doorway of the house where the ceremony was being held was jammed with people, so we went around to an open window to look in. The interior was filled with pungent smoke and dancing bodies; arms joined, the dancers circled the room, singing. A pile of dirt that looked like a grave was heaped on the far side of the floor. In the center of the room, the sick man lay in a hammock hung from the ceiling. He was wrapped in a white sheet; he wore a bright scarlet sash across his chest, and his hands and feet were tied with strips of red cloth. Enisia stood close by him, holding a chicken by the feet. She cut its throat and held it over a small bowl on the floor to collect the blood. There were six drums, all carried by men who led the dances. The women did most of the singing. Braulio was squatting near the head of the sick man, smoking a large cigar and blowing huge lungfuls over him. Against one wall stood several tables piled with food and bottles of what looked like *kasusa*.

"So that's the *walagayo*," Baldwin whispered. "First one I ever saw. They say that by the end of three days, the sick will stand up well and will dance with the people, even the ones that the doctors give over. Obeah supposed to be stronger than the real doctors, but Indian bush medicine is stronger than both."

We watched for a couple of hours: the dancing and singing were mesmerizing. It was getting late, though, and we wanted to reach the sea that night.

"They're waving, Mr. Barney." I looked back toward Orinoco.

Braulio and Enisia stood alone at the end of the long wharf, saying good-bye across the widening distance between us. We waved back.

"Now they are nice obeah people," Baldwin told me before turning back to face windward and the darkening eastern sky.

After leaving the Wawashan, Squier and his two Indian companions, accompanied by four canoes of Miskito from Wasswatla, went to the Set Net (Pearl) Cays, which lie close to the mainland just northeast of the bar.

> Off the mouth of Pearl-Cay Lagoon are numerous cays, which, in fact, give their name to the lagoon. They are celebrated for the number and variety of turtles found on and around them. . . . I became eager to witness the sport of turtle-hunting, which is regarded by the Mosquitos as their noblest art, and in which they have acquired proverbial expertness. . . .
>
> We went, literally, with the wind; and in four hours after leaving the shore, were among the cays. These are very numerous, surrounded by reefs, through which wind intricate channels, all well known to the fishers. Some of the cays are mere heaps of sand, and half-disintegrated coral-rock, others are larger, and a few have bushes, and an occasional palm-tree upon them. . . . It was on one of the latter, where there were the ruins of a rude hut, and a place scooped in the sand, containing brackish water, that we landed, and made our encampment. [pp. 105–107]

It was dark by the time we came to the mouth of the bar. Since there was little breeze, we had been running with the motor, and our churning wake left a rippling triangle of molten silver. The saline lagoon waters had a heavy concentration of bioluminescent marine organisms which flashed with a cold light when agitated. The Miskito call it "burn water." This was true; our canoe seemed to float through incandescent water. I pulled the motor up so that we could drift with the outgoing tidal current. We dipped our paddles into the black lagoon, leaving silver J-stroke signatures on the waters. Beneath us at various depths and traveling in different directions, fast-swimming fish left luminescent meteor tails that marked their ghostly passage through the black water universe. A huge, fiery shape sped toward us like a burning torpedo. Almost as wide as the canoe, it passed beneath the hull, and I peered down on a cocoon of organic light that outlined a gigantic form.

"Manatee. Very scarce now, not like before," Baldwin said.

Long minutes of stillness, then he continued: "We'll paddle through the bar and then put up the sail. Don't be afraid. This bar is safe, faces southeast away from the wind. Most of the time, it's natural calm."

In the darkness it was impossible to see where the lagoon ended and the sea began, but it could be felt. The canoe began to bob up and down as we hit the low sea swells.

"You feel the seas? Steer so we slide over them. You've got to cant the canoe, angle it to the wave. Don't head directly into the seas. Don't fight them. Not too much angle, or we'll catch a sea and broach. Angle, straighten out, angle, straighten out. That's better. Listen to the slap of the bow on the backside of the sea; then you know if your steering is right. Feel the canoe. It's lively; every move is showing the sea. Close your eyes. Feel the roll. Listen to the bow. That's it. That's it. You're going. NO! Too much . . . Easy now . . . better."

This was my first time at sea in the canoe, and it would have to be at night. We'd left the quiet water lagoon, and several stretches of open sea were ahead. Baldwin once more became the teacher, and I tried to learn from his instructions. Our relationship had changed again.

Sail rigged and with a freshening land breeze, we pointed to the cays. At midnight, damp and cramped, we arrived at Crawl Cay, where there was a small shelter.

"Looks like Weddy is here with some other turtlemen. They'll be packed up in the camp. Let's fix a little lodging for ourselves."

Too tired to ask Baldwin any questions, I helped him gather some drift planks from the beach and rig a tent from the sail. Sleep, blessed sleep.

There was a sand crunch noise by my head. I looked up into the morning glare. A Flor de Caña baseball hat was set on a sea-gnarled face with deep eye creases and a white beard stubble; a mouth chewing tobacco was spraying spittle and a stream of words.

"Good thing you slept on those boards, or the soldier crabs would have run off with your teeth."

I got up. The man talking to me—at least I assumed he was addressing me, since there was no one else nearby—was about 5'6", and in his middle fifties. He wore a flour-sack shirt and an old patch-on-patch pair of khaki pants rolled to just below the knees. He stood with feet wide apart, bare toes splayed, arms behind his back. He looked a part of the sea, the way I'd always imagined Hemingway's Old Man.

"Yes sir. Those crab will cut the buttons off your pants. Anything shiny they'll go for. See Ulic over there?" He motioned with his head toward a figure kneeling by a fire thirty yards away. "Some years ago, he put all his turtle money in a new set of teeth. False ones. Pulled the old ones. One night he drank out a bottle on this same cay and slept dead drunk right where you're standing. Soldier crabs plucked those teeth right out of his mouth. Next morning he woke up mashing gums just like a hawksbill. He never did find those teeth, but he still worries around this little spot of coral, peering under things, looking for them. You look a little meager. You want something to eat? We're heating up some rundown."

Baldwin, who had long been up collecting wood, joined us at the fire.

"I see you met Uncle Weddy. His boys are out checking the nets for turtle; leave the old man here behind to mind the cooking."

"Old man? Old man?" Weddy was indignant. "I'm seventy and still moving better than a youngster like you, 'Bali.' Neither rum nor women have slowed me down. I'm doing the cooking so that those boys don't humbug the fixin's."

Seventy? It was hard to believe. I later learned from Baldwin that Weddy had twenty-six children and had trouble counting his grandchildren. He was as fit a person as I'd seen on the coast. His only apparent weakness was his fondness for chewing tobacco. He always kept a day's supply in his shirt pocket, which was stained a deep brown from tobacco juice leached by rain and sea spray. If he ever ran out of chewing tobacco, no matter how good the turtle fishing was or what the weather conditions were, he'd head for the mainland to buy tobacco, meanwhile cutting out and chewing the shirt pocket as an emergency measure.

I kept taking side glances at Ulic while he fed the fire with dried coconut husks and sun-bleached wood, but as he never did open his mouth to say anything, I wasn't able to confirm Weddy's soldier crab story.

"Snapper. Fresh off the reef this morning. First quality fish. Can't make proper rundown without snapper." Weddy opened the large fire-blackened pot and placed the translucent fillets on top of boiling pieces of manioc, plantain and green banana. After they had steamed for ten or fifteen minutes, he poured out the water and ladled in a sauce he said was made from coconut cream, lime and chili peppers and closed the pot again.

"This is the rundown part. The coconut cream runs through the fish and down to the ground provisions."

We sat and ate while we watched Weddy's sons sail toward the cay from their net sets.

"Two, maybe three, head of turtle." The craft was still 300 yards out, and I could barely see the men. "See how she's low in the water and not swinging cranky like? They're carrying turtle."

Three green turtles: one big male and two medium-sized females. Each was worth about ten dollars if sold to the Cayman Islanders or to the Nicaraguan turtle company that was just starting to buy, but

Weddy said he'd carry the big male to Corn Island to butcher and sell. "The company is going to pay the same price for any turtle over 125 pounds. It doesn't pay to sell the big ones. The Corn Island people crying for meat, not money."

Corn-yellow belly shells were crossed by pierced and tied fins. Sea fresh and salt water damp, their streamlined bodies glistened in the new morning white heat. Tiny thin salt lines and circles marked the evaporating sea moisture. A frayed and bristled nylon line was passed under lashed fins, and each turtle was dragged belly-up to the coral rock-walled holding pen, leaving damp furrows in the beach sand.

High sun. A cloudless sky. Gentle sea swells. We were with Weddy in his boat, three miles from the cay, watching him set turtle nets.

"Anybody can set a net, but only the real turtlemen will catch. This time of the year the turtle start to pack up on the feeding banks, fattening up for the trip to the Bogue. At night they shelter on the shoals. Long Reef here is the spot where I figure a whole school to be tonight."

It took about three hours to set thirty nets. Made of nylon or cotton cord, the black, wide-meshed nets were fifty feet long by fourteen feet deep. Anchored by a single line tied to a heavy coral weight, the buoyed nets hung from the surface like underwater flags, shifting direction with the currents. He placed them on the windward edge of the reef over likely sleeping holes and ledges so as to entangle a turtle when it surfaced for air. Weddy hoped the set was a good one.

"Come first light in the morning, we've got to be here before the sharks. When the sun is up, the turtle start splashing in the nets, and that brings sharks. Last week I started to haul in a net, when a shark hit. Big hammerhead. Like to pull me over. I let go quick when I see that ugly monster. He carried off the turtle and the net . . . little thing like that won't worry shark; he'll burst that net just like string."

That evening, we had turtle steaks, and turtle eggs, roasted turtle flippers, and *callipash* and *callipee* (the two latter in the form of soup—in fact, turtle in every form known to the Mosquito men, who well deserve the name of turtle-men. The turtle conceals its eggs in the sand, but the natives are ready to detect indications of a deposit, which they verify by thrusting in the sand the iron ramrod of a musket, an operation which they call "feeling for eggs."

About midnight, it came on to rain heavily, and continued all the next day, so that nothing could be done. The time was "put in" *talking turtle*, and Harris got so warmed up as to promise to show me what the Mosquito men regard as the *ne plus ultra* of skill in turtle craft, namely, "jumping turtle." He did not explain to me what this meant, but gave me a significant wag of the head, which is a Mosquito synonym for *nous verrons*.

The third day proved propitious, and Harris was successful in obtaining several fine turtles. About noon he laid aside his spear, and took his position, entirely naked, keeping up, nevertheless, his usual look-out. We were not long in getting on the track of a turtle. After a world of maneuvering, apparently with the object of driving him into shallow water, Harris made a sudden dive overboard. The water boiled and bubbled for a few moments, when he reappeared, holding a fine hawk-bill in his outstretched hands. [pp. 110–111]

That night we listened to Weddy's stories of good turtle seasons and bad weather, of the strong women and weak rum in Bluefields after the catch was sold, and of the long months spent each year living on tiny islands—times that really didn't seem long enough when he thought back.

After Weddy and his crew had turned in for the night, Baldwin suggested that we take advantage of what looked like a good low tide and make a run to a reef flat on the windward side of Wild Cane Cay.

I stood in knee-deep water a half mile from the nearest land, on a small coral cay whose palm-ragged silhouette against the night sky provided our only assurance that we were not marooned at sea. Fifty yards away, Baldwin's light swung back and forth, a tiny bright cone moving across the reef flat.

In the darkness we had threaded our canoe through the channels, sand shoals and reefs to this spot. Baldwin stood in the bow, directing with the flashlight and hand signals, while I maneuvered the canoe, running the motor at quarter speed. After an hour we had snaked our way to Wild Cane Cay and the lobster ground. During the day the Caribbean spiny lobster hides under ledges and in caves on the edges of the apron reefs around the cays, coming out at night to feed on the shallow flats at low tide. Armed with flashlights, burlap bags and a cotton glove apiece, we'd come to "torch lobster." They'll freeze for a moment when the light hits them, and if you move slowly into position, holding the flashlight rock-steady until you are crouched right over them, and if you compensate for water refraction, you'll get one try. Grab it just behind the head with a gloved hand to protect against its spine-studded back and antennae. If you miss or move the light, it'll jet backwards and be gone beyond the pool of light. If you manage to grab one, you will have to hold on tight, for in trying to escape, it will buck and snap its body with a strength unexpected in a three- or four-pound animal.

I got two and Baldwin four, which would be sufficient meat to take with us the next day when we headed north.

The tide was changing, so we headed back to where we'd left the canoe. Baldwin stopped, turned his light off and asked me to do the same. "Watch this," he said, and started to jump up and down on the reef flat. Seismic rings of light radiated away from the epicenter, generated by the shock waves from his jumping on the reef flat. The shocks apparently agitated bioluminescent organisms on the reef itself, similar to our experience in Pearl Lagoon. I jumped up and down. More light ripples. We stayed there, jumping on the reef, until the tide raised the waters past mid-thigh and each cold splash further dampened our spirits. It would have been a pretty bizarre sight if someone else had been there to witness the two of us bouncing up and down in the water ten miles from the mainland in the middle of the night.

We woke at dawn to look out on a choppy sea to windward. A fresh breeze whipped at the coconut palms, leaving cowlicks in the fronds. Weddy and the other turtlemen stood at the edge of the cay, toes dug into fine coral sand, hands behind backs, watching for signs of the day yet to come. Weddy, grizzled and seawise, thought the weather was changing for the worse. He was going to pull up his nets to avoid losing any if the winds and currents stiffened.

"Mind you take care on the Squier trip, 'Bali'; the weather's going to come down hard." Weddy paused as he worked the tobacco chew, shaking his head knowingly. "Can't count on April calm anymore, not like first time. Everything changing."

By the time we got clear of the cays and reefs, Weddy's catboat was already a distant speck bobbing over the first net set.

"Those turtle going to have it free and easy tonight," Baldwin said. "No nets on the sleeping shoals and Weddy in camp. That's the good life for a turtle."

Keeping to the route Squier had taken, we went back through the bar into Pearl Lagoon, turned north off Hog Cay, and three hours later had reached Tasbapauni again. It was here that Squier and his companions had dragged their canoe across the narrow waist of land that separated the lagoon from the sea. We arrived about nine-thirty in the morning to find that most of the men and many of the women were gone, away working in their fields, planting. Baldwin went to his house to say hello and to get some fresh bread, while I rounded up a few children to help roll our canoe across the 100-yard-wide haulover. We were anxious to press on, as the wind was increasing in strength and the sea was beginning to look bad. Sando, Baldwin's son, helped pole the canoe through the first beach break into the five-foot-deep *skabrika* gap in front of the outside surf line and then jumped overboard when I got the motor going. The power and size of the breaking surf indicated that we would have a rough trip ahead.

At sea—cays and village far behind, occasional glimpses of the mainland from the crest of a frothed swell, deep water motion to the canoe—we sailed on toward Río Grande Bar. The breeze was picking up. I wanted to reef the sail, but Baldwin said no; he'd rigged a "man rope," a three-fourths-inch-diameter line tied near the top of the mast, forming a crude trapeze, which he took hold of, feet spread on gunwales, leaning to windward, pulling hard on the line and lying almost flat out in the strong bursts of wind. Oftentimes board straight and stiff, his body acted as a human outrigger to offset the keelless canoe's tendency to dip the leeward gunwale into the sea.

> About four o'clock in the afternoon, we came in sight of a knoll or high bank, which, covered with large trees, rises on the north side of the mouth of Great River, constituting an excellent landmark. I was in no wise sorry to find ourselves nearing it rapidly, for the wind began to freshen, and I feared lest it might raise such a surf on the bar of the river as to prevent us from entering. In fact, the waves had begun to break at the shallower places on the bar, while elsewhere the north-east wind drove over the water in heavy swells. The sail was hastily gathered in, and my Indians, seizing their paddles, watched the seventh, or crowning wave, and, by vigorous exertion, cheering each other with shouts, kept the canoe at its crest, and thus we were swept majestically over the bar, into the comparatively quiet water beyond it. Half an hour afterward, the great waves broke on the very spot where we had crossed, in clouds of spray, and with the noise of thunder! [p. 115]

Río Grande Bar. For the last several miles we had sailed against the strong littoral current fed by the river. Brown-water river in the sea, carrying along trunks, limbs, leaves and water hyacinth rafts. The mainland jutted eastward where the river outwash had deposited mud and silt over the years, covered over by plants which helped anchor the river rims against the eroding power of sea and wind. A bar is a place where the river and sea are at odds. Fresh water from thousands of creeks and streams flows into the river channel, each stream adding a little more power and volume to the torrent. By the time it runs out into the sea, it can be an awesome thing—strong currents and eddies, charged with sediment from a huge watershed—with enough force to push out against the power of the sea. Swells driven by winds across long stretches of the Caribbean collide with river currents along the eastern coast of Nicaragua. The result is a cauldron of clashing currents, breaking waves, shifting shoals and channels.

Close to the bar now, we could see the hazy spray corona that covered the entire area. The wind had whipped the seas long enough so that the channels were obliterated under breaking waves. Baldwin took down the sail and stood on the mast thwart, holding the bow line, and surveyed the vaporous scene.

"The small channels are closed out; we'll have to come in the main one," he shouted back and motioned me to head toward the northeast and the channel mouth.

He came back and leaned across the tarp that covered our supplies until he was close enough for me to hear him above the motor sound. "Plenty rough up here, but don't worry; just follow everything I tell you to do. If a wave is going to break, swing off and point back to sea. That channel's going to have some big rollers. Don't rush it. Watch me and go in slow. Let's go now."

About a mile and a half out, the water looked deep enough for us to cut across the mud shoals that lined what we hoped was the channel. It was hard to tell, as small waves and swell crests were breaking all over the place. Heading due west into the distant river mouth, we felt the first of the rolling swells, each one lifting us high up as it passed beneath and sped toward the main. As we got in closer, into shallower water, the swells steepened, their crests toppling over, sending an avalanche of white water cascading down the face. Our canoe suddenly seemed tiny, a small toy against an overpowering, indifferent force that overcame everything in its path. Several times, swells picked up the canoe and catapulted it forward; bow down, the propeller spun free in the foamy crest before catching again. Baldwin signaled to slow down, and each time the swell relinquished its hold and broke ahead of us. Closer inside, the going was even more difficult. A wave crashed just behind us, and a wall of white enveloped the stern before I could turn the sluggish, water-weighted canoe aside. Trying to bail and dodge at the same time, we wallowed through the last breaks and into quiet water.

We headed toward the riverside. Opposing feelings of fatigue and elation, delayed fright and new confidence, overcame me. I spoke to Baldwin in unintelligible sentence fragments, jumbled words that couldn't express thoughts and reactions.

We pulled up at what was left of an old wharf in front of the rusting and rotting remains of Río Grande Bar, the old United Fruit Company town. Tired and achy, I stretched out on the sun-warmed planking. I would have gone to sleep right there if Baldwin hadn't nudged me, offering a cup of still-hot coffee from the thermosful he'd prepared at Weddy's camp that morning. It seemed a miracle that coffee could stay hot during the years I felt we'd passed through since leaving the cays. We dug the boiled lobsters out of the waterproof bag and together finished four of them on the wharf. They were the best food I'd ever eaten.

According to Squier's account, they selected one of the small islands not far from the bar mouth on which to build a temporary camp and wait out a storm. After some debate, Baldwin and I decided that the most likely island was Baboon Cay, named after the common Creole word for howler monkeys, which used to be abundant in this area.

> . . . we dragged the canoe high up on the bank, and while I kindled a fire, my companions busied themselves in constructing a shelter over the boat. . . . So rapidly was all this done, that before it was quite dark the hut was so far advanced as to enable us to defy the rain, which soon began to fall in torrents. . . .
>
> For eight days, it rained almost uninterruptedly. Sometimes, between nine and eleven o'clock, and for perhaps an hour near sunset, there would be a pause, and a lull in the wind, and a general lighting up of the leaden sky, as if the sun were about to break through. But the clouds would gather again darker than ever, and the rain set in with a steady pouring unknown in northern latitudes. For eight mortal days we had no ray of sun, or moon, or star! Every iron thing became thickly coated with rust; our plantains began to spot, and our dried fish to grow soft and mouldy, requiring to be hung over the small fire which we contrived to keep alive, in one corner of our extemporaneous hut. . . .
>
> Finally, the windows of heaven were closed, the rain ceased, and the sun came out with a bright, well-washed face. It was none too soon, for every article which I possessed, clothing, books, food, all had begun to spot and mould from the damp. I had myself a sympathetic feeling, and dreamed at night that I was covered with a green mildew; dreams so vivid that I once got up and went out naked in the rain, to wash it off! [pp. 116–121]

After quickly making camp, we set out to explore the small island to try to locate the spot where Squier might have stayed. It was difficult, for hurricanes and extensive flooding have radically changed the topography of the lower Río Grande and Baboon Cay. The western end of the island is higher than the rest, with a five-foot bank and a small patch of coconut palms affording a campsite. Another likely area is near the island's eastern tip, where someone had made a small agricultural plot containing gourd trees, coconut palms, hone palms, breadfruit and plantains. Except for these two places, the rest of the island is swamp, overgrown with white mangrove, *kowi* trees and various palms.

Exhausted, we crawled under our mainsail tent just as the first rain squall hit. One after another the little squalls came out of the warm sea to the east, moving westward toward the darkened mountain forests. The sail overhead billowed and slapped, and the trees crackled with aluminum foil leaves in the wind that preceded each squall. Then came the rain line, a curtain of heavy drops that advanced noisily across the river; first a hissing, open spigot from the skies, then a brief dull pause as it crossed the grass-lined margin of the island; then came the muted sound of rain on trees, and suddenly it fell on us with the sound and feel of a wet drum under a waterfall. There was a regularity to the timing and the various sounds, as if we had a box seat to a symphony in nature.

"Mr. Baldwin, how much will the river rise if this rain keeps up all night?" I had suddenly recalled Squier's description of being marooned on this very spot.

"Not to worry. We're just feeling a little dampness from the sea. In July and August, when the real rains come, the whole lower coast floods. You'd be under water right now. A real top-gallon flood would make this place part of the sea. That's how it is most of the time, except when we get an early flood."

It was comforting to know that the heavy flooding always occurred later in the year, except when it came earlier. With that thought in mind, I fell asleep.

Silence. It had stopped raining, but it was still dark outside. Why was I awake? I was too tired to be awake. Baldwin was still asleep. Then I heard the sounds. Part human, part donkey bray, there were many and they sounded close. My sleep-drugged mind couldn't identify the sound, and it was so strange, so loud and intense that I was a bit anxious. A few of the older Miskito men had told me about some of the spirits and strange animals that supposedly lived in the forest and had to be treated with a great deal of respect, if not outright avoidance. Their descriptions were too fanciful to believe, but the incredible din outside required some explanation. When one knows nothing about them, one is free to speculate *ad infinitum*. The *waula tara* was said to be a large boa that lived up the headwaters of the streams and made the water level fall by sucking up water. Then there was the *wakumbai*, a spirit rider on a mulelike animal which was considered very dangerous. *Patas* was a spirit that lived in the forest and had a light which lured hunters away from trails and whose beam, if it hit one directly, could cause sickness or death. There was also a mermaidlike animal spirit called *prahaku* that lived in the rivers and lagoons; similar to the *li lamia*, or water tiger, said to live in the sea, it would often tip over canoes and drown everyone aboard. Some very old Miskito had told me about an anthropoid ape, the *ulak*, which sounded similar to the *Sasquatch* of the northwestern United States and was said to be seen occasionally in the forests of eastern Nicaragua. None of the descriptions I had been given of these mysterious spirits and creatures, however, mentioned anything like what I was hearing now.

I nudged Baldwin awake and asked him what was making that noise.

"*Kungkung,*" he groaned in Miskito and went back to sleep.

Howler monkeys. So that was the sound they made. Squier had described them, but even his vibrant account did not do justice to their booming uproar. Identification reduced my fight-or-flight feelings, and I lay back to listen to one of the truly magnificent sounds in the animal world.

> I at first supposed that all the ferocious beasts of the forest had congregated, preparatory to a general fight, and comforted myself that we were separated from them by the river. There were unearthly groans, and angry snarls, and shrieks, so like those of human beings in distress as to send a thrill through every nerve. At times the noises seemed blended, and became sullen and distant, and then so sharp and near that I could hardly persuade myself they were not produced on the island itself. I should have passed the night in alarm, had not Antonio been there to explain to me that most, if not all these sounds came from what the Spaniards call the "*mono colorado,*" or howling monkey. I afterward saw a specimen—a large, ugly beast, of a dirty, brick-red color, with a long beard, but otherwise like an African baboon. Different from most other monkeys, they remain in nearly the same places, and have favorite trees, in which an entire troop will take up its quarters at night, and open a horrible serenade, that never fails to fill the mind of the inexperienced traveler with the most dismal fancies. Notwithstanding Antonio's explanations, they so disturbed my slumbers that I got up about midnight, and, going down to the edge of the water, fired both barrels of my gun in the direction of the greatest noise. But I advise no one to try a similar experiment. All the water-birds and wild fowl roosting in the trees gave a sudden flutter, and set up responsive croaks and screams, from which the monkeys seemed to derive great encouragement, and redoubled their howling. I was glad when the unwonted commotion ceased, and the denizens of the forest relapsed again into their chronic serenade. [pp. 140–141]

After waiting out the long storm on Baboon Cay, Squier and his two Indian companions went up the Río Grande to an Ulwa Sumu village, a day's paddle away, where they spent two weeks as guests. The Sumu were once made up of ten subgroups who spoke related dialects and lived in small interior riverine settlements in eastern Nicaragua and Honduras. Caught between Spanish-speaking peoples moving eastward into their territory and the expanding Miskito population moving westward up the rivers, most of the Sumu tribes became fragmented, acculturated, assimilated or destroyed, so that only three of the ten subgroups still exist. Gone are the Kukra, Bawihka, Yusku, Prinsu, Boa, Silam and Ku. Small settlements, usually very isolated, of Ulwa, Twahka and Panamaka remain, but the Río Grande Ulwa village that Squier wrote about has long since vanished.

> . . . they entertained a feeling of dislike, amounting to hostility, to the Mosquito men. So far as I could ascertain, while they denied the authority of the Mosquito king, they sent down annually a certain quantity of sarsaparilla, maize, and other articles, less as tribute than as the traditionary price of being let alone by the Sambos. In former times, it appeared, the latter lost no opportunity of kidnapping their children and women, and selling them to the Jamaica traders, as slaves. Indeed, they sometimes undertook armed forays in the Indian territory, for the purpose of taking prisoners, to be sold to men who made this traffic a regular business. This practice continued down to the abolition of slavery in Jamaica—a measure of which the Mosquito men greatly complain, notwithstanding that they were not themselves exempt from being occasionally kidnapped. [p. 126]

After going up the Río Grande for one and one-half days and still seeing no evidence of Sumu villages, we turned around and made for Karawala, a Sumu settlement made up of remnant Twahka and Ulwa Sumu who were relocated by missionaries in the early twentieth century near Río Grande Bar not far from Baboon Cay.

Surrounded by Creole, Miskito and Ladino peoples, the Sumu of Karawala are similar to the Black Carib of Orinoco in that they are a small, isolated cultural enclave who were trapped in a small eddy while the mainstream of history rushed by them.

Eyes, sometimes whole faces, peered at us from doorways and cracks in the split bamboo house walls. Silver-weathered papta palm–thatched roofs; mango tree shade patches on the short-cropped grass; big-eared, thin dogs curled and sleeping in the cool, swept dirt under the houses; dry noon heat, too far from the beach for a sea breeze—these were a few of my first observations as we walked into the village, seeing no one but watched by many. Door-to-door questions and hesitant replies finally brought us to the house of Victor Ebraham, the *sindico*, or "Mayor," of Karawala.

Mr. Victor was about sixty, broad and fairly short, with graying thick hair; he wore old denims, a bowling league shirt from a missionary barrel from the States that said SHAY FUNERAL HOME on the back, and old rubber boots, broken and split but mended with copper wire stitching that closed the larger breaks. We sat in the cool of his front room and told him about our trip, Squier, and our fruitless search for the Sumu settlement that Squier had described 120 years before.

"Those back day places are all gone now. Not even the older heads remember. I was just a small baby when we came to live here. The old Indian ways are gone. Everything pass—the banana companies, Empresa Nolan lumber company, 'Kennedy foods'—all are gone now, too. Anything good never lasts long; so when it comes, you better make much of it while you can."

Refreshed by a drink of young coconut water served in blue plastic tumblers, we excused ourselves to resume the trip north. Then I noticed a stone axe head on a wall shelf and asked Victor about it.

"That is a thunderstone. It comes from the sky with the lightning. Very powerful. Very lucky, too," he said reverently.

He was reluctant to discuss the subject, but he finally told us what the Sumu believe about these stones, which I definitely knew to be ancient axe heads. Of celestial origin, they were transmitted to earth by a lightning bolt which buried them seven feet deep in the earth. They then magically worked their way up until they reached the surface seven years later. Victor said that possession of a thunderstone made the finder lucky, protected his house from lightning, and helped cure sickness. One had to be sure, however, that it was a true thunderstone. This could be determined by tying a piece of string around the stone and placing it in a fire. If the string didn't burn, it was the genuine article. I didn't tell him that it was really a stone axe head, possibly made hundreds of years ago by his own ancestors. The old Sumu way of life was long past; Victor had only dim memories of former times, most of which went back only to the economic heydays when foreign companies offered work and commissary goods. For Victor there was hope for the future as a result of finding a magical stone from the heavens; an artifact would bring no luck to an Indian in modern times.

He walked with us down to the creek landing where we had tied up the canoe. I told him I would try to return to Karawala someday to tell him how our trip went. "*Kaltalwaran*"—good-bye—he said as he took the thunderstone from his pocket and touched it to our bow. "*Kaltalwaran*."

> At the end of two weeks, I signified to my friends that I should be compelled, on the following day, to leave them, and pursue my voyage up the coast. I had supposed that there existed an interior connection between Great River and the lagoons which led to Cape Gracias, but found that they commenced with a stream some twenty miles to the northward, called "Snook Creek," and that it would be necessary to trust our little boat again to the sea. [p. 138]
>
> They stood on the bank until we were entirely out of sight. I left them with admiration for their primitive habits, and genuine, though formal hospitality. [p. 140]

Antonio had cut two trunks of the buoyant *mohoe* tree, which were lashed to the sides of our boat to act as floats, and prevent us from being overturned by any sudden flaw of the wind. We passed the bar without much trouble, and made a good offing, before laying our course for "Snook Creek." The wind was fresh, and the water bright and playful under the blue and cloudless sky. I leaned over the side of our frail boat—scarce a speck in the broad breast of the ocean—and watched the numerous marine animals and *mollusca* that floated past. . . .

As the sun went down, the wind fell, and the moon came up, shedding its light upon the broad, smooth swells of the sea, silver-burnished upon one side, and on the other dark but clear, like the shadows on polished steel. We lowered our useless sail, and my companions took their paddles, keeping time to a kind of chant, led off by Antonio, the Poyer boy joining in the swelling chorus. The melody was very simple, and, like that of all purely Indian chants, sad and plaintive. I have often thought, in listening to them, that they were the wails of a people conscious of their decay, over a continent slipping from their grasp, and a power broken forever! [pp. 142–144]

We sped toward the end of the river, the mahogany hull slicing through the first chop, wake flat behind, sea and bar calm ahead. We paused momentarily in front of the first bar break. Standing in the bow, fresh wind whipping and ballooning his shirt, Baldwin counted the seas.

"*Kaisa*"—let's go—he cried, and we bounced, skittered and churned from crest to crest over the low waves and swells, the small rooster tail fountain in the wake changing from the root-beer-float color of aerated river water to seltzered lime phosphate as we hit the open Caribbean again.

"Did you feel the shoal?" Baldwin yelled above the sound of the motor.

I shook my head no. We had long ago passed the bar and were in deep water.

"Turn around then. Turn around and go over it again," he said and pointed toward the way we had come.

I turned the canoe in a short arc, stern down, prop digging into the water, bow up, swinging across the eastern horizon. This was ridiculous. Why did I have to know how to "feel a shoal"? We'd obviously passed over it, probably with several fathoms to spare.

"What do you feel now? A shoal?" Baldwin looked at me intently.

I couldn't detect any difference in the movement of the canoe, but I said yes, it was the shoal—anything to get on with our trip northward; anything to get away from running in circles.

"No, this isn't the shoal. We already passed it again. Turn

around." I think Baldwin was perturbed, but he didn't show his disappointment in my inability to find the shoal.

We went up and down that short stretch of coast half a dozen times. The bottom must have been at least ten fathoms, and that tiny shoal, a little bump in the underwater topography, couldn't have been closer to the surface than five or six fathoms.

"Feel the shoal. Feel the shoal with the canoe. We're right over it now. Pay attention to how the sea feels. Now turn around and try again."

I'd long since given up trying to take a bearing on the mainland to use as a marker for that shoal. The coastline above Río Grande Bar is low, and the beach and palms go on monotonously. I'd have to find the shoal Baldwin's way. School was back in session again.

Finally, after I had stopped thinking how impossible it was to locate an underwater bump and started tuning in to the minute differences in the canoe's roll and pitch that telegraphed shallow water bottom conditions, I found the shoal and began to feel the sea in a way that was several degrees more sensitive than anything my empirical background had prepared me for.

As we headed up the coast once more, Baldwin came back to me and said, "That's your shoal now. If you can find that one, you'll find the others." He didn't have to yell for me to hear him this time.

The sun was low in the western sky, and we had to hurry to reach the creek mouth before nightfall. I ran the little Evinrude at almost full throttle, and the bow smacked into the swells, throwing out sheets of water that the wind caught and blew back, bathing us with warm sea water. Momentarily suspended, the droplets hung before the wind and then dissolved against me like liquid marbles. By the time we had sighted the creek outlet, my eyes were blurred and stinging from the salt spray. Because it was hard to see the channel in the dimming light, I just pointed the bow into the lines of small breaking surf and hoped for the best. The canoe bumped over one sand shoal and hesitated on another; the motor jumped up and down as the foot hit bottom. We passed awkwardly over the last of the sand shoals, the canoe and motor digging a channel through it.

Through all of this, Baldwin had remained silent, letting me handle what turned out to be a pitiful landing. I muttered some sort of weak excuse about my salt-water-stung eyes and the twilight, but he just looked at me impassively.

"You couldn't see the shoal at sea, but you found it. You could have felt these sand shoals, too. Next time run alongside the break until you feel and see the channel; then make your cut in. Let's get someting to eat now."

I got a fire going, and Baldwin cleaned and roasted the mackerel he had caught trolling while we circled over the shoal. Nearby were some bushes heavily laden with ripe cocoplums. The scarlet-skinned fruit is about the size of a small plum, with a white interior; a dry, slightly astringent taste; and a wet cotton-wool texture. Flavored with an herb Baldwin picked from the beach scrub, a simple sugar syrup poured over the hot, boiled cocoplums yielded a poor man's serving of *icacos*, a famed dessert of tropical Latin America.

Cleaning and checking our equipment was a daily chore regardless of weather or fatigue. The sun, salt water and rough handling could quickly damage camera and film and the engine, despite manufacturers' claims. Already my waterproof exposure meter was broken, the needle frozen on "f 11." Baldwin took off the fiberglass motor cover and rinsed the salt off the motor with a couple of gallons of our drinking water; he cleaned the sparkplugs with an old toothbrush and a little gasoline. I washed off the Nikonos camera with fresh water, changed film, and cleaned and lubricated the rubber O-rings. Exposed film was kept in small waterproof cans, with lids that pressed shut, similar to one-pound pipe tobacco cans. Each can also contained a perforated tin of silica gel, a desiccant that periodically had to be dried out; we heated the tins in a frying pan over the campfire, cooled them in another sealed can, and then replaced them in the film containers. It took at least two hours a day to do this and to inspect the rest of our equipment and food containers for leaks.

The wind had died down and the smoke from our fire rose straight into the night sky. Sand flies. Swarms of them. Without the sea wind to contend with, they descended on us en masse. Clouds of thick smoke from hastily gathered sea grass and green leaves thrown on the fire helped little. So small that they can easily pass through mosquito net mesh, sand flies inflict a powerful bite which leaves a tiny red spot that itches for days. They were in our ears, eyes, noses and mouths. We rolled up in blankets, not even chancing a crack to breathe through, and abandoned the campsite to the sand flies. My body radiated heat from the long day in the sun, and the blanket was unmercifully hot and suffocating, but that was not enough to prompt me to leave the protection of my wool cocoon and face the sand flies.

The sea was calm, its surface flat. A cloud bank on the horizon diffused the early morning sunlight. Dark water from the mangrove swamp gently flowed through the creek channel and into the sea in one continuous sheet of glass-smooth water. A tarpon rolled lazily in the creek mouth, its large scaled body sending out ripples that broke the calm. Air. Fresh sea air, unfiltered by damp blankets, free from swarms of sand flies.

We drank coffee and ate the last of the stale bread, which had a strong taste from the coconut oil that was turning sour.

Snook Creek gave us access to the inland water route of rivers and lagoons that parallel the coast for many miles. We planned to stop at Kuamwatla, a Miskito village, for some food and fresh water and to see the place where Squier and his companions had been forced to flee and fight, killing some of the villagers in the process. I hoped the impression of that visit had faded with time.

> The village was very straggling and squalid, although the position was one of great beauty. It stood on the edge of an extensive savannah, covered thickly with coarse grass, and dotted over with little clusters of bushes, and clumps of dark pines, more resembling a rich park, laid out with consummate skill, than a scene on a wild and unknown shore, under the tropics. As we advanced, I observed that the huts were all comparatively new, and that there were many burnt spots, marked by charred posts and half-burned thatch-poles. Among the rubbish, in one or two places, I noticed fragments of earthenware of European manufacture, and pieces of copper sheathing, evidently from some vessel. . . .
>
> . . . I did not like the general aspect of things. In the first place, there were no women visible, and then the ugly customers with the guns and spears, when not scrutinizing me or my revolver—which seemed to have a strange fascination in their eyes—were engaged in a very sinister kind of consultation.
>
> The head man seemed particularly anxious to know my destination, and the purposes of my visit. My suspicions had been roused, . . . I thought the opportunity favorable to fall back to the boat, now fully convinced that some kind of treachery was meditated. A movement was made to intercept me at the door, but the presented muzzle of my revolver opened the way in an instant, and I walked slowly down to the landing, the armed men following, and calling out angrily, "Mer'ka man! Mer'ka man!" Antonio stood at the top of the bank, with my gun, his face wearing an anxious expression. He whispered to me hurriedly, in Spanish, that half a dozen armed men had gone down the creek in a boat, and that he had no doubt the intention was to attack us.
>
> . . . I at once saw that there was but one avenue of escape open, namely, to take to our boat, and get away as fast as possible. . . . I brought my gun to bear upon them, determined to fire the instant they should manifest any overt act of hostility. They seemed to comprehend this, and contented themselves with running after us, along the bank, shouting "Mer'ka man!" and pointing their weapons at us, through the openings in the bushes. . . .
>
> . . . I counted this a lucky escape from the village, but was not at my

ease about the party which had gone down the creek. I felt sure that they were in ambush in some of the dark recesses of the banks, and that we might be attacked at any moment. . . . We had reached the darkest covert on the creek, a short distance above its junction with the river, when a large canoe shot from the bank across our bows, with the evident purpose of intercepting us. At the same instant a flight of arrows whizzed past us, one or two striking in the canoe, while the others spattered the water close by. I at once commenced firing my revolver, while Antonio, seizing the long manitee-spear sprang to the bow. At the same instant our canoe struck the opposing boat, as the saying is, "head on," crushing in its rotten sides, and swamping it in a moment. Antonio gave a wild shout of triumph, driving his spear at the struggling wretches, some of whom endeavored to save themselves by climbing into our canoe. I heard the dull *tchug* of the lance as it struck the body of one of the victims, and, with a sickening sensation, cried to the Poyer, who had also seized a lance to join in the slaughter, to resume his paddle. He did so, and in a few seconds we were clear of the scene of our encounter, and gliding away in the darkness. [pp. 149–155]

Squier later learned the reason for his impolite reception in Kuamwatla. An American ship, the *Simon Draper*, had run aground and was wrecked at the mouth of the Prinsapolka River. Her surviving passengers and salvaged goods were discovered on the beach by the Miskito of Kuamwatla, who took them back to their village and helped themselves to some of the spoils and the personal effects of the passengers. Fearing worse treatment, the crew and passengers made a "preemptive strike" against the village and burned it down before a ship from Greytown (San Juan del Norte) rescued them.

"*Meriki man. Meriki waikna aula.*" "An American man is coming." A young boy peered over the bluff at us as we paddled the last fifty yards of shallow lagoon to a small landing below the village and announced our arrival to the community which was still out of sight.

We half-crawled up the steep and slippery path from the beach and were immediately surrounded by what must have been the entire population of Kuamwatla. A man stepped forward and welcomed us to his village. Apparently either Squier's story was fiction, or their oral tradition didn't go back that far. Whichever the case, everyone appeared delighted at our presence and extremely interested in why we had come. The village is isolated enough that few visitors pass through, so our sudden arrival presented sufficient reason for a community meeting that night. We were invited to attend.

In response to our request to buy some food and fill our water containers, Mr. Leonardo, the man who had welcomed us, said simply, "It will be done."

For the rest of the afternoon, we had to politely fend off people who wanted to give us presents of food—bunches of bananas, plantains, yams, coconuts, manioc, pineapples and mangos—in quantities that would have filled our canoe several times over. We tried to accept a sample of all that was offered, but when it came to the pineapples and mangos, the choices were simply too numerous; there were so many varieties, colors and shapes that the mind boggled. Previously, pineapples and mangos were something I'd encountered only at the exotic fruit section at the supermarket. The pineapples were always hard and acidic and the mangos soft and stringy. Not these. The pineapples were all juicy and sweet, but each had a different taste. There were *risris*, hawksbill, carib, big eye, black, sugar and *karapitka* pineapples. Some were snow white on the inside, while others had a dark, almost black fruit. There were even more varieties of mangos: common, hard, hairy, Jamaican, Auntie Rich, Number 11, turpentine, hog, cow foot and sugar. Some had the taste and aroma of blossoms; one tasted of turpentine; another was so tart that eating it was like sucking on a vitamin C tablet. I sampled a bit of each; this placated our hosts and gave me the rare opportunity to attain a gourmet merit badge for maximum taste variety with minimum bulk in the category of tropical fruit.

That night everyone gathered in the church. Kerosene lanterns were lit, and Mr. Leonardo stood up and asked us to tell about our trip. I did the best I could with disjointed phrases in Miskito, and Baldwin filled in and elaborated. No one could recall the wreck of the *Simon Draper* or of ever having heard of Squier's visit to Kuamwatla. In fact, their collective historical perspective seemed to go back no further than the 1920s and 1930s when foreign missionaries and businesses began to expand into the area. Baldwin and I were seeking a point in their history which had long been erased by a new ideology and economics. With Baldwin again helping to translate, I spoke of the history of the Miskito people based on material that I'd dug out of old books and journals before coming to Nicaragua. I related descriptions of the Miskito in the early seventeenth century by such buccaneers as William Dampier, Raveneau de Lussan and Alexandre Exquemelin. I talked of the alliances of the Miskito with pirates, the raids and fights against the Spanish, the English settlement and control of the coast, the establishment of a Miskito king, the nineteenth-century treaties, and the transfer of the coast's political sovereignty from England to

Nicaragua. There were many questions and debates and much laughter among the villagers. The lamps had to be refilled; young children went to sleep; and we talked on into the early morning.

Hoarse and exhausted, we finished at last, shook hands with everyone still awake, and got ready to go to bed. The last couple of hours had been sheer torture for me, and I told Baldwin I had to go outside to relieve myself.

"Use the missionary back house; they built it for *Meriki waikna*," Baldwin said, and he directed me to the single outhouse built out over the lagoon.

It had started to rain, so I took one of our umbrellas—luckily, as it turned out, the big, heavy made-in-China one. Built on shaky pilings, the wet, slippery, narrow wooden walkway became increasingly unstable as I inched farther out toward the outhouse, which was perched ten or twelve feet above the lagoon. There was a large bump on the walkway between me and my destination. At first I thought it was a cat, but it was too fat and low for a cat. A rat. The biggest rat I'd ever seen. A world-champion-size rat that wanted to go the way I had come and seemed to be getting a little edgy about being cut off. We stood there awhile in silent confrontation, yards above the water on foot-and-a-half-wide planking, too narrow for us to pass. There was no way that I was going to let that rat inch by me, and it evidently had similar reservations about my passage. It was one of those moments that hang suspended in the air as clear and long as the note of a bell. If anyone else was watching, it must have been an absurd scene: the foreign visitor, wearing high-top tennis shoes and shorts and standing in the night rain with umbrella, frozen on a tightrope by a common rat. Our respective urges for opposite destinations finally reached critical mass, and I used the only weapon at hand, the stout umbrella, to chip-shot the rat off the planking; I lofted it into the lagoon, where it landed with a thin splash. Either the tide was out, or it hit close to the beach; I tried to remember on which side of the outhouse we had left the canoe.

"There are some big rats in this place, Mr. Baldwin," I gasped when I had hurriedly found my way back to where we were to sleep after making sure I wasn't followed by a revengeful rodent.

After I had related the Kuamwatla rat incident, Baldwin observed that Squier hadn't mentioned big rats in his description of the village. "Things changing, Mr. Barney. In back times rats were few. Nowadays, the same quality rat is big and manish."

The next morning the wind had stiffened, and sporadic squalls drove lacy rain curtains across the lagoon. Crouched under plastic ponchos, we left Kuamwatla and the people who'd come to see us off. As we went out into the lagoon, the village began to lose colors; the people on the beach merged into a small thin huddle; the shapes of houses and trees blurred; smoky wisps of rain obscured the last good-bye waves.

Baldwin surmised that it would rain all day and we would have a hard time finding the inland creek channels through the mangrove north of the Prinsapolka River. If we were going to get wet anyway, we might as well go out to sea and bypass the mangrove until the next river bar at Wounta.

"The Prinsapolka Bar is the worst one on the coast, and it'll be a little nasty today, but you should have the experience," he said and went back to the bow.

I thought I'd rather take our chances in the mangrove, where the worst thing that could happen would be to lose our way. And even if we did, which was unlikely, we could always sleep in the canoe. Then I remembered Baldwin's story about the time he had spent a night in the swamp, submerged to his neck in the muck and water to escape the mosquitoes. If they were anything like the Snook Creek sand flies, then it was the open sea for me, too.

Prinsapolka is a small, rusting, rotting, near-ghost town located just inside the bar on the west shore of a small peninsula that divides the sea from the river waters. At the turn of the century it had been a boom town, called the "Gateway to the Mines." It served as a supply center and port for material and gold ore shipments from the upriver mines at Rosita, La Luz and Bonanza. A large store, now deserted and decaying, was once the Silverstein and Kitting Company, its shelves filled with goods from New Orleans and New York. The La Luz and Los Angeles Mining Company dealt in gold ore and mahogany lumber. The Standard Fruit and Steamship Company started cultivating bananas for export in 1934, the same year that Taca Airlines began a weekly flight to the town. By the late 1930s banana diseases, logged-out mahogany reserves, much-reduced gold production, and the occasional loss of a ship or cargo in the treacherous river bar mouth were signaling the decline of Prinsapolka. On September 19 and October 23, 1940, two severe tropical storms hit the Prinsapolka area, destroying what was left of the banana plantings and wrecking the town. Since then the forest had overgrown former banana plantations, and wind, rain and tropical rot had destroyed surviving structures in the town until only a few sagging and tilting buildings remained to mark the evaporated visions of foreign speculators. A few people hung on. But they, like their town, were old. Economic refugees from another era, they waited for the second coming, when the companies would return and the boom days would be reborn.

We stopped long enough to poke around and get some information on the lay of the bar and the side channels, which are continually shifting position.

The bar looked dangerous. But I was no expert; it was my first look at what everyone agreed was the most hazardous river bar on the coast. Baldwin said he'd seen it much worse. I was glad I hadn't been with him then.

The broad, swift river ran into a sea edged with breaking, muddy-white surf. Visibility was poor, but it appeared that the surf was breaking in a continuous crescent that enclosed the river mouth, one set after another, so that white water ran for at least a half mile out. The horizon was obliterated by close-in storm clouds whose gray walls touched the sea. The clouds hid the heaving swells until they suddenly erupted from the vaporous base to roll, steepen and collapse against the underwater silt and mud bulwark built by the river.

Leaving the silent green forest wall behind, we drifted with the river, motor slowed down just to permit steerage. Baldwin held up his hands, palms a couple of inches apart, facing each other, and then pointed at the bar. The swells were closely spaced; the fetch was short from crest to crest. We went over the first swells, which had already broken once and re-formed. They were easy. Conditions soon worsened, however. At the entrance to the bar, the swells were higher and closer, so that after we had cleared one, the bow was still down when the next one steepened to break. By the time we had worked halfway out of the bar, we'd already had some close calls and taken in some water.

We were right in midchannel, almost through the swells, when Baldwin suddenly jumped back from the bow to shift the canoe's center of gravity. Too late. The bow was down, and the wave wall was going to break on us. I twisted the throttle grip full on; the prop dug; and the canoe plunged through the top third of the wave just as its crest fell over us. For a split second we were inside the curling wave, covered by a ceiling of sea water. The break hit me full in the chest and submerged the engine; it immediately started to sputter and cough until only one cylinder was firing. Baldwin signaled for speed to move out before the next set of seas rolled in. Getting no response, he turned around, and I gave him a one-shoulder, arm-bent, palm-up shrug, the universal signal that I could do nothing; it was beyond my control. Baldwin immediately began to paddle, and paddle hard. The way he was moving that paddle telegraphed his conviction that the next set of waves would be real trouble. With the canoe riding low in the water, already partially swamped by that one wave, with the motor "put-putting" like an old Lister diesel, and with Baldwin paddling at the speed of a steam turbine, we lumbered sluggishly through the rest of the bar.

Beyond the mouth of the Prinsapolka, Baldwin turned around again. "That was about as close as you can get and still come away," he shouted through cupped hands.

I guess he was right, but the emotional impact of our close call hadn't hit me yet. I was curiously detached from the entire experience, as if the camera in my mind had backed away from the scene and was aloofly recording the almost-tragedy.

Later that afternoon the weather cleared, the sea calmed, and the wind died down to a gentle breeze. The April dry was finally here.

We entered the inland waters at Wounta Bar, and as we traveled northward the dry-season weather improved. Rivers and lagoons became clearer; clouds disappeared from the sky; and the riverine forests and marshlands began to dry out.

North of the Río Grande the coastal lowland vegetation changes from rain forest to increasingly open patches of savanna. It is almost surreal to be in the humid tropics—an area that receives 100 to 150 inches of precipitation yearly—and see a grass and pine savanna. We often tied up along a creek or river bank and cut our way through the thick vine-tangled forest corridors that line the water courses. We would emerge suddenly onto a vast savanna that looked and felt like a huge golf course: rolling grass-covered terrain, stands of pine on ridges, and clumps of papta palms in the humid depressions. In some areas the savannas stretch away endlessly until the yellows and greens of the grasses and pines merge to dark gray on the distant horizon. After days of travel through confining mangrove swamps and rain forest–lined rivers, it was an amazingly different feeling to be on an open savanna where space and horizons exist. In the forest and swamps one's conception of space is confined to the vertical, from the water's surface and up the tunnel walls of dark green vegetation that enclose the channels. The savannas evoked a feeling of freshness and openness similar to that experienced at sea in a canoe with a steady breeze and an occasional glimpse of the beach from the crest of a rolling sea.

> It would be difficult to find on earth any thing more beautiful than the savannah which spread out, almost as far as the eye could reach, . . . Along the river's bank rose a tangled wall of verdure; giant ceibas, feathery palms, and the snake-like trunks of the *mata-palo*, all bound together, and draped over with cable-like *lianes*, (the tie-tie of the English,) and the tenacious tendrils of myriads of creeping and flowering plants. Unlike the wearying, monotonous prairies of the West, the savannah was relieved by clumps of acacias—among them the delicate-leaved gum-arabic—palmettos, and dark groups of

pines, arranged with such harmonious disorder, and admirable picturesque effect, that I could scarcely believe the hand of art had not lent its aid to heighten the efforts of nature in her happiest mood. [p. 211]

A maze of forest-rimmed meandering rivers stood between us and our next destination, Puerto Cabezas. Serpentine water courses made one mile of progress actually take four or five to cover.

The forest was quiet in the summer heat. Sunlight permeated everything. Colors grew more intense; edges hardened and sharpened in the bright glare. Perspiration dribbled through the hat band dam, trickling salt into squinting eyes. Hot sunglass frames warmed across nose and forehead. Headaches developed from the high-pitched motor whine, exhaust fumes and water-reflected sun glare. The Kukalaya River, blurred by the outboard drone reverberating off green walls, became fogged-in-mind images. We passed by the area where Squier had spent six days weakened and feverish from malaria. We walked along banksides where one of Squier's Indian companions had been bitten by a fer-de-lance pit viper. No wind. Heat. We pushed on, ignoring Squier's descriptions, longing for the sea again. We traveled more rivers: the Slim Slim Bila, Wark Wark, Wawa, and finally a narrow creek to Lamlaya, a small inland anchorage five miles south of Puerto Cabezas with access to the sea via the Wawa River.

Puerto Cabezas, the second largest coastal town in eastern Nicaragua, is the market center for the economically depressed northeast coast. Once a thriving town of sawmill and lumberyard workers and Standard Fruit and Steamship Company personnel, its population grows smaller each year as Miskito and Ladino workers and their families move away, migrant refugees from another economic bust. The pattern repeated. Millions of stems grown and shipped and then banana diseases and company pull-out. Hundreds of thousands of pine trees cut by foreign companies and millions of board feet exported from the mile-long wharf until the pine runs out and the yards and mills close.

In Puerto Cabezas we purchased food, fresh water and gasoline and sent them back to Lamlaya in a broken-down taxi. We had left the canoe in the hands of a watchman who had looked with disdain at the tiny craft, dwarfed by numerous freight boats tied up two and three deep alongside the crumbling wharf. I wanted to send a telegram to my wife and son back in Bluefields, but the generator at the *Radio Nacional* in Puerto Cabezas was broken, so we were directed to the home of Dr. Ned Wallace, who ran the Moravian hospital.

Ned and his wife Emily had operated the hospital for ten years, and they'd become something of a medical legend on the coast. After using their radio to send a message to Bluefields, we accepted an invitation to stay for dinner. It was a very special occasion for us: a grand dinner without any taint of the wood smoke taste and smell that had permeated everything Baldwin and I had cooked, a long talk into the late evening about our trip and what we could expect to find farther up the coast, and hot showers and freshly made beds.

Because we were in a rush to get off, Ned and Emily drove us down to our canoe. Ned gave us a small box of medicine, aspirins, vitamins and ointments for various cuts and sores and asked if we would dispense them along the way wherever we thought they were most needed. Doctors or medical supplies were seldom seen on the upper coast. He also gave us a case of canned Metrecal meals, three flavors, which we accepted even though they seemed out of place on a trip by canoe through mangrove and Caribbean waters. Crazy. As it turned out, we depended on that Metrecal for food several times when rain or fatigue prevented cooking.

Twelve settlements make up what is collectively known as Big Sandy Bay, located on a low, marshy savanna. Scattered 300 to 1000 yards apart, each of the villages is situated on a small low hill, the only elevations in the area. A network of wooden bridges and elevated walkways interconnects many of the villages, which become islands in a shallow inland sea during the rainy season. Then communication and transportation are by canoe or walkway only. At the time of our visit, the dry season, the creeks connecting the villages and the lagoon were low, and exposed mud and sand banks interrupted our passage so that we had to get out and drag the canoe over some of the shallows. It took four hours to traverse the creeks two miles inland to where we could see the settlements.

Hunger. The upper coast was experiencing a severe dry season, and the fields had become parched and the crops were dying. Most of the men were out on the Miskito Cays, forty miles off the coast, turtle fishing. Food supplies in the villages were low, many families subsisting on green coconut water and the jelly interior mixed with corn starch and green mangos. A stingray speared in a creek mouth was half devoured by young children and women while an old man was butchering it.

The turtlemen would sell their catch to one of the last of the Cayman schooners that for more than 100 years have journeyed south to set turtle nets and buy turtles from the Miskito. A Nicaraguan turtle company was also said to be buying. One of the villagers told us that there were at least 400 turtles out on the cays, penned in mangrove-stick crawls. Practically all of these would be sold, and the Big Sandy Bay men would return to their villages rich with money, but they would find little food to buy. The shelves of the three small Chinese-run stores were almost bare, and no supplies had been ordered from Puerto Cabezas.

With almost no other alternatives for earning money, many of the coastal Miskito have concentrated their efforts on catching green turtles from the Caribbean's richest turtle grounds, which center on the Miskito Cays. Traditional activities can no longer produce what is most desired—money—so the men catch turtles for market to make money to buy food and goods.

One man, too old now to go turtle fishing, told us that the turtle were getting hard to catch because they were hiding.

"Anything that's valuable gets scarce. Bananas, crocodile, tigercat [ocelot] and work—all those things are scarce now, like the turtle. The turtle know we're looking for them, and they move off. They're hiding."

From what I'd seen and read so far, the turtle were scarce not because they were hiding or more elusive, but because they were being killed off in unprecedented numbers. They were becoming an endangered species, and commercial exploitation would hasten their demise. But turtle fishing had been a major source and way of life for the Miskito of Big Sandy Bay for hundreds of years. It was inconceivable to them that something that had always been abundant could be depleted. Historically, the Miskito had little experience coping with inadequate resources. Now, however, they were caught between their traditional ethic of plenty and the new reality of shortages.

The old man informed us that there used to be a rock in the shape of a turtle located in the bar mouth leading to the Sandy Bay Lagoon. This rock, called the Turtle Mother, had magical properties. According to Miskito myth the Turtle Mother was a benevolent spirit that acted as the intermediary between the world of animals and the world of humans. When the turtles were moving in close to the mainland to nest on the beach or to feed in the shallows, the rock would swing around and point westward. When the turtles were to move out into deeper water around the cays, the rock turned and pointed toward the east. Besides foretelling the movement of turtles so that humans could more easily catch them, the Turtle Mother also could increase success by controlling both a person's luck and the movement of the turtles. If, on the other hand, an individual or the community did not observe specific taboos and thus restrict exploitation by taking only what they needed and wasting nothing, the Turtle Mother would send the turtles far out to sea beyond the reach of the turtlemen and also cause their luck to turn bad. The Turtle Mother then symbolically balanced relationships between humans and turtles. The belief in the Turtle Mother made the Miskito responsible for maintaining prohibitions against overkill; individual greed would bring retaliation to all through the magical removal of the turtles.

The Turtle Mother story had been told to Baldwin when he was young, but it was all but forgotten on the lower coast. Here in Big Sandy Bay—which along with Old Cape was the cultural hearth of the Miskito—the story had been kept alive, yet no longer did it influence Miskito behavior.

"The turtle used to play around the Turtle Mother rock, thick, packed up close like ants. But my people killed too many, and they moved off, and the Turtle Mother moved, too—went down to Turtle Bogue in Costa Rica. That's the place the turtles lay now. The Turtle Mother didn't want to mess around with that money business. That's why the turtle is scarce today."

The old man gazed across the savanna in the direction of the sea. An occasional puff of sea wind drove ripples across the long grasses to break in invisible waves against the dry island where we sat.

A hummingbird hovered nearby, its long needlebill inserted into a brilliant blood-red flower, its iridescent blue-green body sparkling sun specks—a thousand tiny mirrors. The bird hung suspended in the warm air. The moment held. Then, abruptly, it was gone, darting away to fly eastward toward the forest that rimmed the sea.

The coastal Miskito villages of eastern Nicaragua lie adjacent to one of the world's major green sea turtle grounds and one of the largest sea-grass pastures, where the herbivorous animals feed. From what I'd been able to read in historical accounts and had seen on our trip, the Miskito had long depended on sea turtles for subsistence. Much of their culture, their livelihood, and their diet was predicated on the availability of green turtles. Turtles served many social and cultural functions; they were not just meat to eat. They provided the main symbolic material for exchanges among kin and between the sexes, and their capture by men and preparation by women signified the transformations from nature to culture, from the sea to human society, from the male to the female sphere—those symbolic transformations which were part of the Miskito's interpretation of their place in the cosmos.

The Miskito had been selling part of their catch to Cayman Islanders, whose schooners for years had visited the turtling grounds twice annually to capture turtles and to buy them from the Miskito. We had heard from customs officials in Puerto Cabezas and from the Miskito that the Nicaraguan government had withdrawn the Cayman Islanders' fishing privileges, and their current visit to the Miskito Cays would be their last. At the same time, two turtle processing companies were starting operations, one in Puerto Cabezas and the other in Bluefields, and they would purchase turtles from the Miskito.

I wanted to talk with some of the turtlemen about this to find out what they thought these changes would mean to them and to their patterns of turtle fishing. If the turtle fishery was to be further commercialized, I wanted to know the Miskito's interpretation and the ultimate impact on their society if they did indeed plan to sell most of their turtles to the new companies—as seemed to be the consensus in Big Sandy Bay. If this was true, there would be major problems ahead, for their need to make money would conflict with the traditional use and significance of turtles. Since all of the turtlemen were out to sea at the time of our visit to Big Sandy Bay, it would be necessary for us to go to the Miskito Cays if we wanted to talk to them.

Approximately one-third of the distance to the edge of the vast continental shelf, whose shallow waters, myriad coral reefs, and extensive turtle grass pastures comprise an optimum habitat for marine turtles, are located several mangrove-covered coral cays, collectively known as the Miskito Cays—the center of Miskito Bank. Baldwin had been to the area once many years ago, and he readily refreshed his memory with the help of some of the old turtlemen, now retired, who sketched the location of reefs, channels and cays with sticks in the dirt. The turtlemen wouldn't be camped on the cays themselves because of sand flies. Instead we were to locate two sand shoals: one due west of Big Miskito Cay, called Whipling, used by turtlemen from Auastara and Dakura; and another, northeast of the cay, known as Sukra, used by the Big Sandy Bay men. At these two places we would find the turtlemen camped in houses built over the shoals.

We left early the next morning. Normally it takes twelve to fourteen hours for the turtlemen to sail out because of the prevailing trade wind and the strong currents. We used the outboard, and four hours later we arrived at the Sukra camp. The descriptions hadn't prepared me for the spectacle. There, forty miles from the mainland, the horizon empty except for the tiny smudge that was Big Miskito Cay eight miles away, was a neat, orderly row of houses. Constructed of lumber and poles carried from the mainland and thatched with palmetto leaves from the cays, the little houses were built on pilings sunk in the hard sand shoal. Because tidal ranges in the Caribbean are not large, the elevation of the houses varied from two or three feet above the water level to a maximum of six or seven. Tied up to each of the stilt houses were two or three catboats, the type of sailing craft used by the Miskito of the upper coast. It gave an eerie feeling to pull up to one of the camps, tie up, and then walk into a house that had a 360-degree view of the sea.

We were greeted warmly, and as soon as the men in the camp learned that we'd just come from Big Sandy Bay and brought news and messages from their families, they called out to their next-door neighbors, and the word was passed on down the line. Soon all the Big Sandy Bay turtlemen had pulled up in their catboats. Some managed to squeeze onto the tiny wharf, and the rest, perhaps fifty or sixty, stayed in their boats. There wasn't enough room for all the boats in front of the wharf, so they were spread in a circle around the entire house, gunwale to gunwale, a marina in the round. We couldn't speak loudly enough for everyone to hear because of the breeze and the sounds from the boats slapping together and against the pilings, so we spoke to the men at whose house we had landed. They relayed the information to the men packed on the wharf, who in turn passed it to the men in the boats in the first row; and from there the news went mouth to mouth around each side of the house to those in the back. If perfectly timed, I suppose the men in the center boat at the rear of the house could have heard the news in stereo; most likely they got conflicting information, however, after it had passed through so many people. Since few of the men spoke Spanish or English, and since my broken Miskito inputs only exacerbated the noise-to-signal ratio in the communication circuit, I soon shut up and let Baldwin handle everything.

With little to do but observe, I started to watch the circular information network as messages from those at the head of the wharf traversed the human coil. It suddenly struck me that the center rear boat crew were playing an amazingly important yet subtle role as the keystone in the arch. With the same original information being passed to them from both directions, variations and extemporaneous additions were certain to amplify the content. These men had to recognize their position in the chain and filter out the original news from conflicting messages. If they didn't, and passed on information from the men on the right to those on the left, and vice versa, then the system had a good chance of running for a long period, independent of the new inputs, for each information lap would transform the original message into a new one, on and on, *ad infinitum*.

Watching and thinking about this made me realize that herein was part of the key to understanding the apparent inconsistencies between social rules and actual behavior that I'd witnessed in Miskito village life. Now this needs a bit of explaining, for it might not be readily evident how I arrived at this conclusion from watching a daisy chain of turtlemen. First of all, it had become obvious to me after living in Tasbapauni that many people's behavior did not conform to the stated or mutually understood social rules; in fact, individual acts and failures to act often ran 180 degrees counter to the rules. For example, everyone was to share meat, when he had it, with close relatives, but many did not; at least village gossip claimed they didn't. Similarly, promiscuity among married men and single and married women was not supposed to occur according to the "new rules" laid down by the various mission churches. But it did, as was obvious from the number of "outside children" in the village and the variety of who-was-with-whom stories frequently circulated. Other discrepancies existed between what should happen and what actually occurred in social and economic transactions involving giving, borrowing, loaning and stealing.

In a small society such as the village of Tasbapauni, or any other relatively closed traditional village, everyone seems to know everything about everyone else. However, the information system is constantly suffering from information overload, for not only are stories of everyone's behavior readily shared, but much of the information is false. Therefore, the signal-to-noise ratio is close to 1:1. The system is overloaded with truth and falsity, and it is extremely difficult for one individual to maintain a clean behavioral slate in the face of rampant accusations of misdeeds. Eventually everyone will be blamed, whether he did it or not. Gossip acts as positive feedback; it loops truth and falsity back through the communication system and validates assumed behavior by repetition rather than by verifying what might have been the actual behavior. Therefore, if the system is overloaded with truth and falsity, and you'll probably get blamed for it anyway, you can get away with a great deal.

This gets us back to the rear center boat crew. Judging from the gossip I overheard as it passed and changed from person to person, if it weren't for that one crew, the information would reach critical mass in the social accelerator, and there would be an exodus of some very angry people back to Big Sandy Bay.

Food supplies in the house where we were to spend the night were running low, so we pooled some of our tinned goods, and we all dined on hot johnnycake, rice and beans, Metrecal beef stew, and heavily sweetened coffee (Baldwin was particularly pleased with the latter, as he claimed that when I made the coffee it was too "brackish").

Late afternoon calm—wind down, sea glassy gray. Catboat and canoe tugged on mooring lines, then drifted in to knock against wharf pilings until the gentle current caught them once more and their lines snapped spring-taut. One man repaired his torn net, tying and splicing-in new diamond meshes made from nylon cord, black from soaking in tar and gasoline. Baldwin read Squier's book; the rest of the men slept. Embers from the midday meal's fire grew white beards as they cooled on their thick ash bed in a cut-off oil drum. The day's catch had been average: three turtles among the six men who were our hosts. Untangled and reset over coral shoals hours ago, their nets drifted with the current, waiting for the nightly return of the turtles from sea pastures.

I examined one of the catboats at the edge of the wharf. The design was the same one used by the Cayman Islanders for the turtle-fishing boats they carried on board their schooners. The hull was about twenty-six feet, tapering sharply at both ends, and it had a four-and-a-half-foot beam and a shallow keel. Empty, the catboat had one and a half feet of freeboard. These boats were fast sailers, stable and capable of carrying a heavy load. There were thirty of them from Big Sandy Bay; most of them had been built by Peter, a retired Caymanian turtler who lived in Kaka, one of the Big Sandy Bay villages. He had told us that it took three months to build one with the help of an apprentice. A single boat required 450 board feet of mahogany for the planking—so finely fitted that no caulking was used—and 45 yards of cloth for the jib and mainsail. These catboats were beautiful pieces of workmanship. They were also expensive for a Miskito: labor and materials cost $450, which, added to the price of turtle nets—$250 for materials for thirty nets—meant a significant investment for a Miskito turtleman.

Darkness. The strong, harsh smell of cheap Valencia cigarettes hung in the calm. More coffee.

The Cayman turtle schooner was soon due back from the southern cays. Some of the men had been away from their villages for two months or more. They wanted to sell their catch and return home. They had heard rumors that this might be one of the Cayman Islanders' last voyages to Nicaragua for turtle. In the still summer sea they waited and slept and talked while the end of the past approached.

Two men who spoke English discussed their expectations for the future as I listened.

"The company people say they'll treat us better than the Caymonsmon. Every week one of their ships will come right here for the turtle . . . won't have to wait for the schooner. They are going to come every week, too; not just once or twice a year."

"I say never trust a Sponmon. They going to rob us for sure. Captain Allie and those other captains treat us good. But the Sponish push them out. Now we left with what? You think dealing with Creole and Sponish going to make we Indian come up in the world? Sponiard? No, papa, Indian don't consort with them."

"That's foolish talk. Who you going to sell your turtle to now if not the company? All the money comes from turtle. If you don't feel to sell, then how you going to make it? No work in this country. . . . everything coming tighter . . . everyone wants to live off money. You'll catch and sell."

"That's to you. Things running on the new plan now, not like when the real companies were here. Those days there was plenty of work, cutting banana, cutting pine, mahogany. Full time. Can't fish turtle like that."

"Company going to get rich again. When company come, you've got to make your move. When leave off, everything go blank. They not going to look for you then."

"You think you can catch money? Turtle change over to big money something. These hours they all pack up on the far shoals, trying to keep away from turtlemen. They know about company."

Their loud remarks attracted the rest of the men, and the discussion continued in Miskito. Every so often Baldwin translated some of the best parts, especially those comments that brought hoots of laughter. No one viewpoint was agreed upon. There was no arbitration, no consent, no yielding. Perhaps the only consensus was that they really didn't have much choice in whatever was going to happen.

The next morning we headed back for the mainland and Big Sandy Bay Bar. The light breeze was too weak to get any speed by sailing, and there was a pervasive smell of exhaust and gasoline. Dark and light blue of water and sky seesawed up and down as the swells rolled. With no wind or spray to keep us cool, the sun baked our backs. A man-o'-war bird glided on sharp black wings in the hot, cloudless air. A shark's dorsal fin moved close by, gray and ominous in the azure waters. A mako. The thin land line grew larger, darker, and more ragged as we neared the coast.

Passing easily through the bar, we followed the long, sinuous mangrove creek to the lagoon and turned north.

> By morning we were clear of the lagoon, and in the channel leading from it to Wano Sound, lying about fifteen miles to the northward of Sandy Bay, and half that distance from Cape Gracias. We reached the sound about ten o'clock in the morning, and stopped for breakfast on a narrow sand-spit, where a few trees on the shore gave shade and fuel. The day was excessively hot, and we waited for the evening before pursuing our voyage. [p. 230]

Wani Sound is the old name for what today is called Bemuna Lagoon, after the Miskito village located at its western edge not far up a small creek. We stopped at the settlement, hoping to talk to one of the last of the Miskito shamans, an old woman whose powers were known the length of the coast, but she wasn't there. She was said to be out on a "mission" to the Río Coco. The savanna to the west of the village grew hot in the sun, and the air hung warm over the yellowing grasses. We felt dulled and lethargic and soon said good-bye to the growing group of people who had gathered to hear of our trip. Near the bar mouth we made camp on a small beach and refreshed ourselves with coffee, mangos from Bemuna, and a view of the sea. We rose before dawn to pack and ready the canoe for the last sea leg to the Cape. We left with the first light and headed NNE out to sea, rather than follow the curving coastline.

The Cape at last—dead ahead, the bow bobbing up and down on the point. Baldwin's inertial guidance system had once again brought us across a long stretch of water to our exact destination.

> Cape Gracias a Dios was so called by Columbus, when, after a weary voyage, he gave "Thanks to God" for the happy discovery of this, the extreme north-eastern angle of Central America. Here the great Cape, or Wanks River, finds its way into the sea, forming a large, but shallow harbor. It was the favorite resort of the buccaneers, in the olden time, when the Spanish Main was associated with vague notions of exhaustless wealth, tales of heavy galloons, laden with gold, and the wild adventures of Drake, and Morgan, and Llonois. Here, too, long ago, was wrecked a large slaver, destined for Cuba, and crowded with negroes. They escaped to the shore, mixed with the natives, . . . with subsequent additions to their numbers from Jamaica, and from the interior. . . . Supported by the pirates, and by the governors of Jamaica, as a means of annoyance to the Spaniards, they gradually extended southward as far as Bluefields, and at one time carried on a war against the Indians [Sumu], whom they had displaced, for the purpose of obtaining prisoners, to be sold in the islands as slaves.
>
> But with the suppression of this traffic, and in consequence of the encroachments of the semi-civilized Caribs on the north, their settlement at the Cape had gradually declined, until now it does not contain more than two hundred inhabitants. The village is situated on the south-western side of the bay or harbor, not far from its entrance, on the edge of an extensive, sandy savannah. [pp. 234–235]

We relaxed prematurely after crossing the shallow bar mouth. The Miskito settlement of Old Cape was visible on the other side of the two-mile-wide lagoon, so we located a minuscule channel that meandered toward the village and started across it. The tide was falling, and the canoe touched bottom after we had gone but a quarter of a mile. We could have waited for the tide to rise, but the sun was so hot that we decided to try to relocate the channel. That was a mistake; we should have gone back to the bar mouth and waited on the beach. The farther we went, the shallower the water got: twelve inches, six inches. . . . We heeled the canoe on its side and dragged it by the bow line. Then we had to unload the gasoline containers to lighten the canoe, carry them ahead one by one, drag the canoe up to the gas, carry the gas ahead, and so on.

A swirl of sand and water and then a winged wake erupted just in front of my bare feet.

"*Kiswa*," Baldwin muttered. "Mind where you walk. Plenty *kiswa* here."

Stingray. I didn't feel like walking much farther. Every step was filled with the anticipation of stepping on a stingray and having a two-inch-long barb slapped into my foot. The water was too murky to see anything, so every time I moved forward, it was with a gingerly probe that fully expected to land on the back of a partially buried stingray. After two more near misses I stopped and asked Baldwin why the rays were always on my side.

"Maybe they like white feet."

It was time for a new plan. Wearing tennis shoes which quickly filled with gritty sand that felt like crushed lava, I sloshed ahead, swinging a paddle from side to side in the mid-shin-deep water to clear a path through the stingray mine field. They were all over the place. I'd blaze a trail for about fifty yards and then carefully retrace my steps to where Baldwin waited. We then hauled the gasoline and the canoe to the end of the stingray-free corridor. For every fifty-yard advance toward the village, I walked 250 and Baldwin 150. In the Lagoon of the Stingrays, the man with tennis shoes walks farther.

Old Cape was once the Miskito cultural center. It was here that French and English buccaneers made the first prolonged contact with native peoples in eastern Central America. Traders and merchants later came to barter cloth, machetes, knives, axes, saws, nails, fishhooks, cooking pots, glass beads, rum, gunpowder and muskets in exchange for hawksbill shell, green turtles, dried turtle meat, sarsaparilla, gums, chinaroot, indigo, canoes and paddles, annatto, and silkgrass. English support and guns made the small Miskito population disproportionately powerful, and they began to expand their territory and influence. Their population grew rapidly from the capture of Sumu women and children; large canoes—each carrying twenty or more armed men—made raids along the Caribbean coast as far north as Yucatan and south to Panama. By the eighteenth century the Miskito dominated much of the western Caribbean and were the major deterrent to Spanish settlement along their western flanks. After a series of treaties and agreements among England, Spain, and later Nicaragua, the expansionist Miskito were contained, and they subsequently became a primary source of labor for foreign enterprises.

Old Cape made a profound impact on Baldwin. He had never been this far north before, but he had long heard descriptions of the "old Indian ways" from his parents and grandparents. To him Old Cape was the symbol of "first time Miskito." This was where the real Miskito people lived, where "real Miskito" was spoken rather than the adulterated language of the lower coast, which was liberally sprinkled with English and Spanish words and phrases. During our stay he spent most of the time comparing the way of life in Old Cape to that in Tasbapauni. In a way he was doing an ethnographic survey of his own people. He sought to validate his childhood memories, to compare village histories, and to immerse himself in stories from the "older heads" about former times.

Old Cape still followed many of the traditional Miskito values, beliefs and customs. Subsequent economic boom and bust cycles had largely bypassed the village, which was once the focus of cultural contact with Europeans. The nearby lower Río Coco was too shallow for larger boats to pass; miles of river-delta mangrove and swamps almost encircled the village. Their only contact with the outside was via twice monthly trips to Puerto Cabezas for supplies in exchange for animal skins and for the sale of rice, bananas, plantains and pigs. Food was abundant. The people lived largely on crops they grew on their narrow beach plots—rice, manioc, bananas, corn, sugar cane, sweet potatoes—and fish from the lagoon and inshore waters. They hunted ducks, white-tailed deer and paca with .22 rifles. Turtle fishing was infrequent and done for subsistence only. It was too far to go to the turtle grounds, and the returns were so poor that only a few of the men still bothered with it at all. Other than one small store where dry goods from Puerto Cabezas could be purchased, there was little cash-based exchange in the village. Food and labor were exchanged among kin and friends.

Old Cape was a cultural outpost for the coastal Miskito, much like Karawala for the Sumu and Orinoco for the Black Carib. Pirates, traders and the foreign companies had come and gone, and the turtles were far off and scarce. To Baldwin what remained were the old ways. At Old Cape not only was the past not dead, it wasn't past.

Almost 600 people lived in the narrow, half-mile-long village. Most houses were of split palm and bamboo, thatched with plaits of *kaka* palm. A few were open-sided, their interiors sparsely filled with hammocks and mosquito nets, a stool or two, an old calendar from a Puerto Cabezas store, a homemade wooden suitcase, cooking utensils, a stem of green plantains or a bunch of *supa*. The smell of cooking fish. Strips of meat drying in the sun—provisions for the meatless rainy season ahead. Tamarind, orange, breadfruit and mango trees. Groups of men, women and children returning in canoes from clearing new fields across the lagoon. River and sea canoes and four catboats in thatched waterfront sheds. An old man poles a long, narrow river canoe toward the village from the small channel that connects the lagoon to the Río Coco. A woman sits in the stern, steering with a paddle, a cloth tied around her head, a pipe in her mouth.

This was as far as we would go retracing the route Squier had taken. After leaving Old Cape, he traveled up the Río Coco for several days and then went north by canoe and foot across Honduras to the Caribbean again.

Baldwin believed that a storm was coming, and some of the men agreed with him. The dry season usually lasts well into May, but no one is sure about the weather anymore. Still, it was too early for the heavy rains to begin. If there were a storm, it shouldn't be too strong.

We decided to keep to our plan and leave the next morning. Another mistake.

The sky to the south and southeast was black. We were going to go directly into it. At this time of year a severe storm was rare, but when one came out of the southeast, it meant trouble. We decided to try to make Puerto Cabezas, where we would stay with the Wallaces and wait it out. If we had had a radio, we would have heard the warnings: tropical storm, stiff winds, all boats seek shelter.

I wondered if the Big Sandy Bay turtlemen were still camped out at Sukra. If so, they were in for some really bad weather.

The next hours were wet hell. Only Baldwin's dexterity in refilling the almost-empty gas tanks kept us from turning over or swamping. In those winds and breaking seas, paddles would have been useless. The motor gave us enough steerage and power to avoid the biggest seas. It was dark by the time we got to Puerto Cabezas; but despite the name, there is no port or harbor other than the long wharf.

The beach was dark and probably closed out by heavy surf, but it was land, and we were tired. There was no use counting the seas, trying to pick a pause between sets, for there were no pauses. We came in close to the beach; a big wave broke just ahead, and we followed behind the break in a kamikaze landing on the beach.

We waited three days in Puerto Cabezas for the storm to pass and the sea to calm down.

After some 1,000 miles, several weeks filled with refreshing and rewarding experiences, some bizarre incidents, long stretches of tranquility and close companionship, we arrived in Tasbapauni. Happy with how the trip had worked out and proud of the canoe, we put on something of a show before landing on the beach. We made a few runs along the beachfront just outside the surf line, cutting a figure eight, surfing partway in on some small waves and then pulling out just before the beach break. By then a crowd had gathered on the beach near Baldwin's canoe shed, and after a few near wipe-outs in the surf, we thought it best to land before we blew our grand entrance by capsizing.

Baldwin was home. We were surrounded by people. At first they looked incredulous that we had returned, and then Baldwin was overwhelmed with embraces from his family, handshakes and questions. Those who had been the most skeptical said they had known all the time that we would make it.

Well into the night, Baldwin recounted the trip place by place, emphasizing details about how people lived, what they ate, and what plants and animals he'd seen. I was too tired to contribute more than an affirmative grunt now and then. I fell asleep on the floor in his front room, waking the next morning covered by our mainsail. Even though I had a cot and blanket in the next room, Baldwin hadn't wanted to wake me, preferring instead to allow me to sleep hard under the sail as we had so often slept on the Cape trip, as if he didn't want it ever to end. I still have that sail, and in restless, landlocked moments I sometimes take it out to look at the travelogue of stains, and smell the sea and the trip once again.

> Gradually my thoughts recurred to the past, and I could hardly realize that but little more than five months had elapsed. . . . And yet what an age of excitement and adventure had been crowded in that brief space! I felt that I had entered upon a new world of ideas and impressions, and wondered to think that I had lived so long immured in the dull, unsympathizing heart of the crowded city. It was with a pang of regret that I now found myself drifting upon a civilization again. A few days would bring me to Belize, where I knew Antonio would leave me, to return to the fastnesses of his people. Where then should I go? [p. 327]

Early the next day we got ready to leave for Bluefields. Although Baldwin had been away from home a long time, he still wanted to finish the trip with me.

Many things happened as a result of the trip to the Cape. Baldwin gained much that was personally important to him, but he also lost much, too. Because of the close relationship that had developed between us, his position in the village was never the same again. Many people thought that from our friendship I would make him rich. Thus, he became the object of jealousy. Sometimes he was cut out of socially based, noneconomic exchanges involving communal labor or gifts of food. Rather than freely give with the implication that he would reciprocate in kind when needed, people often asked him to pay for things with some of the considerable sum of money I was supposed to have given him as a "reward" for making the trip. It was no use denying it; few would believe him—or me, for that matter. It was something that he coped with quietly. It saddened me to think that in helping me, he had ended up with strained and envy-filled social relationships. This was something he had to live with, while I could leave with what I had gained from Baldwin.

While Baldwin's social stature in the village was decreasing, mine was increasing. Tales of my supposed exploits circulated with so many extemporaneous additions that it often became pop theater.

Through it all, Baldwin and I became even closer. Once in a while, late at night, we'd sit on his porch, the sea breeze stilled but the feel of the Caribbean still fresh, and talk of our trip to the Cape. Those were private moments. The things we shared and relived, the perceptions gained and reexamined, and events that happened but were never related, these have been kept between us. Much of our journey to the Cape was never finished.

Two years later, on September 9–10, 1971, hurricane Edith hit the upper coast. The village of Old Cape was wiped out. Many people were killed; all their crops and fruit trees were destroyed. The same hurricane killed six Big Sandy Bay turtlemen who were out at the Sukra camp just north of Big Miskito Cay. We later learned that two of the men with whom we'd stayed at Sukra died in the hurricane; their bodies were never found.

Mr. Baldwin and the author share memories of their 1969 trip to the Cape. Tasbapauni, 1975. Photo by Judith Nietschmann.

3. Tracing Drift Coconuts

Seventy-five yards from the beach, just at the edge of the first surf break, an almost-submerged coconut bobs and rolls in the water. Borne by currents and winds, it has drifted from an unknown source, perhaps far distant—or not so far—until by random chance it has arrived near a mainland shore. It is a self-contained, long-distance drifter. An impervious green skin shields it from marine elements; its thick, fibrous husk provides positive buoyancy; and its well-protected seed can retain germination powers for several months.

Closer to the beach, a large swell catches the coconut and sucks it into the water wall as the wave form builds and breaks and sends the husked flotsam into foam-speckled shallow waters. Each breaking wave carries the coconut a little closer to shore. Stranded partway up on the beach by the ebbing tide, it glistens and dries in the tropical sun. That night a full-moon spring tide and wind-generated heavy surf carry the drift coconut high onto the debris-strewn beach, beyond the limit of normal wave reach. It has finally come to rest on the eastern shore of Nicaragua after an uncharted journey.

Lodged in loose sand at the edge of wind-sheared cocoplum and sea grape thickets, long trailing runners of beach morning glory, and strand-line rows of domesticated coconut palms, the sea-fresh pioneer is tenuously established in its new environment. Days of wind, rain and hot sun pass, and the young green colors fade to earth brown.

The coconut is a self-potted plant. Some four months after it falls and drifts from its parent tree, a leafy shoot may emerge from the dark brown desiccated husk while the roots continue to grow inside. If undisturbed, the roots will eventually break through and start to anchor the palm to its new site.

Coconuts are extremely adaptable, thriving under difficult conditions where other pioneer species would perish. Sun-loving, they do well in constant winds, salt spray and impoverished sandy soils. A dense root network provides secure anchorage. Yet even with their capacity to float long distances, germinate and become established in marginal environments, drift coconuts and natural means of dispersal are believed to be responsible for only a small part of the world's coconut-fringed tropical beaches. The vast majority were deliberately planted by humans, from ancient voyagers to contemporary cultivators.

The morning after a strong storm, the drift coconut has disappeared from the beach. Damp sand and sea flotsam mark where storm waves undercut the beach berm, scalloping cutouts in the margins of strand-line vegetation. Carried out to sea again before it could be anchored, the drift coconut may soon be washed up on another shore by tides, winds and currents. Its brief spell on this beach left no indication that it had ever passed this way.

In the Miskito language a drift coconut is called *kuku awra*, a term that is also used to refer to any foreigner who has come to their shores. Vagabonds, transient visitors, culturally and economically displaced persons are all *kuku awra* to the Miskito. These people suddenly appear from unknown places, transported by chance and strange fates, to lodge with the Miskito. Most stay but a short time before drifting on to another place. Yet these drift coconuts leave a wake, a trail and memories. And even though only briefly established on Miskito shores, they take with them something, too. The vacant place on the beach is unmarked; the images and reflections are carried away.

Since 1968 I have made several research trips to eastern Nicaragua along with my wife and son. We have studied the Miskito subsistence economy: how it was, how it is changing, and the consequent impact on its social and economic relationships; agricultural, hunting and fishing productivity; diet and nutrition; use of resources and impact on fauna and flora; and the effects of economic inflation and out-migration on village livelihood. We have also spent a good deal of time studying sea turtles—their behavior, ecology and exploitation. In turn, the Miskito have studied us and drawn their own conclusions—thankfully still unpublished.

It takes a lot to surprise the Miskito, but then we often did a lot of surprising things. Equipped with scales of various shapes and sizes, we weighed food crops, food in the pot, and food just before it went into their mouths. It's amazing that they put up with us. With tables and chemicals we analyzed water, food and soil samples. We caught and purchased what to the Miskito were valuable sea turtles, weighed, measured, tagged them, and then let them go. We brought big aluminum cases filled with gear: still cameras, underwater cameras, 16mm cameras and videotape cameras. Things were weighed, photographed, categorized and filed.

Questioners gave questionnaires to questionees: household budgets, household composition, births, deaths, social relationships, and the like. Back home, copious field notes were cross-indexed, tabulated, key-punched, fed into computers; significant relationships were analyzed and conclusions drawn. But what we really learned isn't contained in the books and papers that resulted from this research. For the first time I'm going to try to tell how it really was.

The first Miskito Indian I talked with was about forty-five years old; he had been eyeing me curiously as I walked up the trail to his village. The little diesel boat that had brought me from Bluefields had pulled away from the landing and chugged off across the lagoon. I gathered up my belongings and cautiously navigated the muddy path. Sitting on the porch of the first house in the village, legs swinging back and forth, the man watched my every move and to my embarrassment, every slip I made in the mud. I was apprehensive about meeting the Miskito and wanted the first encounter to be socially correct. I wanted to explain to someone in authority, a respected leader in the village, why I had come to eastern Nicaragua and why I would like to visit this particular village.

"How is it?" I asked him, using the Creole phrase for hello.

"Right here," he answered impassively.

"That's good. Tell me, where can I find the oldest man in the village?"

"Oldest man? Oldest man? Oldest man, him dead!"

I cherish that moment. It was one of the many philosophical rewards of living with the Miskito. I wrote about that encounter some years ago, but I didn't learn until recently that the Miskito of that village had also recorded that first meeting as part of their own verbal chronicles.

I ran into my first Miskito on a subsequent trip.

"So you come again, Mr. Barney."

"That's right. How is it this time, Mr. Clemente?"

"Fine. Right here, same as always, life spare. You still looking for the oldest man?"

Studying the particular topic at hand is the easiest part of doing field research. What is difficult is to reorient your cultural load, establish some sort of perceivable role, and maintain body, mind and equipment. It is impossible to prepare for the many cultural, philosophical and psychological challenges to your preconceived notions of doing fieldwork. One must cope with frequent frustrations, blind alleys, misgivings, disenchantments, boredom, startling contradictions, and unexpected setbacks. Nor can one prepare adequately for the specific problems that will be encountered: how to deal with a situation in which a person who you thought was your "good friend," the personification and embodiment of the "noble savage," is really cultivating an economic relationship aimed at acquiring the watch your parents gave you for graduation; how to maintain and repair exposure meters, cameras, typewriters and additional discipline-related mechanical contrivances upon which your research depends but whose reliability factor is nil outside of the place of purchase; or how to live in a fishbowl where privacy doesn't exist, where your every act, mistake and relationship is immediately known by all, and strange explanations for what you are really up to are manufactured and disseminated with great imagination and speed.

Providing for cooked food, transportation, good health and occasional private moments creates the most time-consuming and frustrating problems involved in field research. But one quickly learns to adapt and cope and persevere. There are other things more bothersome.

Living in the rainy tropics right next to the sea, as we did, brings with it a host of small-scale challenges. You soon discover that you have been raising secret zoos and gardens. All leather materials quickly begin to sprout greenish fungal patches, and cockroaches delight in living in and dining on the insides of radios and tape recorders. In the high humidity books start bowing and ballooning; writing paper takes on the structural rigidity of a wet dishcloth; envelopes self-seal; hinges rust and separate; cameras turn into expensive paperweights; and clothes are always damp and mildewed.

During most of the year, too much water is the problem, but the opposite is true during the short dry season. Then, the wells run dry, and available water has to be carefully and judiciously used. For example, I learned how to do the following with the same three cups of water: brush teeth, wash hair, sponge bathe, and shave. There is a secret to this, involving split-second timing, taking out a cup of water at one stage and adding it later, and exercising great restraint so as not to look at the water. These are but insignificant nuisances. They give character to a place and make every day a little bit more interesting. I often think I miss them.

There were two things I will never miss. I didn't cope with them very effectively, nor did I ever adapt to them. I believe that much of my inability to become accustomed to these things results from strong childhood impressions left from reading about the rat torture in Orwell's *1984* and about the pigs running things in his *Animal Farm*.

Every house in Tasbapauni has a few rats living in its thatch roof. There in the thick palm fronds they burrow, cut tunnels, raise families, and do other rat things. During the day they are usually quiet, confining themselves to the safety of their elevated perches. Nighttime is another thing entirely. They scurry about—apparently playing tag—squeak, search for food, and generally take over the house. Every so often their enthusiasm exceeds their ability and they slip off one of the narrow poles that cross-brace the roof. This is why I don't like rats. The second night I spent in a Miskito village coincided, unfortunately, with the "Rat Olympics" held directly overhead. I listened to their activities for a while, but fell asleep partway through the jousting event, in which two rats run headlong at each other from opposite ends of a rafter pole. A sudden heavy thump on my chest awakened me, and I looked down to see a groggy three- or four-pound rat clenched to my T-shirt, staring back at me, whiskers at my neck, heart racing in its warm rodent body. Dazed and frightened, it held desperately to the cotton cloth, resisting my efforts to roll it off. I couldn't take the T-shirt off. Envisioning a death lunge at my throat, I took the only alternative left: panic—sheer, unadulterated, glorious, screamy panic. The rat departed.

The room I slept in was only seventy-five yards or so from the beach, and the sea breeze was strong enough to keep mosquitos away, so there was no need to sleep under a net. Nevertheless, I did from then on, just to keep the rats off. Every so often, a rat would fall, hit the net, and scamper down the sides. It happened often enough that I began to wonder what was happening in other houses. I decided to do a study.

A house-to-house survey revealed that although there were plenty of rats, they seldom fell. I began to feel singled out. Perhaps the rats enjoyed the trampoline I'd put up for them.

Various people told me they'd noticed an increase in the number of rats. They complained that some of their cats died after each visit by the SNEM malaria personnel (Servico Nacional de la Erradicación de Malaria), who sprayed the houses with a solution of DDT, water and kerosene. Cats are extremely sensitive to DDT; in their constant preening and cleaning they had probably ingested small but deadly amounts of the insecticide picked up from around the house. Fewer mosquitos and less malaria also meant fewer cats and more rats.

Several weeks later I went to clean out the rain barrel we'd been using for drinking water, only to discover a complete rat skeleton at the bottom.

I started to take a definite dislike toward rats. I sent to Bluefields for large spring traps and passed them out to all who wanted to reduce their household rat population. I experimented with various baits and found that the best was guava jelly. Some Miskito remember me only from those spring traps and guava jelly. My first tangible role in the village was as a rat exterminator.

The anti-rat campaign was fairly effective, enough so that one Miskito family got mad at me. From their point of view, it was a case of "just when you really need a rat, you can't find one"; and they couldn't find a rat because of me. The reason they wanted a rat was that one of their children had whooping cough, and rat soup was a surefire cure for it. I tended to disagree, but they would have none of it. They wanted a rat. A live one. I checked my rat-frequency map of village houses and suggested they try a particular house not far from theirs.

After all furniture had been taken out and placed on the grass, a platoon of young children armed with sticks and brooms came into the house. The mother and father of the sick child then began to beat and poke the thatch roof with long poles, driving the rats from their lairs down the walls to confront the gantlet of child-held, poised sticks. After a great deal of running about, everyone yelling instructions, children colliding with one another, near-misses, a rat was finally cornered, dispatched and handed to the grateful father.

To make rat soup, you need a freshly killed rat. The first step is to singe the hair in a wood fire and then scrape the remaining charred hair from the body with a dull knife. Next, place the rat at the edge of the fire but not in it. Slowly turn the rat until a clear oil begins to collect on the skin. Scrape this off and save (you'll get about one-half to one teaspoonful from the average-sized rat). Now the carcass can be eviscerated, cleaned, and chopped into one-inch pieces. Place the meat in a pot of boiling water over medium heat, and cook until it's reduced to a thick soup. Before serving, float a few drops of the rat oil on top of each portion.

Later the parents told me that the soup had worked; the child had recovered from their diagnosed whooping cough. If so, then rats can't be all bad after all.

Pigs posed a more personal problem for me. There were many pigs in the village: young ones that ran in packs and large ones, 100 to 175 pounds, that sometimes roamed by themselves and other times grouped together for safety and cooperative ventures. Few of the pigs were penned despite the complaints of non–pig owners; pigs simply eat too much for a family to supply all their food. Instead, they are allowed to roam at will, feeding on whatever they can find. They are free-foraging, self-maintaining bank accounts. The Miskito keep pigs not to eat, but to sell.

A full-grown pig is a valuable animal. Buyers from Bluefields often come to "look pig," and a big pig can be sold for as much as fifty dollars. A Miskito is quick to sell a pig for money, but he won't eat it, even in times of severe meat scarcity. This is because a pig is worth too much money to eat and because pigs are rather indiscriminate foragers. To the Miskito not only is a pig a dirty animal; its meat is also considered unclean. When they sell a pig to a Spanish-speaking buyer, they are happy to get the money, but they may grin and wink a bit more than would be expected over just another economic transaction. That's because they know the pig's feeding history and its ultimate fate: the restaurants and family tables of what they consider unsuspecting Bluefields folk.

I was most repulsed by pigs' dining habits. There were only three outhouses in the village, all built under the direction of different missionaries for the "mission houses" where they stayed during visits. As visitors ourselves, we were offered the use of one of the nearby outhouses. For this we were grateful, as one of the most difficult things we were trying to adapt to was the nocturnal scheduling of Miskito toilet habits. Ready access to an available toilet is so common in our society that we were quite unprepared for a different waste regime among the Miskito. One went at night either on the beach or in the bushes. If mischance should befall you during the day, it was a long, exposed walk to the bushes. That's why we were happy for access to the outhouse, which served as an emergency safety valve during our time of adaptation.

It was because of the outhouse that I became interested in pigs. The outhouse was about twenty-five yards from where we were staying. Built in the style of all Miskito buildings, it stood on wood pilings some two feet off the ground. This elevation, I soon discovered, offered some protection from more than just the wet ground during the rainy season.

An accidental discovery soon became a testable hypothesis: pigs can tell the difference in your intent before you reach the outhouse. For the sake of the more puritanical readers, I will use the common euphemisms to illustrate this: number one (N1) and number two (N2). If our intent was N1, the roaming pigs displayed no interest. However, if it was N2, they came running. They seemed to be able to tell from within five or ten yards of our walk to the outhouse. And pigs are fast; they'd beat us there, crawl under, and be waiting. Some would stand on their hind legs, snouts thrust through the wooden hole. That was a bit disconcerting for two reasons: somehow they were able to decipher our body language, and they aggressively infringed on the sacred private sphere. I began to try to fake them out. I imitated what I thought was a good N2 walk when it was really an N1 mission. Nothing. Oh, perhaps a grunt or two from one of the larger pigs and a halfhearted trot from a young one, but nothing of any consequence. Try as I might, they never fell for a fake walk. Unerringly, they knew the difference.

To cope with their amazing discriminatory ability, each of us devised different defensive strategies. I made a club, a "pig stick," one and one-half inches in diameter and two and one-half feet long. With this I could strike from within the outhouse and inflict enough damage to discourage pig congregations for periods of up to five minutes, especially if I added my loud imitations of aggressive pig sounds. Judi hit on an alternative strategy. She posted me outside the outhouse as "pig guard." I'd go ahead of her, carrying the pig stick, and signal when the field was clear. It was my job to keep the pigs at bay. Our son probably coped with the situation best. He fancied himself a bombardier and enacted modern versions of *Thirty Seconds Over Tasbapauni*.

One night I brought up the pig problem to David McCallum, the Anglican priest in the village. Our sentiments on the situation coincided exactly. In fact, at the time, he was answering a letter from his church in the States that had inquired if there was anything he needed. His reply was concise and to the point: "a pig-proof privy." He got it, too.

I finally decided to follow the pigs rather than have the pigs follow me. Anything is grist for the inquisitive mind. I took notice of their group behavior and dynamics, their home and foraging ranges, and their territoriality. The thing that interested me most was their foraging patterns and range. During the day, the pigs concentrated on the village itself, making sweeps in small bands around every back kitchen, where refuse and vegetable wastes were thrown at fairly predictable times. Their only competitors for this food supply were chickens. Pigs fared poorly, however, when competing with dogs for waste from butcherings of turtles, deer and other wild animals. The dogs took the best; and the rest, which wasn't much, was up for grabs between turkey vultures and pigs.

The periphery of the village was one of the most important foraging zones for pigs. Surrounded on three sides by bush-rimmed forest and on the other by the beach, the village edges were used by the Miskito as nocturnal dumping sites. Pigs patrolled these areas at dusk, two or three times during the night, and in early morning. During these times, most of the pigs continually circled the village, around and around on the Tasbapauni Beltway.

Pigs make the major contribution toward keeping the village clean, but turkey vultures, dogs and chickens also help; consequently, waste materials do not last long on the ground; there are no waste disposal problems. All organic debris are recycled. The

Miskito have no problem with cans, bottles, papers and the like, because these items are rarely used—and even more rarely thrown away. My still-unpublished study came to the conclusion that pigs were the most important consumers in the detritus chain. Despite my squeamish feelings about pigs, they were obviously effective garbage engineers, providing a valuable service for the villagers that was ecologically and economically sound. They made day and night pickups, didn't belong to a union, never went on strike, were extremely efficient, and could be sold before retirement age.

Displayed on the wall was an odd but insightful collection of paper images from afar: old and new calendars given away at Christmas by Chinese merchants in Bluefields, one showing a Vargas-like girl with a bottle of Coca-Cola and a cocker spaniel puppy; another depicting a white middle-class American family washing a 1955 Buick; ads and pictures from old *Time* and *Life* magazines, the recycled flotsam left by shrimp boat captains, missionaries and itinerant academics; a 1961 *Farmer's Almanac*, dog-eared, hanging by a string from a rusty nail; and a collection of photographs and postcards, neatly mounted and framed, positioned in the center of the wall, all the rest relegated to secondary importance, mere contrast to the central point of interest. There were snapshots of a benevolent-looking priest who must have been uncomfortably hot in dark suit and clerical collar in the humid tropics; people lined up in front of houses, standing rigid in front of the camera; a white ship at a wharf; a woman and child building a snowman; a man and child walking in the snow; the New York harbor skyline at night; a schoolboy class photo. Faded, some discolored and marred by fungal growth, reminders of times past and those who had passed this way; captured images of once-known visitors now distant and distant places still unknown; a family history shown without a single picture of the family; brief encounters trapped and verified. This was Baldwin and Alodia's collection of pictures and cards sent back by those who had passed through their lives. A story existed for each; together they made up a larger story.

In a moment by myself I looked at each of the photographs, into the eyes and smiles of those who had once stared into the camera, trying to understand who they were and what they may have left. The pictures didn't resemble the stories; I couldn't match the faces with the memories that Baldwin and Alodia had shared with us. Looking at those pictures was like eavesdropping on a group of strangers: none had a tangible background without reference to the others, including the photo of our son making the snowman.

Photography has made historians of us all. Oftentimes pictures are a more resilient record of an event than words penned or recollections dredged from diluted memories. I used to like to believe this. We used many cameras and shot a great deal of film during our years with the Miskito. It was an easy shorthand. Focus and shoot was faster than think, interpret and write. We felt that less distortion occurred from image to lens to film than from image to mind to words on paper. We shot thousands of frames, but we also wrote hundreds of pages of notes, at last realizing that a picture can't be worth a thousand words if it takes words to say so.

For a while we lost the joy in seeing; perception was through the viewfinder. Sometimes the camera was an intermediary between us and the Miskito; sometimes it was a barrier. At first whatever we saw to photograph became the Miskito to us; thus, each picture also became a self-portrait. The photographs had to be looked at and interpreted, and in the process we saw ourselves on the color transparencies and in the black and white halftones. We became aware of ourselves but not of the Miskito. We talked with the Miskito about our photographs and other visual images. A few simply saw themselves too while others saw things far beyond the restrictive frame. Their interpretations taught us not to cling to our celluloid images, yet we would not have learned without them either. Where we learned the most was between the reality of the event and the captured visual record.

To start to learn about village society, we took pictures. There were almost 1,000 people living in Tasbapauni, so just to associate names with faces was difficult. We also wanted to learn about social relationships—who was family to whom, who gave what to whom and why, and the like. To find out about these things, we took pictures of people: individuals, groups, families; people doing things, or doing little. We then sent the rolls of film to Agfa in Managua via dugout or diesel boat to Bluefields. A few weeks later the prints were back, and we showed them to people, asked questions about names and families, and wrote pertinent information on the back of each photo. Duplicate photographs were given to everyone in the pictures. We learned a lot from talking with the Miskito about the photographs; people seemed more open about discussing individuals in photos than simply gossiping about their relatives and friends.

The bells rang, paused long, then rang again. Someone had died in the village. It was dark, about nine o'clock, with a cool December wind off the sea, and no moon. The bells rang from the church near the beach. The night wind carried the sad news. Several people were sick, and we would soon hear who had died. In a small place such as Tasbapauni, the tragedy of someone's dying is magnified because it affects everyone, for everyone is related in some way to every other family. Tomorrow men close to the family would build a casket while the women cooked food and comforted the grieving family.

The fresh morning had been washed clean by late-night showers. The thick grass outside was wet, green dampness hanging on despite the warming sun. The new day masked last night's death and the hours of sobbing and wailing from the small house not far away. Vicente Prudo's house. Their two-year-old son had died.

Vicente came to see me later that morning. He wanted me to take a picture of his dead son. Perhaps in the afternoon, he suggested, when the mahogany plank casket was finished and the boy dressed in Sunday clothes and placed inside on the white cloth and kapok-stuffed lining. When things were properly prepared and all was ready, he said, he would send for me.

I hesitated. I couldn't conceive of taking a picture of a baby in a casket. I didn't want to. To me it seemed morbid, a violation of a family's privacy just after a death. I had no part of their sorrow. To think of sticking a camera on a tripod over a casket and taking an exposure-meter reading in a room filled with anguished family members was something that I didn't want to do at all. I stammered a few incoherent phrases, trying to think of some way to deny his request.

"We have nothing to remember our baby, Mr. Barney," he said to me, sensing my reluctance. "You never snapped a picture of him. I'd like a picture to look at. When we bury him, he'll be gone except for that."

I had no answer for that. There was nothing to say except that I would take the picture.

Their front room was packed with people. The tiny casket rested on top of two stools alongside a wall. The dead child had been dressed in a new shirt and gaily striped short pants. Pieces of cotton plugged his nose and ears. Several women held tight to Mrs. Prudo and cried with her, arms entwined, bodies racked with grief, mutual comfort and tragedy. No one said anything to me; they just watched as I set up my equipment. A stranger in their midst. Not enough light. Could we move the casket out to the front porch? No words to me, no affirmation, but the casket was moved and tilted up so that the child could be seen. The family, relatives and friends gathered around the casket. I gave no directions. They seemed to know what they wanted. Still no words to me or to one another. The sobbing mother stood next to her dead son and then looked up at me and the camera, bravely holding herself still, waiting.

I tripped the shutter, bracketed the exposure with two more shots. While I unscrewed the camera from the tripod, they went inside, carrying the casket back into the room. There was no need for words from me or from them. No "I'm sorry" or "good-bye" or "thank you for taking the picture." I had taken an image of what was gone. One does not acknowledge these things. They would have a photograph of their child to recall a brief life.

Later I watched the family carry the casket to the graveyard. Many people followed in silence. The sun was low; and long, thin procession shadows rippled over other beachside graves. Hard-edged tropical light outlined the mourners against Caribbean blue haze. A small grave had been dug in the sandy soil near sea grape bushes—beach morning glory runners cut through by shovel and sadness. A tiny, dry sand waterfall spilled into the damp grave to build a small, crystal grain cone on rough-cut mahogany as the lay pastor read from a book.

That was the first of what came to be many funeral photographs.

Two years later we were returning to Tasbapauni. The only village boat in Bluefields at the time was Kukum Julias's old, slow hulk. At best, it would be an eighteen- to twenty-hour ordeal in the cramped, gloomy, diesel-fume-filled hold. But we were anxious to go, and when we saw that one of our favorite old friends, Emiliano Julias, was going too, we knew there would be much to talk about to pass the time.

Just after we had pulled away from the wharf, Emiliano leaned close to me to say something over the noise of the ancient, wheezing Lister diesel.

"Mr. Barney, when we get to Tasbapauni, please for the favor of snapping my boy. I want a picture of him."

Poor Emiliano; his only son must have died, and he was going back to Tasbapauni for the funeral.

"I'm sorry to hear that," I replied. "When did he die?"

"Oh, he didn't die, neither sick. It's not good to wait 'til you're dead for a picture; can't smile."

One summer we brought a Sony ½-inch video camera and recorder to tape village activities and hunting and turtling. Video tape has several advantages over 16mm film equipment; principally, immediate replay to see if you've got usable stuff, and easily synchronized sound recording. We didn't use it very much in the village, however, but recorded only subsistence-related activities in the forest and at sea. All because of Rufus Waggam's trip to Managua.

Rufus Waggam had recently returned from Managua, where he'd gone to sell medicinal herbs and his services as a "bush medicine" doctor. Spanish-speaking people frequently visited the east coast to seek cures for diseases and bad-luck-related illnesses and misfortunes. Miskito familiar with medicinal plants and shaman cures often treated "patients" from the interior, usually for a handsome fee. Mr. Waggam had reasoned that he could increase business and returns by taking his practice to potential patients rather than waiting for them to come to him. Thus, he went to the capital of Nicaragua for the first time. Very few of the Tasbapauni Miskito had ever gone to Managua; most feared it as a dangerous place for an Indian; others, because they spoke poor Spanish or none. The majority simply had no reason to go. Rufus Waggam's return attracted a large, attentive audience. When I stopped by to say hello, a sizeable group had already gathered around him. He was just explaining what he'd seen in a store window in downtown Managua.

"They call it *televisión*. That's in the Spanish tongue. It's a box that shows people doing things. They had one right in front of a selling place, and people packed up to watch what happened. I looked, and I saw a woman hugging up a man. Rubbing and everything. They were talking in Spanish, but I make out enough to know the man was in tow with an outside woman. They were hiding in a room, keeping secret from his woman.

"Then I see the next woman. Look vexed. She find out and burst into the room and catch the man with the other woman. Big trouble. They row, and she get facety with him. She pull out a gun and shoot him dead.

"That *televisión* is a terrible thing, I tell you, people. Wherever you are, whatever you doing, it pick you up and show everybody just what you doing. That thing see through houses. That's how the woman know to look the man. Can't get mixed up with another woman in Managua. *Televisión* pick you up doing business 150 miles away.

"Modern times coming to our little Tasbapauni, but I never want to see that *televisión* here. No, papa, that thing would condemn all the loose goings-on. If my wife catch me on the *televisión*, she'd humbug me, sure; put bush medicine in my food to keep me home."

Laughter. Everyone who had heard Rufus Waggam agreed: television was a dangerous thing.

Within a few hours the story would reach every household. If we had pulled out our video equipment, camera and battery-run monitor, much anxiety and suspicion would have been directed toward us. Worse, we would have brought modern times to Tasbapauni. Anyone we videotaped and showed on the monitor would automatically be guilty of something. And in a highly social environment like Tasbapauni, it was impossible to hide what we were doing, nor did we want to. Rather than risk exposing the Miskito equivalent of *Peyton Place*, we reserved our video recording for hunting and fishing activities.

Most Miskito had never seen an image that proved false. One's visual experience did not include seeing things that were not real. The Managua love-triangle television soap opera was accepted verbatim, regardless of conflicting information or logical continuity problems. What the program meant to Rufus Waggam was strongly influenced by his past experience and associations. As a shaman he had learned never to question the validity of an event or an image. His account of the power of television would be readily accepted as fact. The Miskito, like most traditional societies, do not search for verification through repeated confirmation. Judgment is synonymous with acceptance; suspended judgment for subsequent validation runs counter to the Miskito concept that something is valid by its very being.

A year later Cromwell Forbes, a store owner in Tasbapauni, purchased a used 16mm projector, built the metal sheet-roofed Teatro Oriental, and showed his first film, ordered from Panama—a 1933 Tarzan movie starring Buster Crabbe and Jacqueline Wells. Modern times had come to Tasbapauni, even if the film was more than forty years old. A Honda gasoline generator provided the electricity to run the projector; tickets had been procured from Bluefields; and an old chalkboard tacked to the front of Forbes's store announced the film's title in Spanish and English: *Tarzan the Fearless* and *Tarzan Sin Temor*. Modern times and Tarzan had come to Tasbapauni without fear.

The Teatro Oriental was filled beyond the capacity of the borrowed church pews. The film, one of the first of the Tarzan sound movies, had many of the scenes which later became clichés: Tarzan swinging on lianas from tree to tree, fighting a lion with only a knife, diving into a turbulent river from a high cliff, falling into a death pit, only to be rescued by a friendly elephant. The Miskito did not sit quietly watching the storyline, waiting while the plot developed; they were vocal, loudly discussing every tree, animal, bush, river—in short, every environmental and biotic feature. They saw a different movie than I did.

Sickness and health often were narrowly separated for us and for the Miskito. We both were living in a new social and economic environment, far from doctors and Western medicine, yet confronted by new and old diseases and worsening nutrition. To care for ourselves, to ensure good health in a setting where such disease prevention and public health measures as we had been accustomed to were nonexistent, meant that we had to become self-sufficient in the prevention of illness; failing that, we had to diagnose and treat ourselves with medicines at hand. Our medical kit contained reference books such as *The Merck Manual* and the *Medical Dictionary and Health Manual*—the latter helped translate the former—and a variety of pills, ointments, powders, adhesive tapes, sterile dressings, splints, needles and threads for sutures, an assortment of scissors, razor blades and tweezers, and an oral thermometer. Aside from malaria we fared pretty well, only having to cope occasionally with colds, intestinal parasites, dysentery, and infected cuts and scratches. Our medical supplies became more important to others than they were to us.

People soon learned that we knew a little about what they referred to as the "doctoring business." We knew enough to take a chance on ourselves in an emergency, but not enough to handle confidently or safely the multitude of medical problems in the village. Often by the time we heard about an illness or a severe wound, traditional remedies had been used, sometimes with success; usually, though, with but poor results. If the wound failed to heal or the person continued to be sick, growing weaker each day, the person administering indigenous cures would "give the sick over," that is, acknowledge that the situation was beyond his control. That's when a member of the family would come to "Father Mac," the Anglican priest, for help; and if he wasn't in the village, they'd come to us. Usually we'd try to get someone who was very sick onto a boat for Bluefields, where they could see a doctor. If it was an emergency, an effort would be made to flag down a passing shrimp boat to persuade the captain to carry the patient to the Moravian hospital in Puerto Cabezas, ninety miles to the north. We were able to do a lot with aspirins, antibiotics, and routine cleansing and dressing of infected wounds. There were several instances, however, when the medical problems were well beyond our capabilities, but absence of transport to a distant doctor or the family's reluctance to allow the person to be sent involved us in situations of gravest responsibility.

During our first long stays in the village, by default we became administers of medicine and medical aid when there seemed to be no other choice. It was hard not to interfere with traditional diagnosis and indigenous methods of treatment, but we had neither the confidence, the training nor the inclination to take on the village's medical problems. It was easier to be the Johnny Appleseed of aspirins.

We didn't give out large quantities at one time—just one or two here and there—but they added up over the months. The extent of the aspirin distribution network became evident when Flannery Knight's eleven-year-old son Frederico came to see me one day. He wanted some aspirin to cure his chicken. He asked me in Creole, and it went like this:

"Mr. Barney, please for a Meyoral aspirin. I going to mash it up and give to me fowl. It's giddy in de head and feeling peckish."

A subsequent checkup showed that the chicken with the giddy head recovered; it was no longer pecking Frederico, and it was back to its old fowl self again.

We gave some medical aid to the Miskito, and they helped us with health problems, too. A couple of times we had cuts which would not heal quickly in the humid environment and began to fester, despite various salves and antibiotics. An older Miskito, reputed to know "much bush medicine," made us a poultice from two plants which, when applied to the cuts, cleared them up so that they healed rapidly. Even though we took Aralen every week for the chemoprophylaxis of malaria, Judi and Barney contracted the disease. Think of the worst symptoms of many diseases, put them together, and that's how you feel with a severe malarial attack: dizzying headache, violent chills and fever, weakness, malaise and overall body-ache. Large oral doses of Aralen, a brand name for chloroquine, the most widely used antimalarial drug, did little to suppress their symptoms. I didn't want to travel with them when they were so sick. A very old woman gave me a bottle of *wrih saika*, malaria medicine, made from pieces of a vine *(kina)* and shavings from a tree called *tru* which had been leached in hot water. The medicine had a strong, bitter taste, much like that of quinine. It suppressed their symptoms long enough for us to make the trip to Bluefields.

Frequent encounters with injured, sick and dying people and with those who were trying to cure by native medicinal means allowed us to learn something of Miskito ethnoetiology and local medical techniques. Much of the village doctoring was an amalgamation of indigenous bush medicine, shamanism, and West Indian folk treatment; a smattering of Western pills and injections; and a reliance on improvisation with materials and conditions at hand.

Among the Miskito, there are various types of specialists who deal with medical and magical problems. A *sukia*, or shaman, is considered the most powerful specialist; and while as herbalists, sukias might do some curing with bush medicine, they are also teachers, diviners, guides, advisors and intermediaries between the Miskito and the spirit world. Very few sukias can still be found; their knowledge and skills are no longer passed on to apprentices, and when they die, so too does their experience. On the upper coast, sukias, usually old women, can be still found in Big Sandy Bay and Bemuna. On the lower coast, however, there are none; only a few people who have had a little *"sukia* training." Next in the hierarchy are prophets, who foretell the future and diagnose ailments through dreams. Then come more specialized but more common practitioners, such as the "bush medicine man," *inmawa waikna,* who is an herbalist and who treats medical-spirit problems with medicinal plants; the *yumu waikna,* or stomach ache man; the *pyuta* doctor, or snakebite doctor; and a person who takes care of toothaches—more about him later.

I observed all of these specialists at work at various times in Miskito communities along the coast, sometimes just watching; other times, minimally participating. The only treatment and system of diagnosis that I really learned anything about was from the *yumu waikna* in Tasbapauni. Every culture has a dominant cognitive interpretation of where in the body most medical problems are centered. For the Miskito the stomach, liver and blood are considered the physical focal points for a majority of their ailments. Stomach pain is a common complaint stemming from possible indigestion or a range of gastrointestinal disorders. The Miskito, however, interpret stomach-related problems as being caused from eating too much of a specific food imbued with animal spirit properties, violation of one of the many food taboos, or possible magical meddling instigated by another villager who wishes them harm. There are various sorts of *yumu,* or stomach pain: *karas yumu,* crocodile stomach pain; *libang yumu,* from a small crab; *kiaki yumu,* from the agouti—a small, commonly eaten rodent; *tutu yumu,* from a species of large biting ant; *wuala yumu,* from the boa constrictor; and *pyuta yumu,* caused by snakes in general.

According to the *yumu* man, each *yumu* causes a specific pain and, once diagnosed, has to be dealt with in terms of that particular animal spirit. To distinguish which *yumu* is creating the pain the *yumu* man asks the person to lie down; the *yumu* man gently rubs the patient's stomach area and then listens, ear pressed to the person's belly, rubs again, listens, and so on. From what he is able to distinguish from touch and sound and from asking the person to recall what he has eaten over the last few days, he identifies the specific *yumu.* I learned to treat only a few *yumus,* supposedly the easiest to identify and take care of: *karas yumu* and *libang yumu.*

It may take from one to three hours to get rid of a *yumu* and its associated pain. The treatment generally is as follows: the stomach is continually stroked lightly with an oil—coconut, palm, or *ibo*—while the *yumu* man whistles a soft and pretty melody by exhaling and inhaling so that the whistling is continuous. Occasionally, the whistling is interrupted by short hisses made by sharply blowing through his closed teeth and by commands in Miskito directed to the particular *yumu*, for example, "Crocodile that sleeps on back of river in sea, when frightened, goes in river, away. Now go, crocodile, away. Just like that. Done." Gradually the pain goes away; the stomach muscles relax, and the person usually falls asleep. When the patient wakes up, the *yumu* man tells him the *yumu* is gone—in this case, *karas yumu*—and tells him not to eat specific foods for a short time.

One could easily deduce that the pain goes away from the sound- and touch-induced muscle relaxation and sleep and the positive reinforcement from the *yumu* man that the animal spirit is gone and there is nothing left to worry about. That's certainly a part of it. But it is much more complicated than that. Disease and sickness are seen as having both a natural and a supernatural cause. As an intermediary between the sick person and the source of the particular sickness, the *yumu waikna*, as well as other shamanistic healers, invoke natural and supernatural powers that "cure" because they involve all the perceived relationships in the disease environment: mind, body, ailment, medicine and magical spirits.

A frequent ailment was an abscessed tooth. The closest dentist was seventy miles away in Bluefields, and immediate pain and financial strain meant that all but the hardiest and richest had to seek treatment in the village. Mr. Baldwin had a set of dental tools and did some of the tooth extractions. But he was also gone from the village for days at a time, hunting white-lipped peccary in the rain forest or roughing out a new canoe up a distant river. In his absence tooth complaints were dealt with in the old manner, by using a red-hot nail. A new four-inch-long nail is filed to a sharp point and the head wrapped in string or a strip of cloth; then the nail is placed halfway into a glowing bed of chipped coconut-shell coals, which burn with considerable heat. After a few minutes the point will be red hot, and the nail will be taken out by its insulated head. Meanwhile, the person with the toothache is sitting close by, waiting for treatment. The hardest part is to hold the tongue to one side so the nail doesn't burn it. The hot tip is slowly inserted into the tooth cavity. There is a brief shock of pain, the smell of scorched enamel, and then it's over. According to the nail dentists, the heat closes the cavity, and the heat-cracked tooth will come out, piece by piece, over a period of a few weeks. If it's not a serious cavity, the nail dentist may recommend a pain killer instead of the nail treatment. A sap from a rain forest tree called *buksa mahbra* is said to be an effective pain remedy for toothaches.

Not all the shaman-types and bush medicine practitioners accepted our presence and the occasional medical advice we shared with people who asked for our help. As might be expected, several were openly hostile. We tried to keep away from their activities, hoping we could go about our research without interference. Only on one occasion did we run into a problem. It all started when we went to visit Agatha and Cleveland Blandford, an older couple who had taken a liking to us, often sending us pieces of meat and fruit. I had gone turtle fishing with Cleveland and spent many hours listening to him explain the ways of sea turtles. Cleveland was about sixty-nine at the time but still going strong; he did as much work as men half his age and was reputed to be one of the best turtlemen in the village. Agatha (pronounced Agátha in Miskito fashion), his second wife, was much younger, perhaps forty, and she too was extremely fit and strong. The previous night, they had asked us to stop by in the morning to pick up some pineapple that Cleveland planned to bring from his agricultural grounds up the beach.

When we arrived at their kitchen, Agatha was dousing a chicken with water. She was mad; she informed us that Cleveland had clumsily stepped on the chicken and "mashed him up."

"This is my best chicken. I'm going to fix him up. Bathe him and then put him under the pan," she said, pointing to a large metal washtub. "And then you thump the pan. Good thumps. Quick time, the chicken get cured."

I thought that it seemed improbable that a mashed-up, soaking-wet chicken was going to get cured by being subjected to loud thumps while under a metal tub. I asked Agatha if she was sure it would work. She assured us it would. It's hard to develop a close affinity with a chicken—at least it is for me—but I felt sorry for it and tried to persuade Agatha not to thump the chicken.

"What you know?" she asked. "You don't keep chicken or follow the Indian way. This thing works, I tell you. This is the old-time way. I study these things down, and it help plenty of chickens. Help better than giving them pure pill like that time you say you cure that Knight boy's chicken. You only think that give a helping. Not so. Not like thumping."

I must have said something wrong to get her so worked up. Her comments on my chicken cure cut deep, and I said as much, and we left.

Judi thought I'd been too abrupt with Agatha, and she was right. She talked me into going back later to patch over our chicken argument, but we didn't get around to returning until nine o'clock that night.

Their house was filled with people. A kerosene lantern gave the only light. I smelled a strange odor like burning leaves, obviously not coming from the lantern. A smoky haze hung in the air. We looked for Cleveland and Agatha, and someone told us they were in the next room. Agatha was "plenty sick." The sounds of heavy coughing and gasping for air came from the bedroom. We looked in. I recognized two old *kukas* (grandmothers) and a *dama* (grandfather). The women had on "tie heads" (pieces of cloth wrapped around their heads) and old beads, the kind rarely seen anymore; they were smoking pipes. The man was bent over a smoldering pile of leaves, blowing on them. Agatha was sitting on the bed, coughing and wheezing, trying to fill her lungs with air. Cleveland and another man were holding her to keep her from rolling about on the bed. Cleveland saw us and came to the door.

"I'm glad you came, Mr. Barney and Miss Judi. She's sick. Can't catch her wind. Can't get air. She's getting worse."

I asked if there was anything caught in her throat.

"Nothing like that," he replied. "She get sick from being wet up with that chicken. I sent for these people to help. Old Renales there knows bush medicine good, but so far, no help from that."

Renales was the man on the floor with his back to us, lighting the aromatic leaves. He was a bush medicine man who didn't like us. Having had a couple of run-ins with him, we now avoided him as much as possible. He had brought the leaves, something that looked like dried ferns, a powder made from crushed seeds, and a large homemade cigar from which he puffed and blew clouds of smoke over Agatha. The bedroom was filled with a sweet-smelling but harsh smoke. Judi and I coughed and gagged on it. Cleveland asked us to take a look at Agatha.

She was struggling for air, flushed and perspiring heavily. Some ashes had been rubbed on her chest. Renales's work. Every breath took a massive effort. I didn't think the dense smoke was helping much, but kept my thoughts to myself while I looked at her.

I asked Judi what she thought.

"Asthma? An allergy?" she suggested.

Perhaps.

"Mr. Barney, Miss Judi, if you can help her, please," Cleveland pleaded. "She's going down fast."

We weren't sure what she had. She couldn't talk at all. The wheezing and gasping took all her energy.

Judi and I talked for a minute and decided we must do something—they were our friends—but what to do? First we'd have to confront Renales. He became angry when we suggested that the shutters be opened to clear the room of smoke.

Cleveland Blandford, one of the most experienced and knowledgeable Miskito turtlemen.

"You going to humbug this woman. This bush is good medicine," he said and looked at us defiantly.

Miss Agatha was sick; we had little concrete to offer; Renales was adamant about continuing with the bush medicine smoke treatment; and Cleveland was caught between two sets of contradictory advice from relatives and friends: keep to the old ways with Renales, or see what the white people can do. If they hadn't been so close to us, I would have wished he would opt for Renales. Anything we could do would be chancy at best. We didn't want the responsibility, but Cleveland gave it to us.

"Please do what you can," Cleveland said softly.

We worked out a compromise with Renales. We could air out the room and try some of our medicine; he would stay and watch; and we'd leave the the ashes on Agatha's chest.

"Let's try something simple and see what happens. If that doesn't work, we can try some pills," Judi suggested.

"Let's assume it's an asthmatic attack."

The image of childhood asthma came to mind. What had my mother used? Of course: steam, towels and Vicks.

"Mr. Cleveland, put some water on to boil, and get a towel or large piece of cloth."

Judi went to get our jar of Vicks. Renales just glared.

Remembrances of steamy towels and Vicks. Several large tablespoons of the scented petroleum jelly were scooped out of the squat jar and dropped into the pan of hot water. Agatha began to breathe more regularly after a few minutes of inhaling the familiar-smelling vapor. Renales was interested in the method but was trying not to appear so. I'm sure to him it was not a different remedy, simply the substitution of one element for another: steam for smoke. As Agatha began to feel better, the tension in the room was reduced. A half hour later she seemed well enough, and everyone began to leave.

"If Miss Agatha has a hard time breathing again," I said to Cleveland while Renales stood close by, listening, "just heat the Vicks in the water and put the towel over her head again. We'll stop by tomorrow and bring some pills."

The next morning we were surprised to see Agatha up and sitting on her front porch sewing.

"You're looking better this morning," Judi remarked.

"I'm hard to dead," she replied smiling.

"Did you have to use the Vicks again, Miss Agatha?"

"Could only use it once; there wasn't enough to take twice. Mr. Renales heated it up when I started to go bad on the breathing. He gave it to me, and I drank it all down just like you told him, Mr. Barney. That Vicks is a good purge, too, better than senna and shark liver oil."

Either something was lost in the translation, or Renales was trying to sabotage our Vicks treatment. I thought it best to ignore Renales's behind-the-scenes work. Unfortunately, Agatha could not, and she looked a little uncomfortable at the moment.

"Tell me, Miss Agatha, what ever happened to the chicken?"

Agatha looked uneasy, apparently not from my question but from her Vicks treatment.

"I gave it to Renales for his help. You can ask him about it," she said as she hurriedly excused herself and went inside.

The metamorphosis from guest to host and from hospitality to hostility often occurs in the life of a field researcher when a visitor suddenly appears. This usually happens just after the cultural shock waves generated by your initial presence in a tribal village have subsided. You have become an accepted guest, and your research begins. Isolated from appointments, telephones and deadlines, you immerse yourself in the investigation and in village society. The more distant, isolated and involved you are, however, the greater is the attraction; the brighter the beacon for the stream of visitors who have been stacking up in a holding pattern. In they come, short on food and fuel. You too become a host, but why is it so difficult to offer the same hospitality that the village has accorded you? Academic territoriality? Or Nietschmann's Rule that the greater the distance, the kinkier the visitor?

Bent over some soil samples and a booklet called "Know Your Soils," I was explaining to my Miskito host, Baldwin Garth, why a decrease in the fallow period created a reciprocal decrease in soil fertility; Alodia, Baldwin's wife, came into the room and announced, "A countryman of yours come, Mr. Barney, and he's got a Corn Island man in tow."

I looked out the window. Fifty yards away and homing in on the house were two strangers: one a Creole, who must be the Corn Islander identified by Alodia, and the other an American wearing khaki pants, white short-sleeved shirt, a pair of "I-can-see-you-but-you-can't-see-me" silver-colored sunglasses, and an H. R. (Bob) Haldeman coiffure. Baldwin identified the species as missionary: variety, Protestant.

The American was riding a skinny swaybacked horse while the other walked alongside. Two more were in the quest circuit.

I went back to work on the soil samples hoping they would continue their journey, but that was impossible, as they were traveling on Stanley radar locked onto a Livingstone signal.

Baldwin answered the knock at the door. The American spoke first.

"Hello. I'm Brother Thomas, and this is Brother Downs, and we are traveling in the service of the Lord to establish a little kingdom here in Nicaragua."

Before we could introduce ourselves and welcome them, Brother Thomas had glanced at the table, had seen the book and said, "I see you're reading 'Know Your Soul.' That's strange. We had heard that you were a professor, not a churchman."

He had me neatly boxed into a corner. I could either opt for professors and soils or churches and souls. Baldwin saved the day and my reputation by welcoming them to Tasbapauni and to his house. We then asked them what brought them to the village.

Brother Thomas turned toward me—I couldn't tell if he was looking at me because of his sunglasses. "We came to see you. You must have visited many Miskito villages and know the people. We would like you to suggest which place would be the best for us to begin teaching the Bible to these people."

I realized I'd made a mistake by not voting for professors and dirt. I explained that there were already several mission churches in the village, all of which taught the Bible. Perhaps he should consult with one of the Anglican, Catholic or Moravian missionaries or lay pastors. He brushed off my suggestion by saying something to the effect that missionaries usually didn't identify open niches for the competition.

"Brother Thomas and Brother Downs, I'd really like to help you, but this just isn't my field. Besides, most of the people in this village are already members of a church," I told them.

"Oh, we don't have a church. All we want to do is teach the Bible," injected Brother Downs, who had been silent until now. "We plan to live with them in exchange for the teaching."

I explained to them that the Miskito had little money and would find it difficult to support them for their services. In addition, the people had lost a large part of their crops because of extensive flooding and so would be worse off this year than usual.

Brother Thomas grinned and, in an almost conspiratorial tone, informed us that he had the exclusive rights to a franchise for Nicaragua which would permit him to sell products that the Miskito would not be able to resist.

"Biodegradable soaps and organic vitamins, that's the key," he proclaimed. "There's no competition; everyone needs them; and it helps the ecology."

Even though his motivations were probably good, it sounded as if he had said "plastics" to Benjamin in *The Graduate.*

I tried to convince the Brothers that while their intentions might be commendable, most Miskito would be unwilling or unable to purchase expensive imported soap and vitamins.

Brother Thomas pulled out some samples from a canvas bag and placed them on the table. He then proceeded to explain to Baldwin and Alodia, who had been quietly watching us, why his products were superior to the ones they were using. After he had finished, he pushed the samples across the table to Alodia. Everyone was waiting for her reply. She looked at the stuff on her table: biodegradable soap, organic vitamins, cloth bags filled with soil, and several bottles of soil-testing chemicals. Two sets of paraphernalia from the world beyond her experience.

Alodia made her pronouncement: "Soap is soap, and pill is for the sick," she said to Brother Thomas. "Excuse me now, I have to tend to the kitchen." But as she left the room she looked at me and added, "And dirt is dirt."

It was apparent that Brother Thomas's marketing test had failed. He retrieved his samples and told us they would be moving on to the next village, which was on the beach some twenty miles to the north.

Relieved, I watched them depart: Brother Thomas on horseback, his samples in a bag slung over the saddle; and Brother Downs walking beside him. There were no dragons to slay in Tasbapauni, and so they left.

In the weeks that followed, there were several other visitors to Tasbapauni: a French linguist looking for a drum to take home for a coffee table; an animal dealer who wanted the Miskito to capture monkeys, parrots, toucans and boas for his export business; and an advance man from an American southern university who wanted to bring students to the village "to round out their educational experience and let them see how poor people live." It seemed that everyone needed something from the Miskito—or from the environment via the Miskito.

I was the first person the visitors would look for as soon as they got off the small diesel freight boats or the chartered speedboats from Bluefields. They wanted me to present their plans and demands to the Miskito; to act as a procurer of food, lodging, workers, boats; and to tell them the lowest price the Miskito would accept for their labor, materials and—unbelievably—in one instance a flour-sack shirt that a Miskito happened to be wearing at the time.

I didn't cooperate. I was a lousy host. To counter the constant barrage of visitors and requests, I changed from hospitable to hostile. I'm sure my treatment of visitors was considered bad manners by the Miskito. Proper Miskito behavior toward a stranger in the village meant providing food and lodging. One should be considerate, generous and helpful, as the Miskito were to me and my family. Why was it that we did not exhibit these same considerations when strangers came to see us?

Perhaps the Miskito were right. Maybe we were being too harsh to the visitors who came to see us in Tasbapauni. We decided to try to be as good hosts as the Miskito were to us.

This was to turn out to be a tremendous challenge because the next visitor was the embodiment of the ill-mannered guest.

The Miskito called him "Bird Man." He told us his name was Henry.

"Miss Judi say you must come now!" yelled Frederico, one of Flannery Knight's children.

Flannery and I had been cutting palm leaf in the swamp south of the village that morning. His dugout was piled high, and we hoped it was enough to finish thatching the shed on the beach where he kept his seagoing canoe. We had landed at the creek near his house, where Frederico was waiting with the message.

"You to go home now," Frederico added emphatically. "Miss Judi say for me to fetch you."

Now, Judi isn't one to send out an all-points bulletin unless it's urgent. I told Flannery I'd be back in a while and headed to Baldwin's house, where we were living.

"You won't believe it. He showed up at five-thirty this morning looking for you, and it's been a disaster ever since."

I asked her to back up and tell me who had showed up and what the disaster was.

"See for yourself," she said and took me inside to meet Henry.

They had just finished breakfast. Alodia and our son were clearing the table, and Baldwin was talking with someone hidden under a huge straw hat and behind two empty bottles of Fanta Uva and a stack of opened cans of tuna fish. A shotgun stood against the table next to him.

"This is my husband," Judi said with a hint of relief. "And this is Henry," she added, pointing toward the growing kitchen midden at the end of the table.

"Do you have any shotgun shells? I need some 20-gauge shells to collect specimens," he responded by way of introduction.

I told him we didn't have any shells and managed to find something to do with my outstretched hand.

"I'm collecting for a museum. All that these Indians eat is rice and beans, so I bring my own food."

Henry didn't confine himself to normal conversational codes, but I was able to decipher the origin of the soft drinks and tinned food from his non sequitur remarks.

As I was to find out later, Henry had already alienated everyone at breakfast by stating that all Indians would steal if given the chance: that's why he kept all his valuables in a locked trunk. Furthermore, he had remarked that one of the Miskito deck hands was drunk during the trip from Bluefields and that "these Indians drink just like the reservation ones in the States. If that doesn't prove the land-bridge theory, nothing does."

Henry looked a mess. Sunburned, emaciated, dressed in pants two sizes too large and held up by a safety pin, with sockless, blistered feet shod in heavy rubber boots, he needed help. We offered it.

"I need to cash some traveler's checks, find a boardinghouse, and get someone to take me to the offshore islands." Henry certainly came to the point, but his wants would be difficult to satisfy.

"There's no one here who has a boardinghouse, but we'll find a bed for you. You won't be able to cash your checks in the village."

Henry looked astonished. "But they said these traveler's checks would be accepted anywhere."

"Well, they aren't here. You might be able to find someone with a boat or canoe to take you to the cays, but for cash, not checks."

The rest of the day Henry spent haggling with various boat and canoe owners over a price for a two-day trip to a few of the small coral cays twelve to twenty-five miles offshore. The Miskito had difficulties understanding why anyone wanted to hire a boat to go collect eggs and birds. Henry had problems comprehending why few of the men wanted to take him for the wages offered.

One Miskito seaman told me, "The Bird Man doesn't want to pay us enough. The wind is blowing, and the sea is kicking. We aren't going to lose our canoe for any eggs."

Henry finally persuaded two Miskito to take him by challenging their seamanship, saying they were not good enough to handle the rough weather. The wind had increased in strength and registered an average of thirty miles per hour, with gusts up to forty. Whitecaps, heavy surf and black storm clouds made up the view to sea.

We cautioned Henry against going. Even the best seamen had not left the village to catch green turtles that day; it was too rough. Henry was adamant, however. They would go.

Joseph "Uncle Sam" Dixon and his nephew, Riley Carlos, were to take Henry. They were going over their sails and gear when I arrived to talk them out of it.

"Mr. Joseph, why don't you hold up until the weather clears? All the turtlemen stayed home today, and it looks as though a storm will hit tonight," I said, hoping they would back out.

"Mr. Barney, we are going to take your friend to the cays to get his eggs. He says his study is important. We are not afraid of the stiff weather."

I started to tell him that similar nationality did not necessarily make Henry and me friends, but instead I gave up and returned home. Baldwin was waiting for me.

"I think your countryman is a little light in the head, Mr. Barney. He asked where to go to relieve himself, and I showed him the mission outhouse. But he didn't bother with the toilet. He just did his business on the beach. Half the people saw him, and the other half are laughing now." Baldwin looked at me as if I were responsible for Henry's poor toilet training.

Henry's problems were increasing: one at sea, and two on the beach.

About three o'clock the next morning, Henry and his mysterious trunk left for the cays with the two men in a small canoe. We spent an anxious two days waiting for their return to Tasbapauni.

"They're coming in. They're running with the jib and haven't reefed the sail," Baldwin told us while trying to catch his breath.

We ran down to the beach to where a large crowd had gathered in front of Joseph's canoe shed. The small craft was just outside the breakers, bobbing up and down in the huge swells while the men took down the sails, mast and rigging and prepared to come in through the surf. In good weather and with a fairly calm sea, this is the fun part of a return run to the village. The Miskito are extraordinarily good at handling their canoes in the surf, usually catching a big swell and riding it through the first and second breaks until they run aground in the shallow water. Women and children on the beach applaud and cheer the best rides, and everyone laughs and hoots if someone capsizes.

That afternoon, however, the prospect of their getting through raging, six- to ten-foot surf kept everyone on the beach quiet and apprehensive.

They picked the last swell of the set. The stern half of the canoe was hidden in foam and spray as it slipped down the wave face. The ten-foot wall of water steepened. Just as its top curled over and began to envelop the canoe, they made a ninety-degree cut and sped across the crumbling wave face, turned again and rode the edge of the wave to shore. It was a fantastic display of skill.

Henry looked sick. We helped him from the canoe, and two of us carried his trunk. He was trembling, seasick and thoroughly sodden. Henry was taken to his room and put to bed, and soup and tea were put on to heat. His trunk was placed beside his bed.

Judi and I went back to Mr. Joseph's canoe shed to help him carry his things home.

"Your friend doesn't like the sea. First he was manish and said we were afraid to take him. But when he felt the heft of the weather and the roll of the sea, he's afraid."

People packed into Joseph's front room to hear about the trip.

"The Bird Man said we must take that big trunk along. We told him no, it's too big for the canoe, but he said that if it didn't go, he wouldn't. He said, 'Boy, carry the trunk.' But when we got out to sea, he remembered our names. On the cays he did foolish things. Climbed coconut in a storm with lightning sparking all about. Sand fly molested him plenty; he didn't want to stay in the smoke of the fire. Slept on the ground rather than with us in the camp. Soldier crabs bit him during the night. He got his eggs and put them in the trunk and told us he's ready to go home. We said no, we should stay on the cay until the weather passes."

"Then why did you leave the cay?" asked Salvarita, Joseph's wife.

"He jumped up and down yelling to go. We didn't want to stay with him on that little piece of land," answered Joseph.

Everyone wanted to hear more about the two days they had spent on the cay. Joseph went over every event, point by point. Judi thought it sounded as if they had run an insular day-care center.

"Now, people," Joseph said loudly, "I'm going to tell you about the trip home. It wasn't blowing too stiff that we couldn't get a good sail, so we rigged all the cloth and Riley hung on the man rope and we moved right out. The Bird Man told us to take down the sail, afraid to capsize. Now we were busy with the sailing, so we didn't pay any attention to him. So he rolled up his pants and said he was preparing to swim for his life. But he's safe on the main now and has his eggs and trunk."

Before we left, I asked Joseph if he knew what was inside Henry's trunk.

"That's the funny thing. For all his hollering about that trunk, acting as if it was topped off with gold, all that trunk had in it was a little tin with eggs, his chart and a blanket. He treated the trunk better than he did us."

We all went home to ponder the trunk, Henry, and what we had heard about the trip.

By the next morning everyone in the village had heard the story. The saga was elaborated on and retold over and over. It's probably still being told today.

As soon as Henry had recovered from his ordeal, he left Tasbapauni to go home. He didn't say good-bye, and no one said he was sorry to see him go. After the Henry experience, we had to answer many questions about "our countrymen," such as, "Why are they afraid of the sea?" "Why do they want to see Nicaraguan bird egg?" and "Why are they so manish?"

The Miskito could look after themselves. We went on about our study and braced ourselves for the next visitor to Tasbapauni.

One of the most difficult things in field research is to explain to local people exactly what you're doing and why. Working with traditional societies often increases problems of communication, depending on the capacity of the intracultural filter factor: i.e., the ability of the outside researcher to translate an esoteric subject into culturally relevant terms, and the host society's ability to fit that explanation into an existing category of experience with outsiders or to generate a new one. Effective communication of the research topic and rationale is a two-way street, often necessitating resolution of conflicting presuppositions and world views and of the status and roles of visitor and host. You and the host village society both learn much in the process of trying to make sense out of your presence. Once in a while, however, a freak incident may occur which throws your accepted researcher image out of focus for you and others alike.

We thought our research was going well. It was our second trip to Tasbapauni, after an interval of one and a half years, and our coming back had greatly increased both our understanding of the Miskito and their acceptance of us. We listened to the many stories about our first visit, the strange things we were said to have done and not done, and the variety of explanations for the real reason behind the many months we had previously spent in the village. I had told everyone I was writing a book on the Miskito, about their way of life, which I thought was an easy shorthand way to circumvent explaining what a Ph.D. dissertation was and what led up to doing one. Many of the Tasbapauni Miskito did not accept my story; instead some thought that we were "checking up on Tasbapauni" for the Nicaraguan government; others had it that we really worked for an American "company" and were doing the equivalent of a preliminary analysis of resource and labor availability prior to making a recommendation to begin "company business" in Tasbapauni; still others thought we were interested in "making money" from the "turtle concern"; that is, the reason we were so interested in learning about Miskito turtle fishing and the behavior of turtles was so that we ourselves could exploit them to sell in "the States." Another interpretation was profoundly disturbing, namely that we took photographs and notes to write books and articles to sell for money. This was closer to the truth; we had done this, and we had sent copies to various people in the village. Therefore, some of the Miskito wanted to know where their cut was. These individuals were both perceptive and aggressive, and they had a good point. Furthermore, they didn't accept the answers I gave them for why they hadn't been included in publishing agreements and subsequent royalties. At best, we continued to limp along, following our standard practice of reciprocal exchanges of goods and services with Miskito who helped us.

The mysteries and myths surrounding our work were finally clearing up, and most of the Miskito of Tasbapauni had come to

No longer reciprocally categorized as a "strange outsider" or "village informer," Judi is able to talk with Kuka Martinez about what has happened in the village since our last visit. Tasbapauni, 1975.

realize that I wasn't a missionary, lumber scout, company manager, buyer of skins, potential commercial turtle fisherman, or any of the other categories they had for outsiders they had dealt with.

"Mr. Barney, what's your mission this time?"

"I'd like to learn a little more about how the old plan is changing to the new one and a lot more about turtles."

"That's right; they say you're writing about how we living here, natural booking concern."

The early summer dry was the best time to be on the east coast—Caribbean azure against beach sand tans. Rain, mud, river water had gone from the sea. The air was thick with radiant sun heat, driving out months of dampness—sun glare off water and sand. Shadows were darker, incident light brighter. Sediments settled in slow-moving creeks and rivers; waters became clearer by the day. The tempo of subsistence increased: cutting, clearing, burning and planting to be done before the rains started again; sea turtles to be caught with net and harpoon as they congregated close to the main before heading south to nest at the Bogue in Costa Rica.

In the midst of all this activity, and now with a better-defined role, we became involved in the village as never before, participating in communal agricultural labor parties—called *pana pana* in Miskito, or "hand to hand"—and roof thatching. In addition, Judi worked with

Miskito women collecting shellfish, harvesting and preparing and distributing food, and I went fishing, hunting and turtling with men, dividing meat when we were lucky and going without when we weren't. Besides doing these things, we also made daily measurements of food intake, and time inputs in subsistence, and took weather readings. Our strange requests to weigh what was common and record what everyone else considered obvious were graciously tolerated. Many people even looked forward to our daily visits. Our every move and piece of equipment was scrutinized and the information passed on to become a major link in the village gossip network. They watched us as we did them, each side trying to figure what the other was really up to behind the veneer of illogical behavior.

Research, visiting, data collection, writing up notes, and personal maintenance took fourteen to eighteen hours every day. It was hard work, sometimes discouraging, sometimes elating, but always fatiguing. The Miskito are among the most leisured peoples in the world: subsistence activities take no more than four or five hours per day, often less. Yet here we were—studying a group who were able to visit and rest more than they labored, while we constantly worked to learn how they had so much leisure. From their point of view, we must have appeared slightly "light in the head"—a Creole phrase meaning mentally ill—because we spent so much time and worked so hard to learn what was common knowledge to all of them.

Two graduate students in anthropology from the University of Michigan had offered to help with our research, and we looked forward to their arrival in the village.

When Marianne Schmink and Brian Weiss came, our workload was greatly reduced, and there was an added unanticipated benefit that made our life more relaxed: they became the new objects of Miskito scrutiny and gossip and thus relieved us from the daily pressure of being continually watched, dissected and reported on through the village's information pipeline.

Brian Weiss, in particular, became the focus of casual surveillance by Miskito gringo watchers. He was the best show in town. Everything about him intrigued the Miskito: he had long, unruly, bushy black hair and a beard; he was very animated, even hyperactive, a bundle of high-intensity energy who talked and moved twice as fast as anyone else in the village. Head down, shoulders hunched up, arms pumping in stiff-bent Ls, fists clenched, he would whiz from one house to the next, from one end of the village to the other. Nobody could keep up with him without running.

Byron Blandford was awed by Brian and nicknamed him "The

Jet," after the Miami–San José, Costa Rica plane that flew high and fast over the village on its way south. From Byron Blandford, this was quite a compliment, for he was acknowledged the best walker in the village; but Brian had outpaced, outdistanced and outlasted him when Byron had taken him to see his coconut ground, seven miles down the beach.

"That man move," he told me later. "He doesn't hold back . . . he flies."

Byron shook his head in wonderment. He couldn't fathom how Brian could outwalk him or why he always moved so fast. Byron had walked the equivalent of around the world and then some, so he was in a position to judge these things. Byron was the Moravian lay pastor for Set Net, a Miskito community located eighteen miles down the beach, which he had been visiting for services every week for fifteen years, covering a cumulative distance of a little more than 28,000 miles—greater than the earth's circumference. I had figured this out one day and told him. That's why the loss to Brian's fleet feet hurt so: an around-the-world walker, Miskito division champion, shouldn't have lost to an outsider, especially to a young American "boy."

Brian Weiss wanted to visit some other Miskito villages during his stay on the east coast, so I recommended that he go to Little Sandy Bay, a coastal community twenty-five miles north. Brian wanted to go the next day, and he spent the rest of the afternoon jetting around, assembling traveling gear and enough food to last him for a few days. He didn't have a pack, and his suitcase would be too awkward, so he finally located a large, double-thick plastic bag to carry his things in.

Sunday was a day to remember. Brian left for Little Sandy Bay at five in the morning to beat the heat, and at eleven o'clock the Bloodman came to Tasbapauni.

In Tasbapauni, Sunday is a day to go to church, dress up and walk about, rest, visit with friends and family, and generally relax. Not this Sunday, however. I suspected something was up when I saw a group of men pass by the window of our room carrying guns: .22 rifles, shotguns, and one old 30-06. It was definitely not normal Sunday behavior. Then the church bells started to ring—prolonged ringing, emergency ringing, not the calm, gentle sounds signaling the start of a Sunday service. I looked out the door and saw a large crowd gathering in front of the Anglican Church. All the men were armed, only a few women were present, and no children.

Everyone was talking at once and pointing in every conceivable direction. I asked Granville and Kitty what was going on. As the village "policemen," they seemed to be trying to organize things.

"The old lady saw the Bloodman when she coming here. She give the word, and we're sending out people to guard the place. Maybe we'll kill him this time," Kitty added with a look of mingled fright and menace.

I'd heard many stories about the Bloodman and knew that everyone was terrified of him. But these were just stories; nobody I knew had really seen the Bloodman.

Miskito and Creole peoples believe in the existence of the Bloodman. Which group passed on the story to the other, I don't know, but it is commonly accepted throughout eastern Nicaragua. The Bloodman is an evil person—some say spirit—who lurks on the edges of villages, especially during the dry season. The Bloodman collects blood, mainly from children—once in a while from young women and young men—whom he lures into the bush or surprises when they walk alone. The Bloodman is not simply a local variation of the "Boogie Man" used to keep children quiet and within reach. The Bloodman is a killer. He isn't Indian or Creole but an outsider, a foreigner, possibly "Sponish" or another "variety" of foreigner. He is always described as bearded and carrying a red bag filled with bottles in which he places blood collected from his victims. There are several stories of parents finding their child dead and drained of blood. The Bloodman is said to take the bottled blood to Managua, the capital, and sell it to the *Banco de Sangre* ("Blood Bank") for "several hundred and big odd *córdoba.*" Figures vary, but everyone agrees that the price of blood is "dear" and that the Bloodman probably receives at least $100 a pint, thereby making a "fat fee" from his gruesome trade.

"Who saw the Bloodman, and where?" I asked, thinking that this certainly sounded worth following up; after all, I wanted to get in on seeing what I was sure was a myth.

"Yonder," Granville indicated, gesturing north with pressed lips and outthrust jaw. "Up the beach, they say. Miss Zepora from Río Grande saw him. We're going there right now."

Before going to find Miss Zepora, however, Granville and Kitty organized the troops, sending out men to guard each end of the village and the three creek landings and main wharf on the lagoon side of the village, and "patrols" to go north and south on the beach.

Miss Zepora Matilda was at Antenaldo Carlos's house. I hadn't heard her name before because she lived in Río Grande Bar. Her daughter had married Antenaldo, and Miss Zepora had walked down the beach earlier in the morning to visit, not having seen them for several months.

The front room was jammed. Granville and Kitty pushed through with all the aplomb of two detectives investigating a case. I followed in their slipstream.

Miss Zepora was sitting in a rocking chair, flanked and worried over by Antenaldo and his wife. A white-haired deeply wrinkled old woman, she was trembling and moaning. At Kitty's and Granville's prodding, she told her story again, even though it obviously frightened her to do so. Gradually, between moans and "God spares," the story came out.

She'd left Río Grande Bar around four o'clock to walk the twenty miles of beach to Tasbapauni. About two or three hours after sunrise, she had seen a figure approaching from the other direction. As it got nearer, she saw that it was a stranger, a man, and he was bearing down on her. She'd never seen him or anyone like him before.

"It was the Bloodman, I'm telling you. All hairy-like, no shirt, breathing hard. He rush right up to me. I'm too old to run, but I tried to get away. He followed me right into the water."

Visibly upset, Miss Zepora broke off telling her story at this point, clutched at her daughter's hand and moaned again.

"The Lord saved me. Saved me from the Bloodman."

I knew then who the Bloodman was, but I couldn't get anyone's attention. The family was busy trying to calm the old woman; Kitty and Granville wanted the story; and the rest of the people were listening in stunned silence.

"I tried to get away in the sea, but I fell down. I looked up and he was standing close, reaching for me. He had a sack, and I could hear the blood bottles inside. He was reaching to take my blood, life spare. I tell him please not to kill me and take my blood. He looked funny like, backed off then. Then he got all hunched up and leave me."

"That's the Lord's work," Antenaldo concluded. "The Lord saved her from the Bloodman."

Antenaldo was studying to become an Anglican priest with Father Mac, and his judgment on religious matters was unquestioned.

I finally pulled Kitty over to the side and got him to listen to me.

"I know who the Bloodman is."

His eyes narrowed.

"He's not a Bloodman at all. The old lady saw Brian Weiss. You know, 'The Jet.' He left for Little Sandy Bay this morning. She must have met him on the beach."

Kitty still looked suspicious. I elaborated, describing the similarities: beard, red bag, a stranger—at least to Miss Zepora.

"That was Mr. Brian, no doubt about it." I hoped he'd believe me and call off the search.

A smile grew on his face.

"You mean that Mr. Brian scared this old woman?" He started to laugh.

One person laughing in a room filled with frightened people tends to attract attention. Kitty tried to explain, but collapsed against the wall in waves of body-shaking mirth. It was funny, but his reaction was unreasonable, and others probably thought it rude. I suppose he was reacting in relief to finding out that he wouldn't have to confront the Bloodman after all.

Granville got the story out of Kitty, and soon everyone in the room was giggling and laughing. All, that is, except Miss Zepora.

"You people crazy down this side. Carrying on and fooling around. That was the Bloodman. Up Río Grande way, they'd do something."

Miss Zepora was mad. She didn't know who Brian was, and I guess she thought people were laughing at her.

"The man you saw is a friend of mine, Miss Zepora. That wasn't the Bloodman."

"What you know? I know Bloodman when I see Bloodman." She screwed up her face, crossed her arms with a defiant flair, and glared at me.

"What Mr. Barney's saying is that he knows the man. He traveled here just to visit Mr. Barney." Granville's explanation seemed to dampen her outrage but not her conviction, and she pointed at me.

"And who to say this white man's not the Bloodman, too?"

"No, Miss Zepora. He's not the Bloodman neither. He's just writing about we Miskito people, how we making life here."

Suddenly Kitty jumped up and ran for the door.

"We got to stop those boys. They'll run him down on the beach and shoot him dead."

Kitty started up the beach after the men he'd sent to look for the Bloodman. I wasn't worried about Brian, however. He had several hours' start, and he was, after all, the fastest thing to hit Tasbapauni in a long, long time. They'd never catch him.

Brian returned to Tasbapauni on Wednesday. His entrance into the village was a memorable one. Small children pointed at him and then ran in mock fright. Others smiled and laughed. Bewildered, Brian came immediately to me to ask what was going on.

"Did anything unusual happen to you last Sunday on the way to Little Sandy Bay?"

"No. Not really. Oh, I did run into some old woman who acted strange. But nothing unusual."

"Well, Brian, you're now known as the Bloodman, and you scared the hell out of that woman. Come on in, and I'll tell you about it."

Being mistaken for the Bloodman is a heck of a way to start a professional career as an anthropologist. Weiss would always remember that Sunday. But I'd been implicated, too. The old woman had all but accused me outright of also being a Bloodman. However, Granville had stuck up for me, telling her that I was only writing a book. Thinking back on it, maybe Granville was wrong. Perhaps there's a little of the Bloodman in us all.

That was the only Bloodman Emergency we experienced during our stays with the Miskito, so I was never able to verify whether or not there really is a blood-collecting Bloodman. Symbolically there is, of course. Foreigners, outsiders—some bearded, others not— had for years taken things from the Miskito: labor, resources, the old ways, and things scribbled in books and exposed on celluloid, leaving behind a little less each time, draining some of the indigenous spirit and traditional life with each encounter. Some things were taken for profit, while others were taken to preserve what was once there. Whether it was mahogany, jaguars, turtles, souls, photographs or writings, each export contributes toward draining the passing corpus. To have something taken or captured, whether by axe, turtle net, Bible, pen or camera, whether tangible or intangible, inevitably changes that which is left. What is obtained is always lost in the conversion, so the pressure is greater the next time. Roles mix and switch from actor to spectator. What happens to them happens to us.

The Miskito have an amazing ability to roll with adversity, to integrate new things in Miskito terms and to keep an overall humor. To my thinking, they are the best stand-up comics and one-line philosophers around. In a small way, that's part of why they are still Miskito and haven't gone the way of so many other disappearing and vanished indigenous peoples.

For example, the Bloodman incident didn't end after everyone found out it was only Brian Weiss, an anthropologist in unintentional drag. The "Mr. Brian and Miss Zepora Bloodman Encounter" lives, instituted in village lore, albeit in a much-modified form and with frequent improvisational additions and deletions. Nevertheless, the story is still going strong; the context resilient, the content malleable. I've seen it reenacted. If things are slow, "nothing new," someone might suggest doing the Bloodman number. It doesn't matter who plays whom—that's part of the fun in it; someone will play Brian, someone else Zepora. The stage is set, spectators already giggling. "Mr. Brian, The Jet" comes hustling along, arms pumping, head down, an imaginary sack over his shoulder. "Zepora" stops, trembles and falls down, pleading for mercy, imploring the Bloodman to spare her. A running narration from the audience adds to the documentary feel of it all. It's either high camp or low theater. Whatever it is, it's a damned good show.

For the Miskito of Tasbapauni, the Bloodman remained "something dangerous," to be feared, despite their discovery of the inadvertent imposter. To me, the Bloodman was a symbol of the Miskito's past experiences with outsiders: a myth I first learned about in 1968, but a reality with which the Miskito had coped for generations. It was unsettling for me to learn later that the Miskito may have been correct about a real Bloodman after all. Their old belief foreshadowed the exposure of a real Bloodman. The present had caught up to the past.

In 1978, information began to be uncovered in Managua that indicated the presence of an actual Bloodman, one who may have been tied to the Somoza family, and one who figured importantly in the widespread uprisings and popular dissent against the Nicaraguan government.

The Somoza family had controlled Nicaraguan politics and economy since 1934. In 1967 General Anastasio Somoza Debayle, following in his father's and older brother's footsteps, won the presidential election against token opposition, which set off short-lived street demonstrations and small-scale guerrilla raids. The new government survived and began expanding the family's holdings and fortunes through continued dictatorial rule of Nicaragua's people and resources.

The only effective opposition to the Somoza regime came from Pedro Joaquín Chamorro, the owner of La Prensa, Nicaragua's largest circulation newspaper. Chamorro frequently published accounts charging President Somoza and his political associates with graft, payoffs, kickbacks from foreign investors, exploitation of poor urban and rural peoples, and the looting of international emergency relief supplies sent to Nicaragua after the 1972 earthquake that destroyed Managua. Chamorro and La Prensa were suppressed until September 1977, when government censorship of the media was finally lifted. Chamorro immediately began running stories on a scandal that involved the Bloodman.

In 1971 a company in Managua called Plasmaféresis began to buy huge quantities of blood from poor Nicaraguans for export to the United States. The company was the sole FDA-licensed foreign source of blood plasma and supplied 10 percent of all the raw plasma used in the United States. Plasmaféresis was open six days a week, from six A.M. to eight P.M., and handled a hundred donors an hour, some 38,000 pints per month, 400,000 per year—the equivalent of more than one pint per year from every person in Managua!

Writing in *La Prensa*, Chamorro condemned the blood trade as "an inhuman tariff in the blood of Nicaraguans" and charged that the company was making an immense profit off the poor, who were forced to sell their blood to buy food. Chamorro accused President Somoza of having invested in the company.

On January 10, 1978, on his way to the *La Prensa* office, Chamorro was assassinated. His murder and funeral touched off the first mass protests and violence against the Somoza government in a decade: Plasmaféresis was burned to the ground, as were several Somoza-owned buildings. There were two days of street demonstrations and riots, and a general strike was called by businessmen.

Somoza denied having had anything to do with Chamorro's murder. Five men were arrested and confessed to having been hired to kill Chamorro by the manager of Plasmaféresis, Dr. Pedro M. Ramos, who had left Nicaragua the day before the assassination and who still has not returned. The assassins' confessions also implicated several close associates of Somoza.

Chamorro's death galvanized the nation and gave widespread popular support to the Sandinistas, Nicaraguan rebels who later stormed the National Palace in August and held hundreds of government officials hostage, and who led the September Insurrection that battled Somoza's *Guardia Nacional* from several barricaded cities.

Although the blood bank was destroyed and the oppressive government weakened, the regime of the the Bloodman survived the first round of armed rebel opposition. Further insurrection will follow.

And from their vantage point on the isolated east coast, the Miskito remain aloof from *this* Bloodman trouble. Each people must cope with its own Bloodman.

4. Bottlemail and Apollo 11

The tide is running out slowly, leaving a widening damp sand corridor behind the receding sea. A light drizzle cuts the early morning gray glow to the east. There are no footprints on the virgin beach at five-thirty in the morning. In the village people still sleep after the night-long heavy rain and wind. On the beach beyond high water traces, wind- and surf-piled debris litter the loose sand. Limbs, leafed branches, tree trunks, brown mats of torn sea vegetation lie tangled and half-buried. It is *pastara kati*, high-wind month, July, and the height of *li mani*, the rainy season. It is a time of flooded rivers, rough seas, wind, storms, black skies, sodden forest, and chilly, wet nights. Food supplies in the village are meager; the first harvest is still months away, and nothing is left over from last year.

A solitary figure walks north along the beach. Barefoot, pants rolled above the knees, the man carries a machete, a burlap bag and an old, wired-together .22 rifle. His eyes are alert for a late-feeding deer or agouti at the beach-forest edge. Damp, cold and hungy—not even a cigarette to cut empty stomach pangs—he walks on, picking his way through jumbled drift, following the high-beach soft sand where the going is harder but luckier.

Pungi had wanted to stay in bed, too, but Ena wanted to make coconut oil, enough to sell; then they could buy some flour and coffee. It was a six-mile walk to his *cocal*. If he worked fast, he could pull, husk and carry home the forty needed coconuts before eleven. Six hours to make the oil; they'd eat by sundown. And with any luck, he'd get a shot at an animal or find something washed up on the beach. The first one on the beach always had the best chances at that.

A light bulb, one torn rubber sandal, an empty aerosol spray can (Fresh-Aire room deodorant), various plastic fragments, a worn piece of bristly nylon rope, a tar-covered doll's arm—nothing of use in the first mile. To find anything of value was sheer luck, but there was always hope, especially if no one had gone up the beach earlier.

Each tide brought new things in from the sea. Just two days ago, Cleveland, Pungi's neighbor, had found a large orange plastic float which he'd already converted into a water canteen for trips to the cays. Plastic and metal floats were the best, or plastic bottles or larger containers. The cast aluminum ones could be cut in half for cooking pots and the plastic ones used to store water or coconut oil. Once in a while, serviceable pieces of shrimp nets, nylon ropes and lines were found. These could be taken apart and remade into turtle nets and anchor lines. Hatchcovers, sheets of plywood, board lumber were rare but among the luckiest of finds. The really big and good things were seldom found anymore, not like in the back times during the "Hitler War" when the older heads used to find plenty of fifty-four-gallon drums, lifeboats, crates of food and clothes, and once a drum of alcohol that had been good for a week-long big drunk. What he'd really like to find, Pungi thought, was a nice piece of that white plastic foam. With a little gasoline or kerosene, he'd burn and melt it and patch the leaking nail holes in his canoe.

Some people could walk the beach day after day and not find anything. There was more to finding than just trying to find. When the priest came to hold services, some of the people prayed for luck to find things on the beach—enough lumber to finish a house, a fifty-four-gallon drum to catch rainwater off the roof, or something really valuable to sell to an American shrimp boat captain, like the plastic sailboat that Meshek found last year. But praying wasn't finding. Meshek never went to the services.

Beach drift came from the "outside" or a "next place" beyond the horizon and beyond the bounds of personal experience. Far-off places that lost good things to the sea. Places unknown to Pungi but often thought about and pondered over in reflective moments, such as after finding something on the beach or hearing the "latest" news brought by a returning villager from Bluefields.

Each day the beach looked different to Pungi. This morning it had changed slightly from the day before. It was a July beach and showed the cumulative effects of the heavy weather months of June and July: storms and squalls, heavy surf, wide and powerful longshore currents fed and driven by brown river outwash; all of these together altered and re-formed the narrow sand strip that was the thin elastic buffer protecting the land from the sea. The smooth, flat dry-season beach was gone, replaced by a wave-cut, debris-piled, jumbled sand topography, made even narrower by the wind-driven high water that cut the beach width in half. As a result, walking was slow and more tiring in the high-beach deep sand. And if you were keeping an eye out for a lucky find, the going was even slower.

[6:00 A.M.]

Pungi was hungry. He wished he'd had a piece of johnnycake and some coffee. But there had been none in the house; no food and no money. It was chilly, and the drizzle cut into his body to where he could feel it against the hunger. Maybe he should have stayed home and tried to get some food from a relative. One and a half miles walked, more than four to go; might as well keep going, he thought.

The single figure walked slowly along the vacant beach, his eyes ranging from side to side, alone and searching at the far edge of the Caribbean, long sea and rain forest miles from other places. The eastern horizon gradually turned light in the new-day sun still masked by cloud banks and rain. The start of another day, but one that was to affect peoples everywhere, even those as remote as Pungi Perez.

[6:00 A.M., CDT, 7-20-69, Apollo 11 Mission Commentary]

PAO   This is Apollo Control, 93 hours, 29 minutes ground elapsed time. Some 5 minutes away from loss of signal of the *Apollo 11* on this revolution. And a wake-up call is expected from the spacecraft communicator, Ron Evans, here in Mission Control just prior to the time the spacecraft goes into the . . . goes over the hill on the lunar far side. Standing by as we wait for him to make his call. Presently, *Apollo 11* is in an orbit measuring 64 nautical miles apocynthion, 55.5 nautical miles at pericynthion. Present orbital velocity around the moon, 5,370 feet per second. Spacecraft calculated now to weigh 70,321 pounds. Still standing by for wake-up call. Standing by for Ron Evans's big moment as he makes his call to the spacecraft. As for being the sleep watch, his job has been rather easy, or at least he hasn't had too much conversation with . . . here we go.
CAPCOM   *Apollo 11. Apollo 11.* Good morning from the black team.
SC   Good morning, Houston.
CAPCOM   Good morning. Got about 2 minutes to LOS here, Mike.
SC   Oh my, you guys wake up early.
CAPCOM   Yes, you're about 2 minutes early on the wake up. Looks like you were really sawing them away.

[6:00 A.M., CDT, Pearl Lagoon]

Baird Lewis was tired. The trip from Bluefields had been long and rough, fifteen hours so far, and they still had to cross the upper lagoon from Kisuta Point to the Tasbapauni Creek mouth. As owner of the boat, Baird had stayed up all night to help his captain steer the boat through the heavy rains. Nobody slept much, but at least the others could sit down in the passenger compartment behind the wheelhouse.

Diesel vibration and exhaust sounds pulse-beat passengers into a half-sleep amid damp moldy-smelling blankets. The humid air is choked with fumes and stale odors kept in by the heavy canvas tarp curtains rolled down and lashed against the rain. The tiny boat rolls in the lagoon swells. Baird hangs by one arm outside and unties the tarps. Light and air cleanse the cloistered interior in a rush of cool twilight freshness. Blankets folded, a stray shoe located, the passengers sit and stretch cramped legs and drink cold, sweet coffee. Animation returns gradually to contorted, numbed bodies. Occasionally a burst of wind blows an edge of the rain wall into the open compartment.

A wave slaps the hull, and the prop spins free for a moment, churning the rain-dimpled wake. Baird turns the wheel to bring his boat back on course. The tiny boat trudges slowly across the lagoon. Inside, the passengers again turn to discuss the news heard in Bluefields.

"Can't figure why they want to go." The red ember of the relit cigar moves back and forth like a small neon, emphasizing the old woman's shaking head. "Rocket is pure chance, not so?"

"They going to get rich off rocket. Carry passenger, build hotel on the moon, and open up cantina. That's what it's all about—money business."

The old woman looks distastefully at the young man who has just spoken. "All the time you thinking about money. Money can't get you down from the moon. You think that money . . . "

"Judgment day. That's what's coming," interrupted the lay pastor, holding up a Bible. "High science and rockets going to . . . "

"They're going to find something on the moon, big money something. Rich, ain't ya know . . . they going to get a five-hundred-*córdoba* reward. They study down these things. Know where the money is." Finished speaking, the young man shoves his sockless feet into narrow, pointed shoes whose small size miraculously absorbs the wide, thick-callused soles.

"Worldly things. Money . . . " The man with the Bible again tries to make his point.

"What you know about these things? I'm telling you money and rocket is pure chance," the old woman says and flicks the cigar butt out into the rain.

I watch the Indian woman's bobbing homemade cigar—a reference point to mark our passage. Lost from view on the backside of a wave, it reappears, and then is gone again as currents and our forward motion widen the gap until the cigar is lost in the gray of our wake.

[6:53 A.M., CDT, 7-20-69, Apollo 11 Mission Commentary]

PAO   This is Apollo Control. 94 hours, 21 minutes ground elapsed time. Should have acquisition of signal as *Apollo 11* comes around on the front side of the moon on the tenth revolution. AOS is confirmed. We'll stand by CAPCOM's call to the crew. We have data coming in now. After having breakfast and getting all squared away after the night's rest period, the crew will have a rather busy day, including the first man landing on the moon. Some of the preliminary time's being generated now for maneuvers of the day . . . will include separation at . . . a separation burn at 100 hours, 39 minutes, 50 seconds. Here goes the call.

CAPCOM   . . . standing by.

SC   Houston, *Apollo 11*.

CAPCOM   *Apollo 11*, Houston. Go.

SC   Roger. How do you read the biomed in the LMP with the LCG on? Over.

CAPCOM   Roger. Stand by *11*.

CAPCOM   *Apollo 11*, Houston. We have good data on all three crewmen. We'll play that . . . the commander we do not have yet. . . .

[7:30 A.M., CDT, Tasbapauni]

Baird's boat pulls up to the wharf behind the village, a long, wet trip from Bluefields over at last. The diesel continues to roll over, refusing to stop.

"Shut that thing down," Baird shouts to the engineer below. "You going to drive us right up on land."

A last chug and the motor stops. The passengers stand in the rain, waiting for their things to be unloaded from the hold. Small boxes of dry goods and clothes purchased with money from the sale of pigs, chickens and coconut oil in Bluefields are passed up from below. Hunched against the rain, each person makes his or her way over the flooded path through the swamp toward home.

[7:31 A.M., CDT, 7-20-69, Apollo 11 Mission Commentary]

PAO   This is Apollo Control. Still F line with the air-ground circuit on the tenth revolution around the moon. The crew reported that the commander had 5½ hours of sleep during the night; command module pilot, 6 hours; lunar module pilot, 5 hours. Now 95 hours and 5 minutes into the mission. Another 27 minutes remaining in this pass. Still loss of signal continuing to monitor air-ground circuit. We'll leave it up live until loss of signal.

CAPCOM   *Apollo 11*, Houston. Over.

SC   Houston, *Apollo 11*. Go ahead.

CAPCOM   Roger. The Black Bugle just arrived with some morning news briefs if you're ready.

SC   Go ahead.

CAPCOM   Roger. Okay. Church services around the world today are mentioning *Apollo 11* in their prayers. President Nixon's worship service at the White House is also dedicated to the mission, and our fellow astronaut, Frank Borman, is still in there pitching and will read the passage from Genesis which was read on *Apollo 8* last Christmas. The Cabinet and members of Congress, with emphasis on the Senate and House space committees, have been invited, along with a number of other guests. Buzz, your son Andy got a tour of MSC yesterday. Your Uncle Bob Moon accompanied him on the visit which included the LRL. Among the . . . .

SC   Thank you.

CAPCOM   Roger. Among the large headlines concerning Apollo this morning, there's one asking that you watch for a lovely girl with a big rabbit. An ancient legend says a beautiful Chinese girl called Chango has been living there for 4,000 years. It seems she was banished to the moon because she stole the pill for immortality from her husband. You might also look for her companion, a large Chinese rabbit, who is easy to spot since he is only standing on his hind feet in the shade of a cinnamon tree. The name of the rabbit is not recorded.

SC   Okay, we'll keep a close eye for the bunny girl.

CAPCOM   Roger. You residents of the spacecraft *Columbia* may be interested in knowing that today is Independence day in the country of Colombia. Gloria Dies of the Philippines was crowned Miss Universe last night. She defeated sixty other girls for the global beauty title. Miss Dies is eighteen with black hair and eyes and measures 34½, 23, 34½. First runner up was Miss Australia, followed by Miss Israel and Miss Japan. While you're on your way back Tuesday night, the American and National League Allstars will be playing ball in Washington. Mel Stottlemyre of the Yankees is expected to be the American League's first pitcher. No one is predicting who will be first pitcher for the National League yet. They had nine on the roster.

[7:30 A.M., CDT, On the beach six miles north of Tasbapauni]

High up on the beach at the edge of the tide traces, Pungi sees a bottle. He stoops to pick it up. A one-liter Pepsi bottle, made in Norway, with a screwdown cap, and some papers inside. Pungi fishes them out with a stick, unrolls the papers and shields them from the rain.

Poem to a Finder of Bottlemail

This brief little note
I'm meaning to send
With a bottle along
to a distant friend.

I certainly knew
That a violent gale
might carry astray
with my bottlemail.
By sending it off
with the howling miles
To be washed ashore
On some distant isles,
—and never be found
By anyone else
Than the singing sand
and ocean shells . . .

But as it was dropped
On a sunny day,
I got reason to wish
All luck on its way;
—and look! on the ridge
Of the ocean blue,
My bottle has drifted
From me to you!
—so far and so long
Has it floated by,
That I hope you will write
An early reply.

For sure can you send
A bottle to me;
I'm the song of the sands,
I'm the shells of the sea.
                              11 February 1969
                              Islestone Reed

Written on the Caribbean Sea the 11th of Feb., 1969. Islestone Reed, 3414 Skjåstad, Norway.

To the Finder of this Bottlemail!

Carried along with a million wishful waves, this letter has finally reached you—you lucky finder of bottlemail! What a magnificent feeling must it be to discover such a rarity flowing on the top of the sea, rushing to the beach where you stand—just waiting with excitement to pick it up from the water.

You don't know who has written these lines, but we might come to know each other—if you want to—by just sending a letter to me in return. You will surely get an answer.

So I wish this bottlemail will bring you luck and success throughout

Pungi Perez, the finder of the bottlemail, and his wife Ena. Tasbapauni, 1975.

your lifetime, and always remember that glorious day at the seaside—the day you found this bottlemail.

Greetings from a distant friend across the ocean

Pungi read the poem and letter several times, picking out those words he knew from the few years of schooling he'd had as a boy. *Luck* and *friend* were the ones he looked at most closely. Carefully replacing the papers inside the bottle, he stowed it in his bag, marked the spot on the beach, and continued on toward his *cocal.* Regardless of his interest in the bottle and its contents, he still had to get those coconuts for Ena.

It was through the bottlemail and *Apollo 11* that I met Pungi and later, his family. It was midafternoon; the rain had stopped; and I rolled groggily out of the damp sheets and off the cot to answer the knock at the door. Still exhausted from the boat trip from Bluefields, I stumbled to the door, turning on the portable shortwave radio on the way.

"Excuse for the bother, Mr. Barney, but I came to look you for help," said the man who later identified himself as Francisco (Pungi) Perez. I vaguely remembered having talked with him a couple of times weeks before, but I didn't know him well. He asked me to help him "overhaul" the message found in the bottle and to explain where the sender lived.

I read the poem and letter to him and was just starting to tell him what an amazing thing it was to find such a bottle after it had drifted so far and come to rest on that particular stretch of isolated beach, when the announcements on the radio attracted my attention: the *Eagle* was about to descend to the surface of the moon. I brought the radio outside for better reception, and Pungi carried his bottle and papers. Judi rounded up Barney, who was under his cot playing with the margay, and brought them outside. From the isolated village, our temporary home and Pungi's world, we listened with people all over the world to that moment in history. We looked up into the July sky, and our thoughts and best wishes went out to the men in the *Eagle* and the *Columbia*.

[3:15 P.M. CDT, 7-20-69, Apollo 11 Mission Commentary]

CAPCOM   Houston. You're go for landing. Over.

EAGLE   Roger, understand. Go for landing. 3,000 feet.

CAPCOM   Copy.

EAGLE   12 alarm. 1201.

EAGLE   1201.

CAPCOM   Roger. 1201 alarm.

EAGLE   We're go. Hang tight. We're go. 2,000 feet. 2,000 feet into the AGS. 47 degrees.

CAPCOM   Roger.

EAGLE   47 degrees.

CAPCOM   *Eagle* looking great. You're go.

PAO   Altitude 1,600. 1,400 feet. Still looking very good.

CAPCOM   Roger. 1202. We copy it. . . .

CAPCOM   60 seconds.

EAGLE   Lights on. Down 2½. Forward. Forward. Good. 40 feet, down 2½. Picking up some dust. 30 feet, 2½ down. Faint shadow. 4 forward. 4 forward, drifting to the right a little. 6 [garbled] down a half.

CAPCOM   30 seconds.

EAGLE   [garbled] forward. Drifting right. [garbled] Contact light. Okay, engine stop. ACA out of detent. Modes control both auto; descent engine command override, off. Engine arm, off. 413 is in.

CAPCOM   We copy you down, *Eagle*.

EAGLE   [Armstrong] Houston, *Tranquility* Base here. The *Eagle* has landed.

CAPCOM   Roger, *Tranquility*, we copy you on the ground. You've got a bunch of guys about to turn blue. We're breathing again. Thanks a lot.

That was a moment to be remembered and savored. For a brief time, different peoples throughout the world shared a similar

Pungi Perez contemplates the letter and poem he found in the Norwegian Pepsi bottle on the day of the Apollo 11 moon landing, July 20, 1969.

concern: the continued safety and success of the *Apollo 11* astronauts. In a few days the men of *Apollo 11* would be on their way back to planet Earth; in a few months we would return to our world; but Pungi and the rest of the Miskito would stay in Tasbapauni, a place and a condition apart but nonetheless changed by the events of that day. For us the discrepancies between living in this village and the landing on the moon highlighted our appreciation of two worlds: one highly technological and modern; the other highly social and isolated.

Pungi's world view changed that day. All at once he was flooded with information from distant places beyond the limits of his experience. He asked me about the Apollo Mission, Norway, and messages from the moon and in bottles. I spoke of rockets, spacecraft, ocean currents, Pepsi, and astronauts. It was an unusual day. We both marveled at the chance circumstances that had juxtaposed communication in a bottle and from a spacecraft in one village, on one day, on a remote Caribbean shore.

I went with Pungi to his house to help him compose a reply to Mr. Reed, the originator of the bottlemail. Pungi changed into his best clothes and met me on the front porch; he called out the entire family to witness the writing of the letter. It was a serious occasion, and all were wearing their best. Pungi's wife, Ena, a very pretty woman, held Dempsey, four months old and extremely thin. Fluvia, twelve; Anita, six; and Sidney, one, gathered around their father on the sagging wooden porch. Several neighbors joined us. Other bottles with messages were produced, but none so fine as the one he'd found, Pungi assured us. One bottle contained an address: John J. Johnston, Universal Travel Agency, 515 Audubon Building, 931 Canal Street, New Orleans, LA 70112. Sent 12-23-68. There was also a bottle with a note dropped from a Russian ship off Dakar, Senegal, West Africa. The finders all claimed that their bottles would bring them great wealth as soon as they notified the senders that they had been found.

While I was looking at the New Orleans and Russian messages, Byron Blandford, Pungi's neighbor, told him to be sure to hold onto the luck of the bottlemail.

"Last year one man bucked up a bottle with some American money and a note in it, down the beach halfway to Set Net. He carried it to a next man in Set Net who could read, and that one sent it in. Quick time he get an answer, and every month he gets a check for five dollars, American gold. The one who found it gets not a thing. He was the one who had the reward coming, but he turn over his luck through ignorance."

"That's the thing, Mr. Barney; that's why I asked you to help with my letter and carry it to Bluefields. I have to be sure," Pungi added.

I took out some paper and asked Pungi what he wanted to say.

"Tell him where you found the bottle," Ena injected. "Maybe he never hear of we Miskito people."

"Put that in the letter then," Pungi confirmed.

"Tell him about the hard times here in Tasbapauni, how we making life here," offered one of the neighbors.

"Mr. Barney, just write down that I find his bottle, and I'm glad for that, too. We get to understand about the poem, and all my family look on it. You tell him that I have a wife and four children; write down their names and how old they are . . . "

"Tell him how you came back from the dead, Pungi. Give him that story," Byron suggested. As I later found out, he referred to the time when, coming back from Bluefields at night, Pungi had fallen off Sam Francis's boat in the middle of the lagoon. His absence had not been discovered until the boat landed in Tasbapauni. A search party sent to look for him found nothing. Meanwhile, Pungi had stripped off all his clothes, swum to the closest shore, and was walking the twenty miles through swamp and forest. He arrived at the village at nine P.M., slipped from shadow to shadow to his house, and walked in nude at his own wake. According to Ena, all the friends and relatives began screaming, thinking their songs and lamenting had brought him back from the dead.

"Let's save that story for another letter, Pungi. What other things have happened to you that you'd like to put in the letter?" I asked.

Many people helped compose that letter. Most of it was a straightforward description of finding the bottle, of Pungi and his family, and of what they did for a living. To a person living in Norway, the letter may have seemed as bizarre as the one Pungi had found. But I think it was more poetic.

With the letter collectively finished, conversation turned to the moon landing.

"How much is your government going to give them for being so brave?"

When I explained that they would get their regular salary, nothing more except for the fame of being first on the moon, everyone was incredulous.

"No reward? How much money will they be paid for going to the moon?"

I couldn't answer that one, but when someone asked how far the moon was, I felt more confident about a reply. After all, I was a geographer.

"The moon is about 240,000 miles from earth, or almost equal to ten times around the earth."

Puzzled looks.

"That is, if you were to travel between Tasbapauni and Puerto Cabezas about 2,700 times, it would be the same distance as from the earth to the moon."

Nobody said anything. They just looked at me in a strange sort of way. Conceptual analogy wasn't going to do the trick. I thought I'd try to use a scale example, where they could actually see the relative distance.

"I need a green coconut and an orange." These were quickly obtained. With a ballpoint pen I drew a crude outline of the continents on the smooth, light green coconut. I then put in the boundaries of the Central American countries and measured the length of the Caribbean coastline of Nicaragua, an exaggerated one-quarter inch, as I recall. Now came the time for the orange and some computations on paper. If one inch on the coconut equaled about 1,118 miles on the ground, then 219 coconut inches would be the equivalent distance of the earth to the moon, or, in my example, from the coconut to the orange. I measured off eighteen feet from the coconut and asked a little boy to hold the orange at that mark.

"O.K. If the earth were the size of this coconut, the east coast of Nicaragua would be this big," I said, passing the coconut world around. "The orange is the moon, and it's located where the moon would be. No, let me say that again: the orange represents the moon if the coconut is the earth. So the distance between the earth and the moon is as far as between the coconut and the orange. Got it?"

Something was lost in the translation. I couldn't tell from the way people looked at me whether it was awe or pity they were expressing. I spent the next hour trying to explain the relationship. I blasted tiny twig rockets off the BIC ink spot that represented Cape Kennedy, Florida. I piloted rockets around the coconut and put them into lunar trajectory. I landed mini-LMs on the orange. In a last-ditch effort to make the experience more relevant, I also drifted matchheads across the Atlantic and across the Caribbean to show them how the bottles had been caught up in currents before landing on the beach near their village.

Right in the middle of a very difficult maneuver in which Armstrong and Aldrin were going to blast off the orange to rejoin the *Columbia* Command Module, Pungi interrupted me. I looked up to find everyone else gone, leaving the boy with the orange, Pungi and me. It was almost dark.

"Mr. Barney, you sure you'll mail my letter?" Pungi asked,

peering at me quizzically as I tried to reunite an orbiting seed and a matchhead.

"Sure. You can count on it. No problem," I replied, my assurances doing little to soothe his evident doubt about my reliability and my sanity.

"Well, then, I'm going in. Me and Burnell are going hunting tonight, and I've got to get some sleep before." Pungi went inside, leaving me, the coconut, and the boy with the orange, which he immediately ate, as it was obvious the show was over.

Looking back on that experience, I wish I'd kept the coconut as a teaching aid for my university classes in physical geography. Some very good potential lectures were traced on it.

Tired and hungry from my Houston Control South efforts, I turned for home. As I walked along the beach in the fading light of that July day, I mulled over what I'd said and should have said, and thought of better examples and analogies to explain part of my world to the people in this village. I wondered what they were doing on the moon and if any of the astronauts could have explained where they were and what they were doing to the Miskito.

[6:12 P.M., CDT, 7-20-69, Apollo 11 Mission Commentary]

EAGLE Houston, *Tranquility*. Over.

CAPCOM *Tranquility*, Houston. Go ahead.

EAGLE Roger. This is the LM pilot. I'd like to take this opportunity to ask every person listening in, whoever and wherever they may be, to pause for a moment and contemplate the events of the past few hours and to give thanks in his or her own way. Over.

CAPCOM Roger, *Tranquility* Base.

EAGLE . . . is about ready to fall off. As a matter of fact, it just doesn't look like it sunk any at all.

PAO This is Apollo Control, Houston, at 105 hours 42 minutes into the flight of *Apollo 11*. You have heard that statement in our tapes transmission from lunar module pilot Buzz Aldrin. Our projected time for extravehicular activity, at this point, is still very preliminary. I repeat, it could come as soon as 8:00 P.M. Houston time. We won't know for sure about the time, with reasonable certainty, until about an hour before the event. Meanwhile, as we'll soon be progressing toward man's first step on the lunar surface, we have an interesting phenomenon here in the Mission Control Center, Houston. Something we've never seen before. Our visual of the lunar module, our visual display now standing still. Our velocity digitals for *Tranquility* Base now reading zero. Reverting, if we could, to the terminology of an earlier form of transportation, the railroad. What we're witnessing now is man's very first trip into space with a station stop along the route. At 105 hours 43 minutes, continuing to monitor the loop, this is Apollo Control, Houston.

Later that night we listened to the radio with Baldwin, Alodia, their children and several neighbors. Armstrong was soon due to step on the moon's surface, and Baldwin took over translating into Miskito the AFRTS-relayed broadcast to the group. He was in top form. I could almost imagine him working at one of the consoles at the Houston Mission Control.

[9:47 P.M., CDT, 7-20-69. Apollo 11 Mission Commentary]

ARMSTRONG   Okay, Houston, I'm on the porch.

CAPCOM   Roger, Neil.

ALDRIN   Okay right now, Neil.

CAPCOM   *Columbia, Columbia,* this is Houston. 1 minute and 30 seconds to LOS all systems go, over.

ALDRIN   Stay where you are a minute, Neil.

ARMSTRONG   Okay.

ALDRIN   Need a little slack.

PAO   Neil Armstrong on the porch at 109 hours 19 minutes 16 seconds.

[9:52 P.M., CDT]

CAPCOM   Houston. Roger, we copy, and we're standing by for your TV.

ARMSTRONG   Houston, this is Neil. Radio check.

CAPCOM   Neil, this is Houston. You're loud and clear. Break, break. Buzz, this is Houston. Radio check and verify TV circuit breaker in.

ALDRIN   Roger, TV circuit breaker's in. Receive loud and clear.

CAPCOM   Man, we're getting a picture on the TV.

ALDRIN   Oh, you got a good picture, huh?

CAPCOM   There's a great deal of contrast in it, and currently it's upside-down on our monitor, but we can make out a fair amount of detail.

ALDRIN   Okay, will you verify the position, the opening I ought to have on the camera.

CAPCOM   Stand by.

CAPCOM   Okay, Neil, we can see you coming down the ladder now.

ARMSTRONG   Okay, I just checked . . . getting back up to that first step, Buzz; it's not even collapsed too far, but it's adequate to get back up.

CAPCOM   Roger, we copy.

ARMSTRONG   It takes a pretty good little jump.

CAPCOM   Buzz, this is Houston. F 2 1/160th second for shadow photography on the sequence camera.

ALDRIN   Okay.

ARMSTRONG   I'm at the foot of the ladder. The LM foot pads are only depressed in the surface about 1 or 2 inches. Although the surface appears to be very, very fine grained, as you get close to it. It's almost like a powder. Now and then it's very fine.

[9:56 P.M., CDT]

ARMSTRONG   I'm going to step off the LM now.
ARMSTRONG   That's one small step for man. One giant leap for mankind.
ARMSTRONG   As the . . . the surface is fine and powdery. I can . . . I can pick it up loosely with my toe. It does adhere in fine layers like powdered charcoal to the soles and sides of my boots. I only go in a small fraction of an inch. Maybe an eighth of an inch, but I can see the footprints of my boots and the treads in the fine sandy particles.
CAPCOM   Neil, this is Houston. We're copying.

"This is the dangerous part," Baldwin said to me, looking very stern. "That's all new land up there, like going deep into the *selva*."

Alodia giggled at Baldwin's seriousness. He ignored her and moved the kerosene lamp closer to the radio.

A garbled message from Armstrong at nine fifty-six; he's on the surface of the moon. Baldwin beamed.

"Now he's going to take a good *pasear* on the moon," Baldwin commented. "See what strange kinda things he can buck up."

A short time later Judi, Barney and I went to bed. I left the radio with Baldwin, who was sitting alone on his front step, listening and looking up at the moon.

[10:21 P.M., CDT, 7-20-69, Apollo 11 Mission Commentary]

ARMSTRONG   . . . find the purple rocks?
ALDRIN   No. Pretty small sparkly [cut out] . . . fragments [cut out] . . . on in places [cut out] . . . I would take a first guess, some sort of biotite. We'll leave that to the Lunar Analysis, but [cut out].
ARMSTRONG   Bio compacts underneath [cut out] . . . completely [cut out] . . . no, I say you don't sink down more than a quarter of an inch.
PAO   Biotite is a brown mica substance.
ARMSTRONG   Okay, Houston. I'm going to change lenses on you.
CAPCOM   Roger, Neil.
PAO   Life Support Consumables still looking good.
ARMSTRONG   Okay, Houston. Tell me if you're getting a new picture.
CAPCOM   Neil, this is Houston. That's affirmative. We're getting a new picture. You can tell it's a longer focal length lens, and for your information, all LM systems are GO. Over.
ARMSTRONG   We appreciate that. Thank you.
ALDRIN   Neil is now unveiling the plaque [cut out] . . .
CAPCOM   Roger. We got you foresighted but back under one track.

ARMSTRONG   For those who haven't read the plaque, we'll read the plaque that's on the front landing gear of this LM. First there's two hemispheres, one showing each of the two hemispheres of the Earth. Underneath, it says, Here man from the planet Earth first set foot upon the Moon, July 1969 A.D. We came in peace for all mankind. It has the crew members' signatures and the signature of the President of the United States. Ready for the camera? I can . . .

ALDRIN   No, you take this [garble]

ARMSTRONG   That's the LEC length.

ALDRIN   Now I'm afraid these barbed materials are going to [cut out] . . . The surface material is powdery, but [cut out] . . . how good your lens is, but if you could [cut out]. Very much like a very finely powdered carbon, but it's very pretty looking.

Miss Alodia gave us the news with coffee the next morning; Burnell Taylor and Pungi had killed a jaguar last night. It was barely sunup and hardly anyone was walking around the village, so it was difficult to see how she had heard this; but getting a jaguar was headline billing in Tasbapauni, and Miss Alodia had undisclosed sources that kept her informed even though she, like most of the women, rarely left the house.

"They kill it down Set Net way on the beach. Burnell shot it, but Pungi was along, so they're partners. Rinielius carry it on horse from Set Net—too heavy to back. Granville's going to skin it for them after coffee. They'll be going to Burnell's soon."

Miss Alodia was a top investigative reporter. She wouldn't reveal her sources, but even Baldwin was amazed.

Several men were already at Burnell's when Baldwin and I arrived: Pungi, Granville Garth, Humberto Martinez, Juan Martin, Masaball Wilson, Kitty Blandford and Ocian Martin. The best hunters in the village were among these men.

"You see, Mr. Barney, that bottlemail brought us luck," Pungi said when he saw us, pointing at the dead cat on the grass. "Things are changing for the better now."

It was a medium-sized jaguar, a female, about 130 pounds. Massive head and paws; big white fur belly; thick, beautifully patterned skin—still a thing of grace and power, even in death.

The Miskito knew a great deal about the spotted cats—margay, ocelot and jaguar, several varieties of each—even though they had only started hunting them a few years ago, "when they started buying," as Masaball remarked. Formerly, the hunters never bothered the cats, other than occasionally delighting in sneaking up on them while they slept in a tree. No one would eat a jaguar—the thought was repulsive to the Miskito; there were several taboos and food prohibitions against it. They claimed that the Orinoco Black

Carib frequently mixed salted deer and jaguar meat and tried to sell it in one of the Miskito villages.

Jaguars used to be seen often in the forest across the lagoon, in the beach swiddens, once in a while coming into the village to take a pig or chicken. At night they often came out on the beach to hunt and, according to a few Miskito, to play a tag game in which two cats would run around chasing each other, bounding and cavorting in the sand. They used to follow people walking on the beach at night. The Miskito pretty much ignored them; if one got too close, they'd pick up a stick and toss it back, sending the cat crashing into the sea grape thickets.

According to Baldwin, "First time they were common. Some places pure tigercat."

But since the skin dealers had started purchasing spotted cat hides, the Miskito's live-and-let-live attitude toward the cats had changed. At first many cats were killed by rifles, deadfall traps and large baited hooks hung from chains, jump-high off the ground. Within three years the cats had become scarce, hence the high interest in the one Burnell and Pungi had caught. It is generally accepted by the Miskito that the spotted cats are harder to get, not because they are fewer, but because they are valuable. A source of money is a rare thing, whereas an uneconomic animal is common. Thus, it takes more than just skill to bag a money-yielding animal; it takes luck, and luck is perceived as being as scarce as jaguars. That's why Pungi believed the bottlemail had brought him luck.

While we were watching Granville skin the jaguar—Pungi and Burnell were afraid if they did it they'd nick the hide, thereby greatly reducing its value—Juan Martin asked me why the skins varied so much in selling price. A large jaguar skin was worth almost $140 in Bluefields, while an ocelot skin brought $100; but a margay, which was only slightly smaller than an ocelot, sold for $10 at most. The markings of margay and ocelot skins were very similar, especially if it was a large margay and the hunter cut off a piece of the long tail to make it more closely resemble an ocelot's.

"I think the *krubu* fur is thicker and wears better than a *limwiata*. That's why there's such a price difference." I thought this was the reason; I wasn't sure; there was probably also a factor of recognition built into the price—very few people have heard of a margay.

"What do you mean, wear better?" Ocian asked me. "What do they do with these hides? How come they're so dear?"

Everyone else added further questions, hoping to clear up the apparent mystery of what was done with spotted cat skins after they were sold. I suddenly realized that the Miskito did not know what happened to the skins after they were exported from Nicaragua. No one had ever told them, and they had no models of their own. They were hunting for what was the most valuable of all animals, but they were unaware of how the hides were actually used. To fill the information void, they made speculative estimates based on their own world views. The Miskito were great speculators, and from their explanations I learned much that day.

"I tried to study this down," Granville offered as he worked, cutting the skin from a paw. "And it look to me that they buy those skins for being so slippery. You rub this skin, and it's smooth and slippery. They must use them for rocket bearings. That Apollo rocket carry those bearings."

"The Americans buy them to make bombs," added Humberto, with an inflection that made his statement more of a question.

"It's that air business, Miami jets. They use hides in those." Kitty made his pronouncement emphatically, leaving no doubt that he considered the Miami–San José, Costa Rica flights that passed over the village to be of sufficient consequence to deserve expensive skins.

Pungi's suggestion turned out to be closer to the truth, and he elaborated upon his idea so confidently that most of the men agreed with him.

"The space people are making astronaut suits from the skins." Pungi had arrived at this conclusion from our earlier discussion about the costs of the Apollo 11 Mission; he reasoned that only "NASA, Texas" could afford to buy skins.

He picked up a fold of the jaguar skin and examined it. "This is a fine skin. Pretty. Someday it'll be going to the moon."

I think Pungi saw himself as contributing to the space effort.

All of their suggestions and explanations had one thing in common: they placed the Miskito in a contributory role in world affairs. News from Bluefields, the shortwave radio that was always on in Cromwell Forbes's store in the village, and information shared by various visitors to Tasbapauni had all helped to form the Miskito's view of their productive relationship with current world events. Whether it was jaguar skins, mahogany lumber, hawksbill shell or green turtles, the Miskito interpreted their resource-producing efforts in positive terms, directly linking themselves with the "outside" and the most prominent newsworthy stories, such as Vietnam, Apollo 11, and "the war on hunger," in which they believed themselves to be actively engaged by selling green turtles for export.

It was a major letdown when I told them that the spotted cat skins were made into coats for rich ladies to wear. They were shocked. Why would anyone pay so much just for a coat? Their disbelief was heightened by the fact that they themselves didn't need to wear coats. When they found out the price for a jaguar or ocelot coat, their shock was compounded.

"No one in Nicaragua could afford to buy one of those coats. They are too dear. That's for pure rich people," Granville remarked with a mixture of envy and disgust.

Although that conversation taught me many things about the Miskito, I felt tremendously bad over it. I hated to deflate their enthusiastic explanations for jaguar skin use, but I was also worried that they might misinterpret my silence as confirmation and become even more enamored with killing jaguars for subsequent NASA missions.

But the pseudo-dilemma I posed was patently ridiculous. Whether or not I kept my fairy tales or they theirs mattered not at all to what happened to jaguars or, parenthetically, to the Apollo program. The Miskito's exploitation of jaguars was geared to high prices from available markets. Because they were increasingly dependent on outside foods and materials, they were locked into the few available means of securing cash. Within the village, transactions between people involving labor or materials were becoming more and more based on money and less on social relationships and need, formerly the traditional basis for all economic exchanges.

Pungi and Ena were counting heavily on the money from the sale of the jaguar skin. Food was scant, and they often had but one small meal a day. Extensive lowland flooding had ruined many of the village's crops; store-foods were expensive; and in the middle of the rainy season money was hard to obtain, and relatives could not share what they themselves did not have. So for the time being Pungi and Ena were economically, socially and nutritionally destitute. The jaguar money would help a great deal.

Tracing what happened to that skin was instructive, even more so than learning about jaguar-clad astronauts, when it came to the economic realities of everyday Miskito life. The skin was average size, fifty-two inches from the back of the head to the base of the tail, and should have brought a minimum of $90 in Bluefields. Pungi and Burnell were hunting as partners, so they were to split the profits. However, several others had to be paid off as soon as the skin could be sold. Since Pungi and Burnell did not want to waste any of the hide money on a trip to Bluefields, they asked Halstead Wilson to carry it for them and sell it. It took seven weeks and three trips to sell the skin. According to Wilson the buyers didn't want to pay enough on his first two trips. Finally, pushed by debts incurred while waiting for the skin money, Pungi and Burnell told him to sell it for what he could get, which turned out to be $50. This is what happened to the money:

Use of horse from Set Net to carry dead jaguar to Tasbapauni	$ 2.10
"Gun share"—price paid to owner of gun that Burnell borrowed to kill the jaguar	$10.00
Skinning, drying and curing (Granville)	$ 2.10
Charge for labor to sell skin in Bluefields (Halstead Wilson)	$ 7.00
Burnell's share of balance	$14.40
Pungi's share of balance	$14.40
	$50.00

After almost two months Pungi received quite a bit less than he'd planned on. And during the interim he had purchased food from Cromwell Forbes on credit, based on the security of eventually selling the skin.

July 20, 1969, was a day like November 22, 1963; wherever you were, you probably remember what you were doing when you first heard the news. Located in one of the back eddies of the tropics, physically cut off from the rest of the world by miles of forest and sea and years of cultural isolation, the Miskito of Tasbapauni recall that day vividly. Rarely before had so many strange and new things occurred at one time. Things that drew attention to both economic disparity and affinity between the Miskito and the "outside world."

For Pungi Perez, learning about *Apollo 11*, the LM touchdown, a distant bottlemail friend, and the probable destination of the jaguar skin marked what he considered one of the most significant days of his life. There was another day that was also of major gravity to him and in a way also part of this story, the terrible day he had to bury two of his children.

Family tragedy, sickness and death are constant companions in Miskito households. Far from doctors and modern medicines, their body resistance weakened from intestinal parasites and poor nutrition—especially among the children—and in living conditions that invite accidents and injuries, almost every family had recently experienced severe illnesses and death. Pungi and Ena Perez, however, had experienced more sorrow than most other families. In 1967 Ena's mother was drowned when a boat carrying a top-heavy load of corrugated metal roofing overturned in the turbulent Río Escondido on its way from Rama to Bluefields. Three months later, two of their children died a day apart, each from a different sickness; they were buried together in the graveyard on the northern edge of the village. Only four of the nine children that Ena and Pungi gave birth to were living; the others had died at ages three months, ten months, two years, three years and five years. Pungi and Ena attributed the deaths to sicknesses of natural and supernatural origin. Frequent illness had absorbed most of the money the Perezes had been able to acquire, making them among the poorest families in the village. Through the years, though, Pungi and Ena had remained hopeful that things would get better, their children would stay healthy, and they would finally be able to build a new house to replace their sagging, rotting and leaking home. The year before, they had almost made it. Pungi had found some drift lumber on the beach and had saved enough money to buy roughhewn boards and enough nails to construct their new house. It was then that their youngest child, Dempsey, got sick—first a cold and fever, next diarrhea and vomiting followed by weight loss. Pungi sold the nails and some of the lumber to get enough money to go to Bluefields to see a doctor and buy needed medicines. Dempsey survived that sickness.

While they were waiting for their share from the sale of the jaguar skin, Pungi and Ena tried to plan how they could use the proceeds to make enough additional money to buy more nails. Ena wanted to buy coconuts in the village, dry them into copra and sell that to the Bluefields merchants who occasionally visited the village. Pungi wanted to buy a cast net so he could catch the shrimp that came into the big lagoon to breed during the dry season. Sun-dried, these too could be sold in Bluefields. But Pungi's share wasn't as large as they'd hoped, and it came so late that most of it had to be used to pay for food previously purchased on credit.

If one could but hunt and fish and grow food as had been done in the past, subsistence itself would have been no problem. But modern times had come to the Miskito, and store-bought foods were an integral part of their diets; they were dependent on other imported items as well: guns, ammunition, tools, clothes, books for children who attended the small church- and government-supported school in the village. Sources of money were few and amounts small. A great deal of the time and energy that previously had gone to provisioning now was spent in seeking items to sell, and most of the Miskito's marketable resources were endangered species: spotted cats, sea turtles, crocodiles, caimans and river otters. As these animals vanished, more labor was required to get them, and thus less effort was made toward internal self-sufficiency. One looked for the big break, the luck that would bring a good catch of turtle and money.

Pungi said the problem was in the changing of the plan. In traditional Miskito society, sharing, generosity and mutual concern for the well-being of others were of primary importance. Under the "Old Plan," food, materials and labor were reciprocally exchanged among kin and friends in terms of socially prescribed and adhered-to behavior. The "New Plan" reflects the increasingly monetized village economy, in which labor and materials now have a price tag. Food now is weighed and sold where it was once freely given; a man's labor, like the forest and sea resources, now has a value. The Miskito have become entangled in their own rules. They can no longer produce enough food or supply enough labor to exchange freely within the village as they would like. Nor can they obtain enough money to support themselves fulltime in a cash-based economy. Therefore, one feels poor in a still resource-rich environment; subsistence foods are bought and sold; and the pursuit of money forces increasing dependence on endangered species. Within the contradictions between the old and the new, one is forced to make choices between conflicting values and means.

One afternoon while Pungi and I were discussing the changing of the plan, Ena's father, Theo Waggam, came to visit. During most of the conversation he was quiet, sometimes making only an affirmative or negative grunt. But when Pungi began complaining that he had to buy a piece of meat from a relative who weighed it but should have given it to him, his father-in-law cut in.

"First time that scale business wasn't here. When it came, we older heads said it was spoiling the place. Now that they're playing with the scale, everyone is selling. Can't study them; they condemn the Indian ways. All their turtling is on the plate. They only catch fat turtle with *córdoba*. You work it first time Indian way, more better. Give that meat away. Can't sell the lifeline of the people."

Anita plays jacks with a homemade rubber latex ball and tiny clam shells on the wooden floor. Young Dempsey squirms in Ena's arms as she tries to feed him some of the powdered milk she managed to buy yesterday. Pungi is down the beach husking coconuts for Halsted Wilson at $1.40 per 1,000. If he gets paid, they'll be able to buy some flour and sugar from the store for dinner. If not, it will be "breadfruit pop" again: boiled and mashed breadfruit mixed with coconut cream. Alan Carlos, the engineer on Denny Julias's boat, stops by the house on his way home. They've just returned from their weekly trip to Bluefields. He has a letter for Pungi. A letter from Norway, Ena places it up high on a shelf away from the children and looks out the window for Pungi. Maybe there will be more than breadfruit pop for the evening meal. Maybe the bottlemail has brought luck and economic help again.

Dear Mr. Francisco Perez,

Thank you very much for your letter! It was almost unbelievable. I see that miracles still happen now and then. When I dropped that bottlemail in the Caribbean Sea, I never imagined that it would be found again. Such things only happen in pirate stories.

So I thought, but yesterday your letter dropped into my postbox. I was really surprised!!! And I was really happy. This will be something to remember as long as I live.

You said you would like to hear of my life in Norway. Certainly I will. You are worth it; Francisco Perez is a name I will never forget. Never!

Early this year I went abroad in a Norwegian ship, *Thermopylae*, to go around the world to see other countries and other kinds of people. I like traveling. My voyage this winter was a great experience to me. After crossing the Caribbean in the middle of February, we crossed to the Pacific bound for New Zealand. Maybe I told you that in the bottlemail, so I'll be short. The ship left New Zealand and sailed for Norway the same way back, also across the Panama Canal and the Caribbean. I returned home one day before you wrote the letter to me.

I'm twenty-two years of age and the son of a beekeeper (there is not a single turtle in my home place). I have two elder brothers, one working at a factory for glassmaking, the other living some way off, in interior Norway, working in some kind of factory too. He is a forest-educated man. Neither of them is married, not me either. (People are not so warmblooded in my country as yours.) But I have loved a girl once, and that's the reason for my greatest interest for the present writing poems.

I can't make my living writing verses, so I'm afraid I have to start working in a factory or in an office soon. Maybe I will start at a school in September. For now I'm enjoying the Norwegian summertime. And it's hot in Norway too. Today it has been almost 30° C.

I did like going around the world in that ship I mentioned,

but sailor life is not for me. It's too rough, too wet and too risky. Have you ever been a seaman or have you ever had a farm while being a turtleman? I should like to hear from you again. Tell me more about yourself and about your country, and can't you explain what a turtleman really is? Is it a man who domesticates wild turtle or is it one who hunts them in the sea? (I saw a lot of turtles when I was on the ship.)

Well, Francisco, have good luck with your wife and your children, and I hope I will hear from you again. You see this bottlemail and your answer was really a great experience to me.

Sincerely yours,
Islestone Reed

P.S. At last just one thing about my name. My real name is Øystein Røed, but Islestone Reed I like to call myself—poetically.

So, if you write (I really hope you do), you can call me which of the names you like. The letter will reach me anyway.

5 January, 1970

My Dearest Nicaraguan Friends,

At first, thank you so much for sending me a letter and Christmas wishes. I've been waiting a long time to have your next letter. It was good to hear from you again.

As so often before, the Christmas time was white here in Norway. Have you down there ever been skiing? If you get the chance once, you should try. Maybe there is some snow on the mountains in your country; I don't know. It is not only snow and ice in Norway in winter; there is also a cold and frosty time. Very cold and frosty. Today it was − 20° C.

I was sorry to hear, very sorry, that you, Francisco, have been ill lately. As for the question of "Help," I really don't know what to do!!! Of course, if I was certain that you are ill, maybe I could help you. But even then it would be difficult. I'm not a rich man. I'm going to school now as I've told you before and that is quite expensive. I'm sure this is not easy for either of us, Francisco. You live so far away. I know you only by the very few letters. That's not much and that's not easy.

If I could afford to do it, I would come and visit you at your house in Tasbapauni someday. I could tell you about myself and my country, and I would like to live as you do. Maybe then I would understand a little more of your life. It's hard for me to imagine. I try to figure up here in the cold how you live in the tropics.

I won't disappoint you, but it's so difficult for me to "help." And "help" means money, isn't it right? I remember you told me that money is hard to come by, and I believe you, but what can I do: Send you all I have (that's not very much) in US dollars, or send some clothes, or . . . or what should I do in helping you? Do you have any proposals?

This I have to say, and I repeat, my intention is not to disappoint you!!!

I hope you'll be able to write again, and I wish you'll recover soon. It is far to your place, but nevertheless, I should like to visit you. Maybe I'll come someday.

Islestone Reed

With a special greeting to your daughter Fluvia.

12 September, 1970

Dear Francisco,

I am just sending you a short letter and beg you to write soon. I'm so excited to hear if my package has arrived or not. I haven't heard from you for such a long time. Please send me a letter and tell me how you are and if my mail and package have arrived.

When you write, please send the letter by air mail; if not, it will take a long time.

You know, I could not break the correspondence with a bottlemail friend.

Yours,
Islestone Reed

5 April, 1974

Dear Friend Francisco,

Perhaps you almost have forgotten me, since such a long time has passed without a letter. I suppose it was my turn writing. On the other hand, I've reason to believe that my letters have problems reaching you. Maybe the state control is more strict in your country concerning mail. The government in Nicaragua seems much more absolute in its control than in most European countries. Concerning the package I sent you, after some 20—twenty—months it was returned to my own address. The package was sent 22-4-70. A few days before Christmas the year after, I had the package once more in my hands. The package had apparently reached Nicaragua because it had stamps from Managua upon it. As you understand, this was very sad—maybe most for you, as the package contained a lot of clothes that may have suited you and your children. After being returned, I guess there is no use in sending another one. But I will carry on writing to you. Shame on me for not writing much earlier!

The last letter from you I received in September 1971. You had sent it through a second person, as far as I could see, a friend in Michigan, U.S.A. After this letter I had another one (and this was the very last I heard from you) in February 1972.

As you understand, writing poetry has been of greatest importance to me. This may have caused the frequent change of occupation during the last years. For long periods I have had no job at all. This may seem strange to you, but I am without a job again, not because of a dismissal or difficulty in finding a job. Labour—mostly any kind—does not suit me anyway. This attitude may involve great problems for me in the future, and I am not—by now—very optimistic in this way. Concerning poetry, I have sent a collection to a publisher, and I await their answer soon; but to be realistic, there is very little hope. Maybe another time I will succeed in publishing my poems. As I said, this is of greatest importance to me!

Now I'd better cut off for this time, and I shall await your answer. Greetings to your family. I hope this letter will find you well.

Sincerely,
Islestone Reed

[attached to this letter was a poem]

The Turtleman

Some gentle blue miles off
they go in dories to hunt 'em,
—the welcome turtles

Returning home
wet and tired on a rainy afternoon
he doesn't bring any turtle—
bringing nothing
except the cold reflections
of an unsuccessful day
into night . . .

Returning home
to meet his little Fluvia in the doorway,
Smiling to father!
—a smile more welcome
than a hundred fat turtle.

24 June, 1974

Dear Francisco,

I was very glad and very satisfied on receiving your last letter a few days ago. This time I shall not let you wait for long, as I did last. My hope, and wish, is that from now on we shall write to each other as regularly as possible. Such a unique way we came in touch—I mean the bottlemail in '69—is really worth a further connection. My hope is, of course, that we can meet one day; there might be a chance. The world of today is not too big. But, nevertheless, I shall look forward to each letter from you. What are your friends saying about your correspondence with a Norwegian friend?

There is much about Norway that I could tell, and maybe something more about myself, but as I see there is another question you want me to answer: about the package I sent you. You never got it, and are sorry to hear that after a year or so the package was returned to me; yes, this was sorry for me and for you, I know. You ask me to try a second time, but I think that will be of little use. Besides, I have no suitable clothes that I want to be quit of right now. Later on, perhaps; but I ask you to look on me as a pen friend, not as a regular helper. I do not consider myself as a miser or anything like that, but concerning "help"—the way you ask me—I must say that it will do best if you didn't. And I ask you to try and see it my way and my problems in a matter like sending a big package. Again, primarily I am your pen friend, and I hope a good one—as I consider you to be. I feel a little insufficient in being asked for help. I hope you understand this and forgive me if I have said something that might hurt you.

I look forward to your next letter. Your friend in Norway,

Islestone Reed

June 4, 1975

Dear Islestone,

Writing you again to tell you that I received your last letter of June 24, 1974, along with a picture of you and your wife. I then sent a picture of my family. It's been so long since then that I thought I'd write again to find out if you received it or not.

We were glad to hear that you married. Congratulations must be years too late.

As always, things are hard here. We are getting along, but even in our village, prices have gone up. This time we are after shrimp in the lagoon. Sometimes we find them and other times, nothing.

The heavy weather has started. The rains will go on until September.

This year I have been working hard trying to plant some rice and corn.

Our daughter Fluvia is studying in high school in Puerto Cabezas. We are trying to keep her in school as she really wants to study. She is in the second year.

My family is larger. Altogether, we have six children: Fluvia, 18 years old; Anita, 12 years; Sidney, 7 years; Dempsey, 6 years; Jean Darlin, 3 years; and finally, Bunder, who is 6 months old. Floyd died when he was almost two.

We are still trying to build a new house for the family but have been unsuccessful so far.

We hope to hear from you soon.

Your friend,
Francisco Perez

P.S. Ena and all the children send best regards to your wife.

Note to Mr. Reed: Once again I write to you for Francisco. He told me what to say and I wrote it down for him. The first letter I sent for him was just after he found your "bottlemail," the day of the *Apollo 11* landing on the moon. B. Nietschmann, Ann Arbor, Michigan.

5. Animals in Our House

I suppose it was inevitable that we end up with wild animals in our house. What we had no way of knowing, however, was how much these animals would affect our lives, how much they would virtually reorganize our everyday activities, even the relationships between Judi and me and between us and our son.

During the first year of study with the Miskito, we maintained a house in Bluefields. It served as a base from which to organize the many long trips to Miskito villages and hunting and fishing territories that took us away for weeks or months at a time, and also as a home away from home for our six-year-old son, thereby enabling him to attend school. Luckily, as it turned out, it was a big house, with four large rooms, plus an inside kitchen for food preparation and an outside one for cooking; a porch and an outside bathhouse. The house was built some five feet off the ground on ironwood stilts, and had an elevated covered wooden walkway connecting it to the outside cooking kitchen in back. The big yard was enclosed by a chain link and flattened oil drum fence; it had a large cement pond, a well and many trees, including soursop (called *guanabana* in Spanish), orange, Barbados cherry, lime, mango, shaddock (which looks like an overgrown grapefruit) and coconut trees. It was an ideal spot for what came to be a micro game park—the house and yard alike—much to the growing amazement and then consternation of our neighbors.

Most of the animals we acquired were of "broken wing" origin: orphaned helpless young; injured, sick, unruly, even ornery animals, first taken as curiosities and then kept as pets by village folk until maintenance and attendant hassles grew to be too much for normal people to worry over. That's when we got them—the animals and the hassles. What was at first only a trickle of a few animals staying with us for short periods until they grew either old enough or strong enough to be released soon became a deluge of furred and feathered houseguests. We wondered, in fact, who was running the house.

Eyewitness reports and rumors spread, and it became known throughout the coast that the crazy gringos in Bluefields not only cared for wild animals but were actually living with them.

Our household soon was organized around a constant flow-through of animals. Some were temporary visitors; others held onto their new niches for longer periods by tenacious adaptation and by finding their ways into the hearts of their faunal hostel hosts. We ended up running a combination halfway house and country club for monkeys, parrots, spotted cats, iguanas, coatimundis, boas, tree frogs, freshwater turtles, and other animals. The yard was taken over by sleeping cages, perches and clothesline-leash runways. The pond was filled with fresh water and aquatic vegetation, and the house subdivided into several feeding and sleeping areas for visitors and residents, leaving us to fend for living space and privacy as best we could. It was a daily challenge to keep predator and prey apart and to keep some personal places and periods void of animals. We considered it a minor miracle to be able to go to sleep together without finding a balled-up coati under a sheet at the foot of the bed, or having a half-grown margay spring down on us from its favorite top-shelf perch just after we had turned off the lights. It was a rare but awesome spectacle to be wakened in the night by the coatimundi and the margay, who had just discovered each other in the middle of our bed while trying to sneak up on our sleeping forms.

Much of our activity, interaction and research time soon centered around the animals. Their daily care involved obtaining and preparing foods (this led to standing orders with local vendors and shopkeepers for specific fruits and meats), giving the animals attention and exercise, cleaning up after them, and keeping them apart—especially separating the two margays from the monkey and the parrots. Squier, the white-faced monkey, was inseparable from Judi, and one of the margays followed me everywhere, circumstances which led to many difficult confrontations. If Judi was coming into the room where I was, she'd have to announce it first.

"Squier's with me. Who's with you?" she'd ask before going from one room to the other.

"Simba's with me. Don't come in here just now." And I'd pick up the margay and move him into another room.

Thus, our life was spent shuffling animals from one room to the next in a Bluefields variation of musical chairs.

In order to carry out the research, we had to make some adjustments in the system. We hired and trained a neighbor's son to help look after the animals in our absence; this took quite a bit of doing, as almost all of the neighbors thought we were out of our minds for living with animals, some of which they considered dangerous. Nevertheless, Neil soon adapted to them and quickly learned the special diets and behavior patterns. When Baldwin and Alodia Garth's son Sando came to live with us in Bluefields so he could attend the Catholic high school, he too learned to care for and play with the menagerie. He had to, for many of them considered his room their own, and he soon found out that moving in with the Nietschmanns meant moving in with the animals. The margays created the largest problems because they didn't readily let anyone else handle them, and they were always stalking or play-pouncing on the parrots or other animals. Therefore, whenever we left the house for extended periods of fieldwork, we took one of them with us. This made life easier for Sando and Neil in Bluefields, but it led to problems of no small consequence for us when we were traveling on crammed passenger-freight boats visiting a Miskito village.

The major conflict that developed out of all this was not the result of the time consumed or the hassles; it was of a more personal nature. As we got deeper and deeper into the research, we realized that the tropical lowland fauna was being impoverished largely by commercial hunters and animal collectors who sell skins and pelts to luxury markets and supply the pet trade, zoos and medical institutions with live animals. One of the major thrusts of our work was to gather statistical evidence showing the frequency of these activities and the resultant impact on the various faunal populations and on the Miskito themselves. Our reports and conservation proposals to agencies and departments in the Nicaraguan government strongly urged the cessation of commercial hunting and exportation of both live animals and animal products. We tried to make a case for complete protection of all the spotted cats—jaguars, ocelots and margays—and of monkeys and parrots. Yet here we were, with these very species in our house as either pets or temporary guests. We condemned the exotic pet trade in the United States, which every year imported huge quantities of depleted, even endangered species, stripping large areas of tropical America of native fauna for the satisfaction of the well-heeled, well-to-do pet market in our country. Many of these animals die during capture, en route, in warehouses, or from well-intentioned but improper care by their new owners. Some are purchased with little knowledge of the inordinate amount of care and attention required by an exotic wild animal. Some are purchased because of the ego boost received—the classic stereotype of the macho walking an ocelot on Fifth Avenue. Yet we kept these same animals in our own house. We brought up, lived with, cared for, became attached to, grew fond of, and loved the very same animals that we sought so strongly to keep from the export trade. Though we didn't actively seek these animals or purchase them, and we did return several to their natural environment, nonetheless, their presence was a constant reminder that our actions were inconsistent with our beliefs, especially when it came to spotted cats.

We learned much from these animals. Some of the things we found out involved ourselves, the Miskito and natural history. Even with all of the problems and inconveniences that resulted from living and traveling with them, we enjoyed every minute of it. The animals that came into our lives and the time we devoted to them were the most gratifying experiences we had. In many respects not only did we bring our work home, our home became our work; for it was the animals in our house that symbolized the spirit and content of what we did and what we most enjoyed.

The introduction of a white-faced monkey (*Cebus capucinus*) into our household created trouble. The fault was partly mine, but the monkey must share some of the blame, too. Our relationship got off to a bad start. Some monkeys might have the makings of a seaman, but this one did not.

I had just finished loading the canoe in front of the beach at Tasbapauni and was ready to leave for Bluefields when a little girl waded out carrying a small monkey. She told me that her father had captured it the day before while hunting and that he wanted me to have it as a gift. I should have looked this gift monkey in the mouth. But one does not decline a gift among the Miskito. The monkey would go to Bluefields—by sea. It was late, and I was tired of trying to hold the canoe off the beach against the push of broken waves. Improvised monkey accommodations were needed. I tied a cord around his chest and waist and fastened him to the canoe in such a way that he could still move around, but would have a lifeline in case he fell overboard. For the first couple of miles, the monkey clutched at the yellow nylon lines that lashed the tarp and supplies in place. The canoe's roll and pitch, and the constant dousing by sea spray and wind-flung sheets of water made him miserable. Whether from fright or chill or both, he trembled; he was a miniature gray-bearded old man, soaked and seasick. He clung to the lines looking at me. Salt water washed over him. Away from the mainland, the sea swells buffeted the canoe, at times violently, making it impossible for the monkey to keep his balance. Finally he dug down under the tarp and hid for minutes at a time, until a loud wave slap against the hull would roust him from his sanctuary and he'd come up to look at me again. Invariably, it was then that a maverick swell would hit, splashing more spray and water over him, forcing him to abandon the hazardous and wet topside for the insecure but dry impromptu monkey quarters beneath the tarp. This went on for three and a half hours, until we passed through the bar at El Bluff and entered the quiet waters of Bluefields Lagoon.

I named the monkey Squier, after the nineteenth-century adventurer whose journey had become part of my life. But Squier never did like me. Throughout his stay with us he maintained an irreconcilable aversion to me, resulting no doubt from having been shanghaied into a rough sea trip. But he took to Judi right away. In fact, he jumped into her arms the first time he saw her. His affinity for Judi was matched only by his rejection of me. We gave him free run of the house, but every time he saw me coming near, he'd scream and rebound off the walls in a state of high panic until he spotted Judi; then he'd make a dive for her, landing on her head, neck, back, waist or legs, depending on the distance between her and his takeoff point. This gave Judi some awkward moments; Squier's flight to safety was quick, unexpected, and often linebacker-powerful. Safe, he'd start screaming what I took to be insults. Each time I tried to approach to reassure him that I meant no harm, he'd grab Judi even tighter and urinate. This too was awkward, besides being a nuisance. Judi didn't take too well to being dribbled with monkey urine, so whenever Squier jumped on her for safety, she would tell me to stay clear—well clear—reinforcing Squier's rejection and reaction at my presence. He clung to her as he would to his mother. Together, they'd yell at me. His tenacious grip and fright-induced discharges made Judi both uncomfortable and immobile. She asked me to build a cage for him in the yard.

Although caged monkeys are the norm in the States, Squier was not one to be caged. I built what I considered a first-class monkey cage. Big, airy, screened on three sides, elevated off the ground, with tree limbs and branches and ropes and hoops from which to hang and swing. He didn't like it. He chattered and screamed for Judi to get him out of what I'd put him into. And if you haven't heard the pleading, beseeching cries of a martyred white-faced monkey, you've been missing a major anthropomorphic emotional input that plays havoc with human feelings of guilt and rejection and other assorted reactions. Failing to crack our emotional defenses (he never knew how close he'd come), he escalated his anticage program by incessantly scraping his metal feeding dish against the wire screen. This was nerve-racking but still not as bad as his urinating on Judi. But when he started to spread his excreta on the ceiling, wall and cage screen—which I had to clean daily—he succeeded. I had a discussion with Judi to decide which was worse—her having to clean up monkey urine or me having to clean up monkey excreta.

There was no easy resolution to the problem; it was a matter of perspective, dependent on who had to clean what. We found an alternative, but the solution called for some cooperation on Squier's part, too.

"O.K. Squier, you win. We're going to let you out. But on two conditions. First, you have to stay outside. You can't come into the house anymore. Second, you have to decide whether or not you want to stay in the yard, where we'll feed you, or if you want to, split."

I wasn't too hopeful that my explanation of the conditions for Squier's parole were completely understood, but it made little difference. He was happy to get out of the cage, and it would be up to him to stay in the yard. He was released on his own cognizance.

Amazingly, he stayed—at least most of the time. Every so often he would try to pry a window screen or shutter open, or turn a door handle to get inside with Judi. Yet his monkey-burglar forays were few and were always accompanied by demonstrations of such agility and ingenuity that they were overlooked. Four things kept Squier outside: abundant food and water, Judi's late afternoon reading and writing sessions on the back porch, the margay take-over of the interior of the house, and the blossoming of Squier's relationship with the dog, Daniel Boone.

Squier had the run of the entire backyard. He had his own feeding area at one corner of the open-sided porch, and it was always supplied with his favorite foods. He was inquisitive, and there was much going on for him to observe: the other animals, life in Bluefields as seen from a high tree, or life in the house as seen from between the slats of shuttered windows. Many were the nights that bedroom noises and activities drew him to the shutter, his shadowed form spread out and clutching, a simian voyeur. His Peeping Tom nature, white-rimmed and bearded face, and strange relationship with Judi confirmed, at least to me, that he was a dirty old man. The morning after, he always treated me with even more disrespect than usual by hurling insults and pieces of fruit. It was then that he would run away from home.

Squier would be nowhere to be found. He'd disappear. Feeling guilty, exactly at what I never asked her, Judi would encourage me to mount a search of the entire town for the missing apex of our triangular relationship. Bluefields was simply too large a place for one person to cover, even if the missing item was a conspicuous, free-ranging monkey. To expedite recovery, I decided to mobilize the legions of small children who always seemed to be gathered around our house looking in on the zoo. I instigated the Squier Recovery Reward, a one-*córdoba*, no-questions-asked reward for his return. Once news of this source of income had spread among the younger folk of Bluefields, Squier was never able to escape very far from the watchful eyes and dexterous climbing ability of the small bounty hunters. He was very tame and could be coaxed from a high place of refuge by one of the fearless monkey trackers with a piece of fruit or candy. One enterprising youngster even went so far as to try to short-circuit the recovery system by enticing Squier from a backyard tree and over the fence with a piece of candy; he then brought him around to the front door to be exchanged for the reward.

Squier's voyeur habits were closely correlated to the frequency of his disappearances and payment of the Squier Recovery Reward. However, even though we had extremely nosy neighbors, I don't think they ever put the circumstances together. After all, who would have thought that the external travels of a white-faced monkey were associated with internal goings-on?

What kept Squier home more than food and the recovery reward was his relationship with Daniel Boone. Although surrounded by tropical animals, our son wanted a dog. Any dog. Preferably a puppy. It so happened that our close friends John and Barbara Giesler, a Moravian missionary couple, owned a female that gave birth to a litter while Barney was over at their house playing with their children. He was offered the pick of the litter on the spot. When he brought the news home, he was not to be denied. He got his puppy and named it Daniel Boone.

Because Daniel Boone was hard to housebreak, he was relegated to the back porch at night. It was there, I suppose, that the equally relegated Squier met him and grew accustomed to his presence. They were just right for each other: the young pup had been taken from his mother, brought to a strange house, and placed outside; and Squier needed a friend. He found the constant companionship he sought and provided the same to Daniel Boone. At first light we'd go out to the back kitchen to start breakfast, and there on the porch would be Squier cuddled up with Daniel Boone, both still sleeping.

The three of them—Barney, Squier and Daniel Boone—went everywhere together. As the dog grew, Squier began to exert more control over him. In fact, Squier became domineering and lazy. He no longer was content to range about the yard on his own, but would instead find or wake Daniel Boone and ride him as a jockey does a horse to wherever he wanted to go. The sight of the monkey riding a dog bareback is a thing to behold. He used the dog's ears as reins and held on with his legs and prehensile tail. Throughout all of this, Daniel Boone remained gentle and tolerant and always served as a ready steed for Squier's leisured country club life.

Squier and Daniel Boone. Preferring to ride rather than to walk or climb, the white-faced monkey and our son's dog became constant companions. Bluefields, 1969.

Two of the first permanent additions to our household were yellow-head parrots *(Amazona ochrocephala).* One was from Twappi, a Miskito community north of Puerto Cabezas, and the other was from the Tasbapauni area. Both were supposedly gifts, but we quickly found out there were good reasons why these birds had been given away. The male we named Dama, meaning grandfather in Miskito, and the female Kuka, which meant grandmother. Their names suited their personalities, for both were older birds, had cranky dispositions, and delighted in meddling in our family affairs.

When we first got Kuka, my visions of research in the tropics were still clouded with hazy myths of intrepid and benevolent Western scientists moving among indigenous peoples and fauna with equal ease. The Miskito family that foisted her upon us assured us that she was tame and a good talker, and that she liked people. As it turned out, giving us the bird must have been their idea of a practical joke. I carried Kuka around on a short stick for a few hours, feeding her by hand and talking reassuringly to her. After what I believed to have been a reasonable get-acquainted period, I placed her on my shoulder in the best Long John Silver–Ivan T. Sanderson style. A trailing ragtag band of Miskito children followed us, giggling and howling with laughter all the way. I didn't see anything funny about carrying the bird on my shoulder, but they certainly did. Finally, one burst of unrestrained mirth sent two of the little demons to the ground in fits of helpless laughter. I stood my ground and confronted them. What was so funny?

"*Rauha tutu,*" one of them told me, and then they all fell down, clutching their sides and rolling about in absolute, unbounded hysteria.

"Parrot crap?" I asked myself. I turned my head slowly to look at the back of my shirt. A long white stripe went from shoulder to waist as if I'd ridden a fenderless bicycle through a huge puddle of whitewash.

I told Kuka what I thought of her actions in no uncertain terms. That's when she bit me on the ear. Not pecked—bit. A parrot's beak has incredible strength. She fastened on my ear, bit down, and then gave an added twist with her head, leaving a deep, bleeding cut which throbbed with physical and ego-damaging pain.

By then the children were beside themselves in laughter, as if they had taken leave of their senses. When Kuka joined in their mirth, they lost complete control and began thrashing about on the grass, gasping for air between howls and choked spasms of giggling. Kuka was still on my shoulder, as I was somewhat hesitant to try to remove her, not wishing another attack on my damaged ear. She began to ruffle and puff up her nape and head feathers and stretch out her wings; and with orange irises dilated, she started to turn around on my shoulder in a bizarre sort of parrot victory dance. This last act brought down the house and closed out the show.

My dignity now shattered beyond redemption, I hastily scooped up a stick and managed to get Kuka to step on it. With new-found respect for parrots and with utter disdain for myths of intrepid explorers, I marched back to where we were staying, holding Kuka at arm's length.

Dama and Kuka stayed on perches we built alongside the covered walkway that connected the back of our house with the cooking kitchen. During the torrential downpours the parrots were in sheer ecstasy. They'd raise a din so loud it could be heard above the drumroll of rain falling on metal roofing. The elevated wooden flooring often became slippery with water and fungal growth in the heavy Bluefields rains; and it was easy to slip. Any fall or even slight misstep would bring forth cackles, shrill laughter, and wheedling falsetto phrases in Miskito from the birds. They expressed incredible delight in watching us at all times, but our falling down made their day; they would spin on their perches, wings spread out, feathers ruffled, in celebration of parrot supremacy.

Dama could imitate a crying baby with unbelievable accuracy. And Kuka could mimic a heavy, racking tubercular cough with such precision and feeling that we often thought we had either a very sick visitor or a very sick bird. Our neighbors often asked us about the state of our family. Is the new baby well? Shouldn't the sickly person see a doctor? Apparently they didn't keep close track of the number of people living in the house but believed any rumors or any noise they heard. Most of them thought we exhibited abnormal behavior and living habits anyway, so if we weren't actually out of our minds, we didn't have far to go—a universally held assumption about all foreign visitors. We didn't take it personally.

In almost all of our interactions with the parrots, they seemed to come out on top. The only one who continually got the upper hand with the parrots was Squier, who spent hours sneaking up on them just to startle them by pulling a tail feather or making a grab for some of their food. My estimation of Squier went up as a consequence.

There were many temporary guests at our house: iguanas, freshwater turtles, lime-green orange-bubble-eyed tree frogs, a rambunctious and mischievous coati, a young hawskbill sea turtle, and other assorted species. Some were sick or injured and required medical treatment. Our veterinary knowledge was close to nil, but shortwave radio-phone patches to vets in the States helped in diagnoses and selection of medicine.

The coati (*Nasua narica*) was a real joy. His curiosity and his acrobatics on curtains, screen doors and clotheslines made him entertaining to watch and challenging to cope with. A coati has a distinctive ramrod-straight tail, which he holds vertical when walking or uses as a balancing rod when climbing; his long, pointed snout modifies somewhat his raccoon-like appearance. We named him Mr. Quash, using the Creole word for coati, and he soon became quite tame and could be easily handled. Even though omnivorous, coatis have a decided sweet tooth and will seek out candy, sugar or any sweet-tasting food. Mr. Quash would come when called, take a piece of fruit or meat from our hand, make a churring sound something like the purring of a cat, and then go to sleep contentedly in one of our laps, balled up, front paws covering his eyes, and long tail wrapped around his paws and snout.

Mr. Quash was suffering from rickets when we first obtained him. We put him on a special diet to correct this, but his fondness for sweets made him cantankerous over his new food selection, and we had to coax him to eat. To keep the candy junkie on the straight and narrow, everything sweet in the house had to be placed in sealed cans and jars. Occasionally, he would discover a poorly hidden and improperly sealed cache of sweets and go on a binge. Momentarily satiated, he'd tuck away in one of his favorite retreats to sleep it off, all the time oblivious to our scolding and dismay. Once again, Mr. Quash had beaten the system.

When we first came to Nicaragua, we were well armored and behaviorally conditioned to a fine panic edge by widely disseminated myths of tropical dangers and hazards: especially, one should constantly beware of snakes, jaguars and sharks. If we had taken this advice to heart, not only would we not have gone near the water, we wouldn't have gone near the forest either. This would have made research difficult, for we worked where the sea and forest abut, leaving little but the high-tide zone as a refuge from the supposed dangers of land and water. Luckily, we soon learned to shed our insulating conceptions of the perils that lurked everywhere ready to attack and kill. Over the years we spent many enjoyable and educational times at sea, diving among coral reefs and sharks; we went deep into the rain forest, where on rare but glorious occasions we were privileged to see jaguars and other spotted cats. We never did see many snakes, other than boas. This doesn't mean that there aren't dangers from these animals, or that we were completely blasé toward them. Instead we learned to separate myth from fact and came to understand something about these animals and then to respect and admire them. Rather than being constantly stalked and threatened by major sea and forest predators, we found that our greatest problems came from sand flies, jelly fish and stinging coral at sea, and from ticks and biting flies in the forests.

Much of our reeducation on tropical predators started with our study of the spotted cats: jaguars, ocelots and margays. One of our major research goals was to examine the natural history and commercial hunting of these cats, so we began talking to Spanish-speaking hunters and skin buyers—generally people new to the forests around Bluefields. Most were deathly afraid of the cats, even the relatively small margay, ascribing to them supernatural feats of bloodlust, cunning and voracity. I suppose they needed to vilify the behavior of the spotted cats to justify their own activities and to prove that they were only doing their duty by courageously ridding the forests of these "man-eaters."

Skin dealers in Bluefields and Managua told us numerous stories of jaguar attacks on rural peoples where the cats had killed for no reason but pleasure. In all our travels, however, we never were able to meet anyone who could verify the killing of a human by a jaguar. It was always the reverse. Therefore, we began to disbelieve the self-serving stories.

We really started to learn something about spotted cats from the Miskito, and then we learned from those we raised in our house.

Miskito hunters did not fear the cats. I remember one time when I went into the forest with two hunters after white-lipped peccary, one of the most sought after game animals, and had the good fortune of seeing an ocelot before it saw us. The tawny, spotted and striped cat was dozing on a low branch some fifty yards ahead. We had been moving very quietly, as the ground was still wet from an early morning shower and the dampness helped muffle our footsteps. Granville saw it first and motioned his hunting companion, Archileius, and me to continue very slowly and softly. We got to within twenty-five feet of the ocelot and watched it for a long time. It was beautiful. Its long, thick body was draped along the limb, and its short, powerful legs hung down. After a few minutes it rose and gracefully stretched, arched its back and tail, and spread its oversized fur-webbed paws to twice their normal dimensions. It yawned. Then it saw us. The series of expressions that came over its face put it in Marcel Marceau's league: bafflement, surprise, caution, and then supersensitive awareness. It crouched, and I could sense that it would soon spring, not at us but away.

Archileius raised his gun and took aim, but Granville put his hand on the barrel and pushed it away before he could fire.

"No, don't shoot," he whispered.

I looked back toward the limb, but the ocelot had vanished. No sound, no vibrating branches or leaves, nothing.

Archileius was puzzled. Granville had stopped him from making a sure kill. The ocelot's skin would have earned them at least thirty or forty dollars each—a great deal of money for either of them. I was glad that Granville had restrained him from shooting because I had been about to tackle Archileius myself. If I had, I would have broken two important rules: first, a guest on a hunting trip should follow explicitly the directions of his hunting hosts; and second, I had vowed to myself not to interfere with Miskito hunting and fishing practices, as I was here to study them, not reform them. Therefore, Granville, not I, took the brunt of Archileius's wrath. Granville ignored him, and soon Archileius lapsed into sporadic, questioning insults. But he was talking to himself.

Later, back in Tasbapauni, I asked Granville why he had stopped Archileius. He didn't want to talk about it. I don't think he himself knew. All he said about it was that "he didn't feel to kill the *krubu*." This was strange, as the lucrative spotted-cat-skin market was in high gear; many Miskito were hunting them, and Granville himself soon started to hunt the cats in earnest. Perhaps it was my presence; perhaps it was the beauty of the moment, or a fleeting remembrance of a wisp of old Miskito lore about the cats. I never did find out.

The Miskito have many folktales about jaguars *(limi bulni)*, ocelots *(krubu)* and margays *(limwiata)*. In times past, according to the older Miskito, the cultural world of the Miskito was linked to nature by a finite amount of life energy that flowed between humans and animals and between society and nature. For example, when a child was born, the life energy often came from an animal, particularly a jaguar; and when the person died, the life energy could go back into the animal world again. The Miskito saw a circularity of life energy flow between nature and humans and an affinity between themselves and the cats. The jaguar, the ocelot and the margay symbolically were to nature what the shaman was to the Miskito: power, protection and an intermediary. In "first time" days there were prohibitions against killing the cats because of their role in nature and with the Miskito. But the Miskito had no reason to kill them anyway, so they were left pretty much alone.

These are old traditions which only a very few still remember. More recent myths tell about the supposedly strong powers of the cats which protect them against hunters. One of the most widespread beliefs concerns the ocelot, or *krubu* as it's called in Miskito. It goes like this: If a hunter is out in the bush and a *krubu* sees him, it will lie on a low limb and hit him on the head as he passes beneath, momentarily knocking him unconscious. Another way a *krubu* can render a hunter unconscious is to urinate on the trail ahead of him. The fumes will make the hunter feel so drunk and dizzy that he will fall down, dropping his sack and gun. Then the *krubu* will come out of hiding and start to cover the hunter with debris, such as fallen leaves and limbs. If the hunter begins to move or starts to wake up, the *krubu* will urinate over his prostrate body. If he is unconscious for a long time or simply stays still, the *krubu* will finally go away and leave the hunter alone.

One of the great things about other people's myths is that an outsider is free to read into them whatever he wishes. In fact, many social scientists make a living at this. I can verify from personal experience that spotted cat urine is powerful stuff, having a high odor and a long range from well-developed spray apparatus. These cats also cover their feces and urine spots by throwing back dirt with their hind legs, as do domesticated dogs. The cats "box" quite a bit with their front paws, too, either in playing or in knocking down small game. Nevertheless, the Miskito story seems a bit farfetched. I never had a spotted cat urinate on me in the forest—although one did do so on a colleague of mine in my office at the University of Michigan. More about that later. Anyway, the point here is that once the Miskito began to hunt the spotted cats, they broke the special bond which previously related cats and humans, and in return they may have supplied the cats with mythical defense powers to try to offset their own violation of former taboos. I don't know if this is the case at all. My interpretation is only an interpretation and one that is shaky at best. But through myths and interpretations we can see ourselves in others.

What I have related about spotted cats up to now has been a rather rambling, eclectic discourse about the stray bits and pieces of information we had begun to pick up, all of which ill prepared us to raise two of these cats in our house. Nor were we prepared for the changes they would make in our lives.

The first night of the margay was memorable. I had just come back from a long stay with some Miskito to the north, carefully timing my arrival to be home to take care of the animals so that Judi and Barney could go to Managua to meet some friends who were passing through Central America on their way south. It was raining, as it always seemed to be in Bluefields. Judi and Barney caught the late LANICA flight that had been stalled for hours because of the rain and mechanical problems. Finally, the pilot emerged, looked at the leaden sky, glanced toward the grease-dipped mechanic, crossed himself religiously, and climbed in and cranked up rickety old C-46; he spun it around, drenching those of us who remained at the edge of the shed, and took off from soggy Bluefields.

Wet, tired and already lonely, I was just starting to prepare the evening meal for our yelling, meowing, screeching menagerie when Seymore Robinson stopped by to see me. He was carrying a small water-soaked cardboard box which he was holding with great respect.

"I made to find out that you just come back to town," he said. He placed the box on the kitchen table and indicated with outthrust lips and chin that it was for me.

The box moved. Mr. Seymore jumped. Then a thin gray-and-black-spotted paw pushed through the wet, weakened cardboard.

"Mind that thing doesn't get out," warned Mr. Seymore, and he took a cautious step backward.

I was surely interested in the contents of the box, but Mr. Seymore was showing a healthy uneasiness for whatever was inside.

"O.K., what's in the box?"

"That's a tigercat. Young tigercat. They are dangerous even when they are young."

By now Mr. Seymore had backed to the far side of the room. A series of raindrop puddles marked his retreat. Given his display of subdued fear, I marveled at his courage in getting the box to my house.

I opened it up. A big-eyed, wet and matted kitten was inside. Trembling either from the dampness or from fright at being bumped around in a small box, it nevertheless climbed readily into my hands and started to gnaw softly on a finger.

"Watch out for that thing. If it tastes blood, it will get manish."

I couldn't believe he could be so scared of such a little helpless cat, even if it was wild. But he was a skin buyer, and he'd worked with spotted cat skins, buying them from hunters and selling them to dealers in Managua, sometimes shipping them abroad himself. Maybe he thought that because his business had led to the demise of so many spotted cats, any still-living descendant would single him out for retribution.

I asked him where he got it.

"One hunter brought it today from down south. The Yolina Selva. Said he found it after shooting a big she tigercat. Found it next to her, backed right up against a big *gamba*, hissing. He brought it to me along with the skin."

It was a fairly common story. The hunter had an easy shot at the female who stayed to protect her young one. And it was still too weak and small to run far.

"I brought it to you, as you are the only one who'd want it. Nobody around here wants a live tigercat. Can't sell that thing in Bluefields. Only you people keep that kind of animal."

Mr. Seymore was right. No one in Bluefields would want a tigercat in his house. If I didn't take it off his hands, he'd probably send it on a freight boat to Rama and then overland to Managua, where one of his business contacts would pick it up and try to sell it to a tourist outside one of the big hotels. I didn't want him to do that. I could feel its rapidly beating heart and warm body against my forearm. It was a small thing. Dirty, matted, it appeared to me all ears, eyes, tail and skinny legs. I was hooked, figuratively and literally, as by now the kitten had wrapped all four legs around my arm and was trying to hold on with its needlelike claws.

When I told Mr. Seymore that I'd take it, he seemed relieved. He hurriedly excused himself and left.

It's hard to tell an ocelot from a margay, especially when they are young. But its long tail, huge ears, and markings suggested that this was a margay, a fairly rare spotted cat, identified scientifically as *Felis wiedii* and locally by a number of names, depending on what language you were speaking: *peludo* or *caucelo* in Spanish; *limwiata* in Miskito; and "tigercat" in Creole English, a nonspecific name which also included ocelots.

It was a male. His fur was dark gray overall with black stripes and spots and large black-rimmed brown markings. On the back side of his large, sensitive ears were the characteristic white "eye spots," or

ocelli, found on both margays and ocelots, from which the latter
derives its common English name.

I'd spent many hours in Mr. Seymore's store, examining the
various skins and markings. He had shown me how to tell the
difference between a margay and an ocelot, but admitted that at
times even he was fooled. Now I wanted to know exactly what cat I
had on my hands. A full-grown ocelot might weigh as much as
forty-five pounds, while even a big margay seldom gets over
twenty-five. I decided it was a margay as much from its markings as
from a personal need to justify acquiring another animal. Hopefully,
he was a margay, the small edition of the tigercat group.

He was weak and hungry and readily got over his fright when I
fed him some warm milk with a couple of tablespoons of chopped
meat. He must have been older than his small, thin frame
suggested. Perhaps the hunter had had him a long time and didn't
feed him, or maybe he was sick. He certainly must have been
maltreated, and he was wary of any sudden move I made.

I talked to him while he ate but made no move to touch him. By
now all the other animals were making it known that they hadn't
been fed, so I left to make the rounds. Our neighbors felt uneasy
when the normal raucous sounds reached critical mass at feeding
time, and I tried hard to allay their growing doubts about us by
keeping the din down.

Though famished, the cat followed me to the screen door, where
he stayed until I returned and then went back to eating. Afterwards,
he went to sleep curled up in my lap while I read. Then the lights
went out. The diesel-run generators that supplied electrical power
in Bluefields frequently broke down, so I was used to the sudden
disappearance of lights, but the cat wasn't. In the darkness I could
feel his body stiffen, and when I got up to look for a flashlight,
candles and the kerosene lantern, he became very agitated. He
jumped around and ricocheted off the walls, frequently leaping up
and grabbing onto my pants and then vanishing in the darkness,
only to strike again unexpectedly from another direction. Each time,
his claws dug through the thin material, enough to make me
apprehensive about the next hit. Margays are nocturnal, and his big
eyes gave him an advantage in the dark. By the time I'd located and
lit the lantern, the cat had somehow knocked over a can of linseed
oil, and soaked his tail and back legs in the spilled mess; he was
running around leaving oily footprints and brushlike splotches on
the floor, table, lower walls—and my pants.

I washed him in soapy water as best as I could and carefully dried
him. He looked a mess. The oil added to his generally woolly and

matted appearance. Until he was cleaned up better, he would have to stay in the kitchen—at least for the night.

He protested by scratching at the door and meowing persistently for hours.

The next morning I found him asleep on a pile of my notebooks I had forgotten to remove from the kitchen.

The margay quickly became the center of the household. His development to maturity was interesting to observe, but filled with problems and often rather trying circumstances, as can be seen in the following extracts from our "margay notebook":

December 13. The margay is much more active today despite its busy first night in the house. He follows me from room to room and howls when a screen door cuts off his progress. He had to wait to be fed and was getting belligerent, but the house rule is that the animals get fed in the order of when we acquired them, and he has the lowest seniority. He ate a surprising quantity of milk and meat for such a small animal.

He is very graceful for a kitten and has extraordinary reflexes. Last night during the melee, he was halfway through making a playful five-foot leap at me from a kitchen counter, when I suddenly turned, and he reversed his body in midair and landed softly on the floor. He is very inquisitive and playful and has the bad habit of sneaking up behind me and then making a rush toward my bare toes. I put on my boots, but the laces fascinated him even more, and he is always underfoot.

He is very tame for all his bad experiences since being taken from his mother. I'll wait until he gets adjusted to the house before trying to housebreak him. His messes and unexpected attacks are hard to handle, but his beauty, grace and friendliness certainly offset these habits. I hope Judi and Barney will like him.

He really likes to be with me. He is curled up in my lap as I write this. I still have no name for him. Perhaps I'll use the old standard, "Simba," even though its linguistic heritage is from another hemisphere.

Took him across the street to Mr. Mitchell's *pulpería* and weighed him on the scale: 2 lbs. 7 oz.

Since last night he has eaten ¾ pound of chopped meat and has drunk one pint of milk.

Judi and Barney returned late this afternoon. They seem delighted with the cat. Barney likes the name Simba and insists that is what he will call him, regardless of any other name we devise.

Simba went to sleep with Barney, but woke him up in the middle of the night by biting on his toes and preening his hair. His nocturnal activities keep our house on the go twenty-four hours a day—the Bluefields Strategic Air Command.

December 14. Simba spent the morning exploring the yard and playing with Barney. He slept all afternoon, high up on a top shelf. He prefers high, flat places.

December 15. I spent most of the day getting ready to go to Tasbapauni. Simba was ignored and protested vehemently. I left in the afternoon with Denny Julias.

December 16. [Judi's notes] Simba has been sick—diarrhea—and won't eat anything. What a mess.

December 17. He'll drink milk, but won't eat and walks strangely. Rickets?

December 18. He's eating chopped meat again, and his stool is normal. He bites playfully, and it's difficult to be in the same room with him, yet it's worse to listen to his protests if left alone.

December 19. I am sick [malaria] and sent a message to B. N. to return to Bluefields. I have to leave the animals in Neil's care. I hope he can handle Simba.

Feeling worse. Fever, chills and ache. Simba has quieted down but will not let Neil touch him. Instead he is watching me while I'm collapsed on the bed.

[Barbara and John Giesler come over and take Judi and Barney to their house so that they can care for her.]

December 21. Barbara said Simba started to meow and cry when he saw her at the house.

December 24. [B. N.'s notes]. Just returned from the Gieslers' with Judi and Barney. Most of my time is split between taking care of her and the animals. Simba was overjoyed to see us again. How could he have developed such close feelings in such a short time?

It's amazing how much he has grown during the few days I've been in Tasbapauni. Perhaps he's only filled out. If so, he is probably older than I first thought him to be. Instead of three months, he may be as old as five months.

He completely dominates the house. Climbs up the screen door and always seems to be lurking somewhere ready to pounce on anyone who passes beneath his high hiding places.

I decided to clip his nails, which should keep him off the screens and from climbing up the mosquito nets at night. He didn't resist at all while I worked with his paws. They are huge for a cat so small. They double in size when spread out.

Christmas Eve fireworks outside have all the animals in an uproar, especially Simba, who is very sensitive to loud noises and either cowers under something or dashes wildly about in complete panic.

December 27. Simba is becoming more dependent on being with someone all the time. This morning he jumped into the shower room with me and balanced on the edge of the bottom Dutch door and watched me intently.

I decided to give him his first real bath. He has no fear of water and likes to play in it. I put some warm water in a metal tub and washed him with shampoo, rinsing him several times. Afterwards, the tub water looked like the Río Escondido.

His fur is still woolly and matted in places, characteristic of young cats, but his coat is changing.

December 28. Simba and I played a game in which he goes off until he's ten to fifteen feet away, and then begins to stalk my tapping fingers. This kept up for three hours. He never tired but I did. During the stalk, Simba keeps his eyes on the finger target, never looking at the terrain itself; instead he feels his way over the bumpy ground. When about three feet away, he stops, front paws together, head and shoulders down, his whole body trembling, back muscles knotted, and then springs and lands with one bound on my hand, paws first and then teeth. He doesn't bite, though. Then he moves away and tries again.

This play and other games we've devised are based on the predatory skills he would normally be learning. He learns everything quickly. It is impossible to fool him more than once with a new game or subterfuge.

January 3. Simba's coat is changing. Clumps and tufts of his thick, fuzzy fur are coming out, showing a short, smooth, beautifully mottled coat underneath. His belly fur is very soft—white with scattered black dots.

January 4. I've started to grow a beard because of Simba. He constantly wants to lick and suck on my neck, and his wide, raspy tongue started to irritate my skin and a large rash developed.

January 28. The beard is still short, but it gives me some protection from Simba's affectionate demonstrations. He spent two hours today cleaning and preening my beard. He takes better care of me than I do myself.

I think that Judi and Barney are getting upset over the large amount of time I devote to Simba. In turn, Simba is getting jealous of them.

Fieldwork takes us away from the house for long periods of time, and when we return, Simba insists on commanding all of my attention. I recall one time that I spent several hours with Simba in one of the trees in the backyard, climbing about the branches with him. Margays are the most arboreal of the neotropical cats, and he prefers to be high up in a tree. Judi called me in for lunch, but I didn't hear her. When we finally came down, she was fuming about all the time I spent with Simba. He is becoming increasingly hard for Judi and Barney to handle, and it's difficult for them to maintain rapport with him. He has made some aggressive moves toward Barney, and I'm afraid he might scratch or bite him. Simba is complicating our life and family relationships.

March 25. Simba went with us today to the forest creek and swimming pool three miles from Bluefields. It's a deep, clear pool, surrounded by smooth rock and shaded by overlapping tree crowns. Simba swam and played tag with us in the water.

June 23. Big Simba scene last night and today. All of Bluefields is in a tizzy over it.

About eight o'clock last night Simba somehow got out the front door. He's intelligent enough to turn door handles and push screen doors open, but he must have learned how to unlatch the catch as well. We didn't discover his absence for an hour or so. We looked for him in the yard, calling his name, but he didn't come. We went around the neighborhood with flashlights and asked everyone if they had seen him. No one had, but they all became frightened at the idea of a tigercat loose in the neighborhood, and soon everyone went inside, locking and boarding up their houses. We stayed out until one o'clock but couldn't locate him.

After a restless night I got up early to try again. Nothing. Simba might approach a stranger—he certainly wouldn't run away; and I feared that someone might shoot him, mistaking him for a wild tigercat from the nearby forest edge. Most people in Bluefields don't like wild cats and are afraid of them, and his hide is worth quite a bit. Even though he's not full grown yet, he is large, weighs almost fifteen pounds, although he looks much larger than a fifteen-pound animal.

Afraid that he might be killed, I decided to take a message to the local radio station, Radio Atlantico, which broadcasts Bluefields news and plays country and western music. They announced my message in English and Spanish:

"The Nietschmanns' pet tigercat accidentally got out of their house last night and should be in the neighborhood. It is tame and will not hurt anyone. A reward is offered for information on its location. They ask that no one try to catch it or shoot it."

This was broadcast several times during the early morning. By ten A.M. the rumors started. Simba's escape had escalated into stories describing the escape of a jaguar, marauding wild tigercats on the edge of the town—some were reported in the downtown area having made attacks on small children and been driven off, and excited demands that the "zoo house" and the gringos had to go.

At last, Mr. Mitchell's small boy came to the door, pushed through the crowd of agitated neighbors, and told us that Simba was across the street, behind his father's *pulpería*, inside an abandoned chicken coop.

We immediately rescued the trembling Simba. Although we got him back unharmed and sent another message over the radio informing everyone to call off the search and general panic, our relationship with the neighbors deteriorated even more. For the rest of the day I noticed that anyone who had to walk by our house made a cautious and wide detour.

In late May I had been in Tasbapauni for some weeks when Judi sent word from Bluefields that she and Barney were coming up on the next boat and were bringing a "surprise." Sure enough, a couple of days later they arrived on Sam Francis's boat, a broken-down old hulk that was so slow the passengers frequently made sails out of their blankets to try to catch a favoring wind and hurry the trip along. Inside a straw basket was their surprise, a tiny bundle of yellow and black, another spotted cat. It was so young that its eyes had been just opening when Judi got it in Bluefields. Seymore Robinson had struck again! Another hunter had brought it to him after having killed its mother.

We named him right away, this time with a Miskito name, *Sabi*, or one who walks quietly, which was a misnomer at the time, as he could hardly stand, much less walk. He weighed one pound, three ounces, and we judged that he was about three weeks old.

We nursed him with an improvised bottle and nipple. As the days passed, we gradually began to wean him, substituting milk and finely chopped turtle meat, which he sucked on.

We had only four months left on the research project and spent almost the entire time in the field, returning only briefly to Bluefields for supplies and to check with Neil and Sando, Baldwin and Alodia's son, who was living in our house while he went to school and helping care for the animals. Simba had become despondent and more difficult to handle because of our long absences. We had decided not to take him with us in the field; he was simply too hard to handle and too demanding. I felt bad about this and knew that he might become morose and even more aggressive; but the research project was more important, so Simba was left at home.

On the other hand, Sabi, being small and young and having an altogether different personality from Simba's, traveled with us everywhere. He readily took to the three of us and was part of our everyday—and even night-time—activities. His sudden pouncing effectively reoriented our attention from one another to him.

The Miskito already thought we were strange, and my walking around with a wild cat in a backpack only added to their amazement.

One old man, Cecil Everil Hebberd, stopped me one day as I was walking along the beach on my way to an agricultural ground where I had a test plot to measure soil fertility and yields. As we talked, the pack began to move, and I could hear Sabi wiggling and scratching inside. For a while Hebberd was too polite to ask what was inside the pack, although his curiosity was obvious. Finally he mentioned the pack, commenting on what a nice one it was and how I could carry all sorts of things inside. I replied that he was correct. He then asked if he could take a look inside such a handsome pack to see how it was sewn together. He went around behind me and opened up the flap. I bent down so he could look into the open pack top. A loud hiss and low growl erupted from the pack. He closed it up again.

He gave me a long, contemplative, calculating sort of stare. Then

Our son ("Little Barney") decides to "do time" with Sabi in our coral cay thatched camp. I had admonished and temporarily chained the margay after he had chased one of the turtlemen into the water. 1972.

he looked at the pack again and touched the side, pushing it in with one finger until Sabi slapped at it from the interior.

"*Krubu* or *limwiata?*" he inquired.

I said it was the latter.

"Aye, *limwiata*. *Limwiata* and *kuku awra*," he said with a sigh and some hint of exasperation in his voice, and he went his way, leaving me with a good deal to occupy my thoughts. A margay and a drift coconut on the beach.

Sabi was devilish, passionate and beautiful. Because of his constant companionship as a member of our household in Tasbapauni, the cat developed a close relationship with the three of us. It's hard to explain the nature and intensity of the very special rapport among us. Sabi watched me continually, staying away when I was grouchy, ambushing me when he sensed that I was in a better mood. We communicated with each other on a wave length different from any I had ever thought possible, frequently without words from me or bites, yells, yowls, howls, meows and the rest of his linguistic repertoire from him. If he was doing something I didn't want him to do, a simple look stopped him. Often he'd take my notebook, pull it under the cot, and start to growl, making me fear that he was going to rip the thing apart. Yet he never did. He was just teasing, trying to get my attention; and taking my valuable notes did the trick every time. The last months with all of us and Sabi together in Tasbapuani were the best of all.

It soon came time to go home to the States. We'd been away for fourteen months, and many things made us reluctant to return to what would now be a strange world. The most difficult task before us was making arrangements for all the animals in our house. All, that is, except Sabi, who would have to stay with us. I had spent some time trying to rehabilitate him so that he could return to the rain forest, but he was too tame—he'd walk right up to the first hunter who passed by him.

We had to release or to find homes for all the animals and birds. The hawksbill's damaged fin had healed, so we released him in the sea. The coati too was released. After some deliberation and much investigation we were able to find a person in Bluefields, a budding young naturalist, to take Simba. Squier was shipped by plane to Pete and Joan Haupert, who ran the Moravian hospital in Bilwaskarma on the Río Coco. There he found excellent accommodations; he even ate his meals with the Haupert family. The parrots went to stay with Baldwin and Alodia in Tasbapauni. Daniel Boone, Barney's dog, went to live with a Rama Indian family far up the Kukra River south of Bluefields. I asked that they keep his name, and they repeated it until they had the correct pronunciation. The dog was in a good home, and by retaining his name, I was able to plant an academic time bomb which didn't go off until two years later. When an anthropologist wrote me to ask about doing fieldwork with the Rama, I advised him to be sure to visit the Rama on the Kukra River. He wrote again later, only thinly veiling his displeasure at having been puzzled for almost a month by an Indian dog named Daniel Boone. Apparently the Rama family had kept secret the identity of the dog's former owners until they finally felt sorry for the exasperated anthropologist and blew our cover.

That left Sabi—and a major problem. We were scheduled to return to the University of Wisconsin, where we would live in Married Student Housing while I wrote up my research. The problem was that Married Student Housing didn't allow any animal larger or noisier than a goldfish, and we couldn't afford a private apartment or house, but would have to stay in the University's partially subsidized housing. We couldn't live elsewhere; we wouldn't part with Sabi; and they wouldn't let him live there. We decided that we could solve all three parts of the problem by going to the university apartment and taking Sabi with us but not telling anyone about him.

Married Student Housing at the University of Wisconsin is called Eagle Heights, but many refer to it as "Rabbit Hill." It is a large apartment complex located on the edge of the campus near Picnic Point on Lake Mendota and a large expanse of forest and fields. It was packed with inquisitive children and adults; thrown together by economic necessity and professional desire, they turned their attention toward two things: academic study and the study of their neighbors. Matched against thousands of attentive eyes, keeping Sabi a secret would require stealth, an external veneer of a "normal" family, and a hidden room.

True, Sabi was just a cat, even though a wild one, but he was already larger than any domesticated cat I'd ever seen, and he didn't make ordinary cat sounds. Frequently vociferous and loud, he often emitted piercing howls, growls and roars. The walls of the apartment were thin, so we had to do something to mask his jungle sounds.

Our room became a combination bedroom, study and sound-proofed cage. We paneled the walls with sheets of acoustical pressboard, bought an AM-FM radio for background noise, installed a floor-to-ceiling screened cage behind the sliding wall-length closet door, trimmed a dead tree to fit into a corner, and moved Sabi into his new sequestered quarters. For the next eight months I wrote my dissertation, we slept, and Sabi careened off the walls. It may have been the first Ph.D. thesis written inside a cage.

We didn't keep Sabi in the room all this time. He needed exercise every day, both to maintain good health and to tire him enough to let me get some work done. Across the street from our apartment was a large open field with garden plots, surrounded by many acres of forest and meadows, overlooking Lake Mendota. The problem was to get Sabi from the zoo room to the forest unobserved. To let the cat out of the apartment, I had to put him into a bag. Well, not a bag exactly, a briefcase. Another special Sabi purchase. I bought a huge leather, accordion-type briefcase, almost suitcase size, cut out the dividers, made some inconspicuous airholes here and there, and carpeted it with a scrap of rug.

Sabi soon learned that the briefcase meant a run in the forest, and he would jump in and wait to be closed inside. To any curious observer I was only carrying a briefcase into the forest. Any place but on a university campus this would have appeared to be unusual behavior in itself, but development of a high tolerance for strangeness is one of the adaptations one has to make to live in academia. A briefcase-carrying person entering the woods was simply put down as another weird Thoreau-type off to read in forest solitude.

Those were fun days. Sabi was running free, and that made me feel better about the impositions to which we were subjecting him. There in the forest and fields we would play hide-and-seek,

Sabi, our margay, relaxing after a run in the woods across the street from his cloistered hideaway in Married Student Housing at the University of Wisconsin, Madison, 1970.

catch-me-if-you-can, chase; and we would flush pheasants, run rabbits, and tree squirrels. Those runs did more than exercise zoo-room-cramped muscles; the forest romps with Sabi kept up my own spirits and helped me cope with the problems of readaptation to my own society after so many months in the tropics with the Miskito and our animals.

Our son had many friends, and the approaching winter soon began to reduce outside playtime and drive them inside. They were perceptive little varmints, and it was quite a challenge to hide Sabi from them. The burden of concealment was really on young Barney, who, if he wanted to bring his friends inside to play, had to make them wait at the door while he came to our room to let me know that the coming of the horde was imminent. On went the radio and in came the children. Barney kept the secret that would have made him the envy of all his friends.

When our friends dropped by or when we invited them for dinner, the radio was always on in the zoo room. If this was disconcerting to our visitors, they never let on. However, when we insisted on escorting them to the bathroom to make sure they didn't open the wrong door, they were somewhat mystified; and they were even more baffled to find one of us still waiting for them when they emerged.

It wasn't until I had completed the dissertation and we were getting ready to move from Madison that we told anyone about Sabi. It was a glorious night—a coming-out party for Sabi. We had invited Bill Denevan, the head of my dissertation committee, and his wife Susie over for dinner. The cage-written thesis was finished, and we were getting ready to move from Madison and Eagle Heights; so when Denevan asked me about a detail on my research, I took him into the zoo room to look at my field notes. Wide-eyed and slack-jawed, he stopped in the doorway. I'd grown so accustomed to the room's appearance that I had completely forgotten what an outsider's reaction might be at first exposure to a padded, soundproofed cell with a few cut-off trees and limbs in the corners. He just stared. Then he must have felt something staring at him, for he turned and looked up to where Sabi was perched, crouched on a high platform near the ceiling, just four or five feet from his head, seemingly ready to spring. I must say that Denevan took it in stride. As an old tropical hand he was as interested in Sabi as Sabi was in seeing a new face after all those cloistered months. By then Susie had come in, and Sabi was undecided as to which was the more interesting to watch.

I explained Sabi's presence and the need for the room's peculiar furnishings.

"So that explains your hands," Bill said. "I always wondered about your hands." Apparently he was referring to my frequently scratched and nicked hands and wrists, one of the by-products of aggressive wrestling and play with Sabi and his needle claws. "They are not the hands of a scholar."

After we left the University of Wisconsin, Sabi was able to come out of the closet and live openly with us.

Travels with Sabi entailed some difficulties and many joys. He returned with us to Nicaragua and the Miskito Coast several times. Without our own canoe we utilized the always overcrowded and overloaded passenger-freight boats to journey from Bluefields to Tasbapauni and other Miskito settlements to the north. Judi and Barney often were crowded into tiny cramped places, but their space miraculously increased as soon as Sabi was taken out of his traveling cage to stretch his legs. The Miskito were not exactly enthusiastic to see him again, but they accepted his presence as part of the strange behavior that they'd long seen us exhibit. I pointed out to our timorous traveling companions that although we were foreign visitors, Sabi was home born, a Miskito Coast citizen and deserving of traditional Miskito hospitality. The cat and the Nietschmanns had become part of the Miskito burden, a load they shouldered with hesitant grace and small expectations.

One summer we had our own boat, this time a large seagoing diesel vessel with a crew and turtlemen aboard. We were doing a study on the ecology and migration of hawksbill sea turtles. Sabi took some time to get his sea legs, and he never did really adapt well to life on the *Glendora*. Luckily, a good part of our work was done among the many small coral islands that dot the waters off the coast. Sabi had the free run of any island we camped at. I was somewhat embarrassed by his behavior, however. He readily sensed that the turtlemen with us were fearful of him; they would immediately retreat, even flee, if he made a playful rush at them. One time I caught him chasing two men, nipping at their heels, circling and feinting, until they ran into the water. Then Sabi pranced up and down the beach as if he were the king of the island. When I scolded him, he sulked for hours in the buttonwood thickets until an empty stomach persuaded him to return to camp.

Traveling by air with Sabi in the States was more difficult and required some of the tactics and equipment that had kept him hidden in Wisconsin. He was too sensitive and high-strung to travel in the baggage compartment as other pets do. If we were to fly, Sabi would have to accompany us on the plane with the rest of the passengers. We surmised that neither the passengers nor the airlines would relish having a wild cat visible on board during a transcontinental flight. Therefore, we would have to either hide him or disguise him. A dachshund sweater and hat not only made him look silly, they didn't cover his seventeen-inch tail or hide his thick forelegs and oversized paws. Disguises were out. Instead, we would try to hide him.

In the winter of 1970 airplane hijacking was not the threat it came to be; airport surveillance was minimal, and there was no mandatory checking of all passengers and carry-on luggage. We were en route from Detroit Metro Airport to Los Angeles International to visit our parents in California. I was wearing my professional tweed sport coat and V-neck cardigan and carrying a pipe, a briefcase and a University of Michigan suitbag. Judi was dressed in similar campus garb. Barney carried a three-week-old Michigan–Ohio State football program. We hoped that our academic cover would ward off watchful government and airline agents who were reported to be stationed in airports and on some of the flights. Sabi was in the briefcase. The only flight we could get was on TWA, with a changeover at St. Louis. All went well until St. Louis.

They were doing a random spot check. Two men—chunky, with short hair, thin ties and humorless eyes—were behind a long table. Metal rails, similar to those on a cattle chute, guided all passengers past them for inspection of carry-on baggage before they could enter the waiting area for our flight to Los Angeles. We stopped, backed around a corner, and discussed what to do. We couldn't get on the plane without passing through the inspection, yet our parents were probably already on their way to the airport to meet us. We decided to straight-face it and hoped we might appear as such an All-American family that they might just wave us through. I asked Barney to whistle "Hail to the Victors" and hoped that they weren't OSU fans.

The waiting lounge was full, and we were among the last passengers in line. Judi went ahead and placed her coat and purse on the table; Barney whistled; and I set the briefcase down on the floor and put the clothes bag, University-of-Michigan side up, on the table. They opened, prodded and examined. Ready to go, I picked up the briefcase and started to move off with Judi and Barney.

"Just a minute, sir. We'll have to inspect your briefcase, too. Place it on the table." The man spoke with a Jack Webb tone and cadence; he was pointing at the exposed briefcase.

It was not one of my better moments under pressure. As I carefully put the briefcase on the table, I imagined the little room we would soon be in: hospital-green walls, linoleum floor, wooden chairs, and the two inspectors telling us that we were violating rule such and such. Undercover Sabi and his field director were about to be interrogated and exposed; the cat who came in from the cold.

"Sir?"

I snapped out of thinking what was in store for us when that case was opened. They were looking at me suspiciously.

"Sir, would you please open the briefcase?"

I didn't want to open the briefcase. Sabi was inside—a taut bundle of muscles. He didn't like strangers much, and I knew he was certainly aware of different voices and peculiar circumstances on the outside of his leather refuge. As I mentioned before, a strong nonverbal communication system existed between us, and I knew that he knew something was up. I was thinking more about how to defuse Sabi than I was about the two men, who by now were tensed; one of them had unbuttoned his coat, exposing the butt of a revolver.

"Gentlemen, there is a margay in my briefcase, and I don't think it's wise to open it up right now."

I realized afterwards that I shouldn't have said that; the word *margay* is not in most people's vocabulary, and they could interpret it to mean anything. But it was too late. The Jack Webb one gingerly grabbed for the clasp, while his partner moved back, reached inside his coat with one hand, and held up the other to signal me to stay where I was. Judi and Barney stood only yards away, but they could do nothing. It was a frozen moment, suspended between apprehension and anticipation.

Ever so carefully he undid the catch and opened the briefcase. Sabi exploded through the crack—a hissing, yowling, claws-out, ears-back eruption of defensive fury. Jack Webb still hung onto the case and tried to close it, pinching Sabi amidships as he stood on his hind legs trying to get at the one who had violated his lair. The resultant jungle howls and outraged cat sounds must have alerted the entire airport, but my thoughts were on Sabi, and I reached for him, no longer caring what the gun-toting partner might do if I didn't stand still.

It didn't take much to quiet him down. Sabi, that is. After a few soft words and caresses he went back into the briefcase. Jack Webb didn't quiet down so easily, however. And I don't blame him. It must have been a hell of a scare. He had a difficult job at best and could have been suspecting the worst in my briefcase. To have an attacking margay on his hands certainly was not part of his expectations or his training.

"That . . . that thing . . . that's an ocelot," he stuttered, still white-faced and shaking.

"No, it's a margay. I said I had a margay in my briefcase. We always travel with him."

"Damn!" That's all he said, "Damn," which I thought showed a tremendous display of personal restraint and control. In his shoes I would have said a lot more.

"Go ahead and get on the plane," he ordered with a weak, exasperated grunt.

We got on the plane, but the other passengers were a little skittish and left a lot of empty seats around us.

They wouldn't be so nice nowadays. But back then it must have been different, or he was one hell of a guy. Wherever you are, Mr. Inspector, I wish you well and apologize for the margay on Flight 91.

I had been teaching in the Department of Geography at the University of Michigan for a couple of months when I decided it was time to introduce Sabi to my new environment. As yet nobody knew we had him. I wanted to do this a stage at a time. I was spending much of every day at school; Judi was working on her degree in anthropology; Barney was in the second grade; and Sabi was home alone and didn't like it. I couldn't take him to class with me, nor could I take him for a walk around campus or Ann Arbor. He was just too unusual and beautiful an animal for anyone to ignore. Besides, one of the diagnostic characteristics of any large university campus is a high ratio of dogs to people, and Sabi and dogs didn't mix well. Therefore, Sabi would come to school with me, but in the briefcase, and he would stay in my office until we went home together.

The first day went well enough. Sabi explored the new office surroundings and left his mark here and there, staking out his claim to the territory. Finals were still several weeks away, and the blood-in-the-water exam-preparation frenzy had not yet panicked students, so none came to see me during my office hours. Perhaps Sabi could remain a secret through finals, when people's curiosity would be blunted by more pragmatic concerns. But that was not to be.

It happened on the second day. And it happened in a big way. Sabi was up on top of a US-Steel bookcase, the highest spot in the room, intermittently dozing and preening himself, when a faculty colleague came in to see me. Unfortunately, he was smoking a pipe. I carried a pipe for show but rarely lit it. Sabi didn't like smoke. In fact, he got very upset over it.

The pipe smoker was sending up clouds of smoke, and Sabi was no longer dozing. He was up and pacing back and forth on the bookcase top. My colleague didn't notice him at first, but when he did, it was a magic moment in the history of the department.

He was sitting in a chair when he looked up into Sabi's huge eyes; with flattened ears and trembling muscles, the cat was coiled and ready to jump. Sabi hissed and spat margay warnings—fearful sounds to the uninitiated. The pipe smoker backed off and tried to exit quickly, but he stumbled over his chair and fell to the floor in a tangled heap. At the same time Sabi showed his disdain for the prostrate pipe smoker by turning haughtily, lifting his long tail, and sending down a spray of urine on the still-suspended smoke clouds and my mesmerized fellow geographer.

Oh, that was a memorable moment in geography: a classic moment, one to be cherished and held on to.

The animals in our house gave us an appreciation for wild things, but also left us with an attendant sadness at seeing wild, sensitive creatures tamed and dependent. Only some were we able to rehabilitate and release back to their natural environment. Those that stayed with us longer and those that became an emotional and social part of our family could never return, for their lives were as inexorably mixed with ours as ours were with theirs. And in the process, they became as maladapted to their former environment as we became to ours. After having animals in our house, neither of us could go home again.

6. When the Turtle Collapses, the World Ends

After delivering a lecture on the solar system, philosopher-psychologist William James was approached by an elderly lady who claimed she had a theory superior to the one described by him.

"We don't live on a ball rotating around the sun," she said. "We live on a crust of earth on the back of a giant turtle."

Not wishing to demolish this absurd argument with the massive scientific evidence at his command, James decided to dissuade his opponent gently.

"If your theory is correct, madam, what does this turtle stand on?"

"You're a very clever man, Mr. James, and that's a good question, but I can answer that. The first turtle stands on the back of a second, far larger, turtle."

"But what does this second turtle stand on?" James asked patiently.

The old lady crowed triumphantly, "It's no use, Mr. James—it's turtles all the way down."

In the half-light of dawn a sailing canoe approaches a shoal where nets were set the day before. A Miskito turtleman stands in the bow and points to a distant splash that breaks the gray sheen of the Caribbean waters. Even from a hundred yards he can tell that a green turtle has been caught in one of the nets. His two companions quickly bring the craft alongside the turtle, and as they pull it from the sea, its glistening shell reflects the first rays of the rising sun. As two men work to remove the heavy reptile from the net, the third keeps the canoe headed into the swells and beside the anchored net. After its fins have been pierced and lashed with bark fiber cord, the 250-pound turtle is placed on its back in the bottom of the canoe. The turtlemen are happy. Perhaps their luck will be good today and their other nets will also yield many turtles.

These green turtles, caught by Miskito Indian turtlemen off the eastern coast of Nicaragua, are destined for distant markets. Their butchered bodies will pass through many hands, local and foreign, eventually ending up in tins, bottles and freezers far away. Their

A turtleman wraps the shaft of his harpoon with cotton twine to make a hand grip and a loop through which will pass the harpoon line. In this way the heavy palm wood shaft will not sink and be lost after it is thrown.

meat, leather, shell, oil, and calipee—a gelatinous substance that is the base for turtle soup—will be used to produce goods for more affluent parts of the world.

The coastal Miskito Indians are dependent on green turtles. Their culture has long been adapted to the once vast populations inhabiting the largest sea turtle feeding grounds in the world. As the most important link between livelihood, social interaction and environment, green turtles were the pivot around which traditional Miskito Indian society revolved. These large reptiles also provided the major source of protein in Miskito diet. Now this priceless and limited resource has become a prized commodity that is being exploited for almost entirely economic reasons.

In the past, turtles fulfilled the nutritional needs as well as the social responsibilities of Miskito society. Today, however, the Miskito depend mainly on the sale of turtles to provide them with the money they need to purchase household goods and other necessities. But the turtles are a declining resource; overdependence on them is leading the Miskito into an ecological blind alley. The cultural control mechanisms that once adapted the Miskito to their environment and faunal resources are now circumvented or inoperative, and they are caught up in a system of continued intensification of turtle fishing which threatens to provide neither cash nor subsistence.

Entangled in the set net sometime during the night, an exhausted green turtle is hauled from the early morning Caribbean. Big Sandy Bay turtlemen near Sukra off the Miskito Cays, 1972.

Big and fat, this female green turtle will be butchered immediately for the turtlemen's families, who have been complaining of "meat hunger." Tasbapauni, 1969.

The coastal Miskito Indians are among the world's most adept small-craft seamen and turtlemen. Their traditional subsistence system provided dependable yields by means of judicious scheduling. Agriculture, hunting, fishing and gathering were organized seasonally according to weather and resource availability and provided adequate amounts of food and materials without overexploiting any one species or site. Women cultivated the crops while men hunted and fished. Turtle fishing was the backbone of subsistence, providing meat throughout the year.

Miskito society and economy were interdependent. There was no economic activity without a social context, and every social act had a reciprocal economic aspect. To the Miskito, meat, especially turtle meat, was the most esteemed and valuable resource, for it was not only a mainstay of subsistence, it was the item most commonly distributed to relatives and friends. Meat shared in this way satisfied mutual obligations and responsibilities and smoothed out daily and

Pungi Perez and Percival Hebberd unloading turtles on the beach at Tasbapauni in 1968. The green turtles were butchered for village kin distribution and for sale, while the hawksbill (in the canoe) was killed for its shell (tortoise shell). Palm wood harpoons and cotton and nylon lines, used to catch these turtles, can be seen in the canoe.

seasonal differences in the acquisition of animal protein. In this way those too young, old or sick or otherwise unable to secure their own meat received their share, and the village achieved a certain balance. Minimal food requirements were met; meat surplus was disposed of to others; and social responsibilities were satisfied.

Today the older Miskito recall that when meat was scarce in the village, a few turtlemen would put out to sea in their dugout canoes for a day's harpooning on the turtle feeding grounds. In the afternoon the men would return, sailing before the northeast trade wind, bringing meat for all. Gathered on the beach, the villagers would help drag the canoes into thatched storage sheds. After the turtles had been butchered and the meat distributed, everyone would return home to the cooking fires.

Historical circumstances and a series of boom-bust economic cycles disrupted the Miskito's society and environment. In the seventeenth and eighteenth centuries, intermittent trade with English and French buccaneers—based on the exchange of forest and marine resources for metal tools and utensils, rum and firearms—prompted the Miskito to extend hunting, fishing and gathering beyond their needs to exploitative enterprises.

During the nineteenth and early twentieth centuries, foreign-owned companies operating in eastern Nicaragua exported rubber, lumber and gold and initiated commercial banana production. As alien economic and ecological influences intensified, contract wage labor replaced seasonal short-term economic relationships; company commissary supplies replaced limited trade goods; and large-scale exploitation of natural resources replaced sporadic, selective harvesting. During economic boom periods the relationship between resources, subsistence and environment was drastically altered for the Miskito. Resources became a commodity with a price tag, market exploitation a livelihood, and foreign wages and goods a necessity.

For more than 200 years, relations between the coastal Miskito and the English were based on sea turtles. It was from the Miskito that the English learned the art of turtling, which they then organized into intensive commercial exploitation of Caribbean turtle grounds and nesting beaches. Sea turtles were among the first resources involved in trade relations and foreign commerce in the Caribbean. Zoologist Archie Carr, an authority on sea turtles, has remarked that "more than any other dietary factor, the green turtle supported the opening up of the Caribbean." The once abundant turtle populations provided sustenance to ships' crews and to the new settlers and plantation laborers.

In the seventeenth and eighteenth centuries, the Cayman Islands,

settled by the English, became the center of commercial turtle
fishing in the Caribbean. By the early nineteenth century, demands
on the Cayman turtle grounds and nesting beaches to supply meat
to Caribbean and European markets decimated the turtle population. The Cayman Islanders were forced to shift to other turtle areas
off Cuba, the Gulf of Honduras, and the coast of eastern Nicaragua.
They made annual expeditions, lasting four to seven weeks, to the
Miskito turtle grounds to net green turtles, occasionally purchasing
live ones, dried calipee, and the shells of hawksbill turtles
(*Eretmochelys imbricata*) from the Miskito Indians. Reported catches
of green turtles by the Cayman turtlers generally ranged between
2,000 and 3,000 a year until the late 1960s, when the Nicaraguan
government failed to renew the islanders' fishing privileges.

Intensive extraction by foreign companies led to seriously
depleted resources. By the 1940s many of the economic booms had
turned to busts. As the resources ran out and operating costs
mounted, companies moved to other areas in Central America.
Thus, the economic mainstays that had helped provide the Miskito
with jobs, currency, markets and foreign goods were gone. The
company supply ships and commissaries disappeared; money
became scarce, and store-bought items expensive.

In the backwater of the passing golden boom period, the Miskito
were left with an ethic of poverty, but they still had the subsistence
skills that had maintained their culture for hundreds of years. Their
land and water environment was still capable of providing reliable
resources for local consumption. As it had been in the past, turtle
fishing became a way of life, a provider of life itself. But traditional
subsistence culture could no longer integrate Miskito society and
environment in a state of equilibrium. Resources were now viewed
as having a monetary value and labor a price tag. All that was
needed was a market.

Recently, two foreign turtle companies began operations along
the east coast of Nicaragua, one in Puerto Cabezas in late 1968 and
another in Bluefields in 1969. Both companies were capable of
processing and shipping large amounts of green turtle meat and
by-products to markets in North America and Europe. They
purchased turtles from the Miskito. Each week company boats
visited coastal Miskito communities and offshore-island turtle
camps to buy green turtles. The "company" was back; money was
again available; the Miskito were expert in securing the desired
commodity; and another economic boom period was at hand. But
the significant difference between this boom and previous ones was
that the Miskito were now selling a subsistence resource.

As a result, the last large surviving green turtle population in the

Caribbean was opened to almost year-round intensive exploitation. Paradoxically, the Miskito Indians, who once caught only what they needed for food, conducted the assault on the remaining turtle population.

Another ironic element in the Miskito-turtle story is that only some 200 miles to the south at Tortuguero, Costa Rica, Archie Carr had devoted fifteen years to the study of sea turtles and to the conservation of the Caribbean's last major sea turtle nesting beach. Carr estimates that more than half the green turtles that nest at Tortuguero are from Nicaraguan waters. The sad and exasperating paradox is that a conservation program ensured the survival of an endangered species for commercial exploitation in nearby waters.

Green turtles (*Chelonia mydas*) are large, air-breathing, herbivorous marine reptiles. They congregate in large populations and graze on underwater beds of vegetation in relatively clear, shallow tropical waters. A mature turtle weighs 250 pounds or more. After a turtle is caught, it can live for a couple of weeks if kept in shade on land or indefinitely in a saltwater enclosure. Green turtles have at least six behavioral characteristics that encourage their exploitation:

Miskito turtlemen returning to their village after several days at sea netting green turtles. As most of their catch was sold to a buyer on the turtle company boat, they bring in only one turtle—hardly sufficient to satisfy kin obligations and their own family's needs. Tasbapauni, 1969.

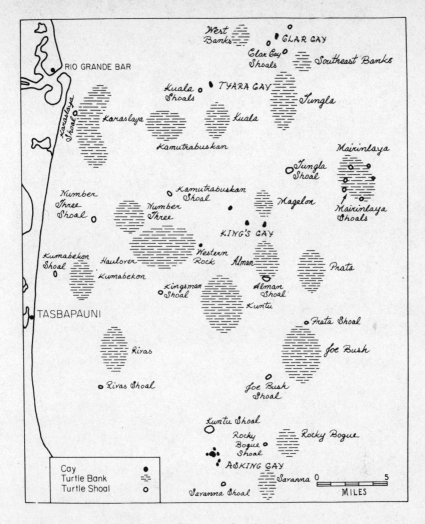

they occur in large numbers in localized areas; they are air breathing, so they have to surface; they are mass social nesters; they have an acute location-finding ability; when mature, individuals migrate seasonally on overlapping and shifting two-, three- and four-year cycles for mating and nesting; and they exhibit predictable local distributional patterns.

The extensive shallow shelf off eastern Nicaragua is dotted with numerous small coral islands, thousands of reefs, and vast underwater pastures of marine vegetation called "turtle banks." During the day a large group of turtles may be found feeding at one of the many turtle banks, while only a few turtles may be found at adjacent marine pastures. The turtles graze on the vegetation, rising periodically to the surface for air and then floating briefly before diving again. In the late afternoon groups of turtles leave the feeding grounds and swim to shoals, some up to four or five miles away, to spend the night. By five the next morning, they have gathered to depart again for the banks. The turtles' precise commuterlike behavior in moving between sleeping areas and feeding pastures is well known to the Miskito and helps ensure good turtling.

Each coastal turtling village exploits an immense sea area containing many turtle banks and shoals. For example, the Miskito of Tasbapauni utilize a marine area of approximately 600 square miles, with twenty major turtle banks and almost forty important shoals.

Because of their rather predictable patterns of movement and habitat preference, green turtles are commonly caught by the Miskito in three kinds of operations: on the turtle banks with harpoons, along the shoal-to-feeding-area route with harpoons, and on the shoals with nets which entangle the turtles when they surface for air.

The Miskito's traditional means of taking turtles was by harpoon, an eight- to ten-foot shaft fitted with a detachable short point tied to a strong line. This simple technology pitted two turtlemen in a small seagoing canoe against the elusive turtles. Successful turtling with harpoons requires an extensive knowledge of turtle behavior, and tremendous skill and experience in handling a small canoe in what can be very rough seas. Turtlemen work in pairs: a "strikerman" in the bow, the "captain" in the stern. Together they make a single unit engaged in the delicate and almost silent pursuit of a wary prey, their movements coordinated by experience and rewarded by proficiency. Turtlemen have mental maps of all the banks and shoals in their area; each one is named and its location determined through a complex system of celestial navigation, distance reckoning, wind and current direction, and the individual surface-swell motion over each site. Traditionally, not all Miskito were sufficiently expert in seamanship and turtle lore to become respected "strikermen," capable of securing turtles even during hazardous sea conditions. Theirs was a very specialized calling. Thus, harpooning restrained possible overexploitation, since turtles were taken one at a time by two men directly involved in the chase, and there were only a limited number of really proficient "strikermen" in each village.

Those who still use harpoons must leave early to take advantage of the land breeze and to have enough time to reach the distant offshore turtle grounds by first light. Turtlemen who are going for the day or for several days meet on the beach by two A.M. They drag the canoes on bamboo rollers from beachfront sheds to the water's

Surfacing for air, this hawksbill turtle became entangled in a net set by Miskito turtlemen. The shell of this endangered species will be sold to the jewelry trade. Miskito Cays, 1972.

edge. There in the swash of spent breakers they load and secure food, water, paddles, lines, harpoons and sails. Using a long pole, the standing bowman propels the canoe through the foaming surf while the captain in the stern keeps the craft running straight by means of a six-foot mahogany paddle. Once past the inside break, the men count the dark rolling seas building outside until there is a momentary pause in the sets. Then, with paddles digging deep, they drive the narrow twenty-foot canoe over the cresting swells, rising precipitously on each wave face and then plunging down the far side as the sea and the sky seesaw into and out of view. Once past the breakers, they rig the sail and, running with the land breeze, point the canoe toward a star in the eastern sky.

A course is set by star-fix and by backsight on a prominent coconut palm on the mainland horizon. Course alterations are made to correct for the direction and intensity of winds and currents. After two or three hours of sailing, the men reach a spot located between a turtle sleeping shoal and a feeding bank. There they intercept and follow the turtles as they leave for specific banks.

On the banks the turtlemen paddle quietly, listening for the sound of a "blowing" turtle. When a turtle surfaces for air, it emits a hissing sound audible for fifty yards or more on a calm day. Since a turtle will stay near the surface for only a minute or two before diving to feed, the men must approach quickly and silently, maneuvering the canoe to a spot directly in front of or behind the turtle in order to take advantage of its blind spots. Once harpooned, a turtle explodes into a frenzy of action; in its hopeless underwater dash for escape it tows the canoe along at high speeds until it finally tires enough to be pulled alongside.

But turtle harpooning is a dying art. The dominant method of turtling today is the use of nets. Since their introduction, the widespread use of turtle nets has drastically altered turtling strategy and productivity. Originally brought to the Miskito by the Cayman Islanders, net materials are now extensively distributed on credit by the turtle companies. This simple technological and economic change, along with the high demand for turtles, has resulted in intensified pressure on green turtle populations.

Buoyed by wooden floats and anchored to the bottom by a single line, the fifty-foot-long by fourteen-foot-wide nets hang from the surface like underwater flags, shifting with the current. Nets are set in place during midday when the turtlemen can see the dark shoal areas. Two Miskito will set five to thirty nets from one canoe, often completely saturating a small shoal. In the late afternoon green turtles return to their shoals to spend the night. There they sleep beside or beneath a coral outcrop, periodically surfacing for air where the canopy of nets awaits them.

Catching turtles with nets requires little skill; anyone with a canoe can now be a turtleman. The Miskito set thousands of nets daily, providing continuous coverage in densely populated nocturnal habitats. Younger Miskito can become turtlemen almost overnight simply by following more experienced men to the shoal areas, thus circumventing the need for years of accumulated skill and knowledge that once were the domain of the "strikermen." All one has to do is learn where to set the nets, retire for the night, remove the entangled turtles the next morning, and reset the nets. The outcome is predictable: more turtlemen using more effective methods catch more turtles.

With an assured market for turtles, the Miskito devote more time to catching turtles, traveling farther and staying longer. Increased dependence on turtles as a source of income and greater time inputs have meant disruption of subsistence agriculture, hunting and fishing. The Miskito no longer produce foodstuffs for themselves; they buy imported foods with money gained from the sale of turtles. Caught between contradictory priorities—their traditional subsistence system and the market economy—the Miskito are opting for cash.

The Miskito are now enveloped in a positive feedback system where change spawns change. Coastal villages rely on turtles for a livelihood. Decline of subsistence provisioning has led to the need to secure food from local shopkeepers on credit to feed the families in the villages and the men during their turtling expeditions. Initial high catches of turtles encouraged more Miskito to participate, and by 1972 the per person and per day catch had begun to decline noticeably.

In late 1972, several months after I had returned to Michigan, I received a letter from a turtleman who wrote, "Turtle is getting scarce, Mr. Barney. You said it would happen in five or ten years, but it is happening now."

Burdened by an overdependence on an endangered species and by accumulating debts for food and nets, the Miskito are finding it increasingly difficult to break even, much less secure a profit. With few other economic alternatives, inevitably the next step is to use more nets and to stay out at sea longer.

The turtle companies encourage the Miskito to expand turtling activities by providing them with building materials so that they can construct houses on offshore cays, thereby eliminating the need to return to the mainland during rough weather. On their weekly runs up and down the coast, company boats bring food, turtle gear and cash for turtles to fishing camps from the Miskito Cays to the Set Net Cays. Frequent visits keep the Miskito from becoming discouraged and returning to their villages with the turtles. On Saturdays villagers watch the sea for returning canoes. A few men bring turtle for their families, but the majority bring only money. Many return with neither.

Most Miskito prefer to be home on Sundays to visit with friends and attend religious services. (There are Moravian, Anglican and Catholic mission churches in many of the villages.) But with more and more regularity, turtlemen are staying out for two to four weeks. The church may promise salvation, but only the turtle companies can provide money.

When they return to their villages, turtlemen are confronted with a complex dilemma: how to satisfy both social and economic demands with only a limited resource. Traditional Miskito social rules stipulate that turtle meat should be shared among kin, but the new economic system requires that turtles be sold for personal economic gain. Kin expect gifts of meat, and friends expect to be sold meat. Besieged with requests, turtlemen are forced to decide who will or will not receive meat. This choosing is contrary to the traditional Miskito ethic, which is based on generosity and mutual concern for the well-being of others; and the older Miskito ask why the turtlemen should have to allocate a food that was once available to all. Turtlemen sell and give to other turtlemen, thereby ensuring reciprocal treatment for themselves, but there simply are not enough turtles to accommodate other economic and social requirements. In order to have enough turtles to sell, they butcher

Villagers demand meat at a turtle butchering. Surrounded and obscured by his kin and neighbors, the turtleman does not have enough meat to satisfy everyone. Tasbapauni.

fewer in the villages. This means that less meat is being consumed than before the turtle companies began operations. The Miskito presently sell 70 to 90 percent of the turtles they catch; in the near future they will sell even more and eat fewer.

Tension is growing in the villages. Kinship relationships are strained because of what some villagers interpret as preferential and stingy meat distribution. Rather than endure the trauma caused by having to ration turtle meat, many turtlemen prefer to sell all their turtles to the company and return to the village with money, which does not have to be shared. However, if a Miskito sells out to the company, he will probably be unable to acquire meat for himself in the village, regardless of kinship or purchasing power. I overheard an elderly turtleman muttering to himself as he butchered a turtle, "I no going to sell, neither give dem meat. Let dem eat de money."

The situation is bad and getting worse. Individuals too old or too sick to provide for themselves often receive little meat or money from relatives. Families without turtlemen are families with neither money or access to meat. The trend is toward nuclear families operating solely for their own economic ends. Miskito villages are becoming separated neighborhoods instead of close-knit communities.

The Miskito diet has suffered in both quality and quantity. Less protein and fewer diverse vegetables and fruits are consumed. Present dietary staples—rice, white flour, beans, sugar and coffee—come from the store. In Little Sandy Bay, for example, 65 percent of all food eaten in a year was purchased.

Besides the nutritional significance of what is becoming a largely carbohydrate diet, dependence on purchased foods has also had major economic reverberations. Generated by national and international scarcities, inflation has hit the Miskito. Most of their purchased food is imported, much from the United States. In the last five years prices for staples have increased 100 to 150 percent. This has had an overwhelming impact on the Miskito, who spend 50 to 75 percent of their income for food. Consequently, their entry into the market by selling a subsistence resource, diverting labor from agriculture, and intensifying exploitation of a vanishing species has resulted in foods that are of poorer quality and are higher priced.

The Miskito now depend on outside systems that are subject to world market fluctuations for money and materials. They have lost both their autonomy and their adaptive relationship with their environment. Life is no longer socially rewarding, nor is their diet satisfying. The coastal Miskito have become a specialized and highly vulnerable sector of the global market economy.

Loss of the turtle market would be a serious economic blow to the Miskito, who have almost no other means of securing cash for what have now become necessities. Nevertheless, continued exploitation will surely reduce the turtle population to a critical level.

National and international legislation is urgently needed. At the very least, commercial turtle fishing must be curtailed for several years until the *Chelonia* population can rebound and quotas can be set. While turtle fishing for subsistence should be permitted, export of sea turtle products used in the gourmet, the cosmetic or the jewelry trade should be banned.

Restrictive environmental legislation, however, is not a popular subject in Nicaragua, a country that has recently been torn by earthquakes, volcanic eruption and hurricanes. A program for sea turtle conservation submitted to the Nicaraguan government for consideration ended up in a pile of rubble during the earthquake that devastated Managua in December 1972, adding a sad footnote to the Miskito–sea turtle situation. With other problems to face, the government has not yet reviewed what is happening on the distant east coast, which is separated from the capital by more than 200 miles of rain forest—and by years of neglect.

As it is now, the turtles are going down, and along with them the

Miskito. Seemingly, this is a small problem in terms of ongoing ecological and cultural changes in the world, but each local situation involves species and societies with long histories and, perhaps, short futures. They are weather vanes in the conflicting winds of economic and environmental priorities. As Bob Dylan sang, "You don't need a weatherman to know which way the wind blows."

The situation steadily deteriorated after 1974, the height of commercial exploitation, until the "turtle boom" threatened both traditional Miskito subsistence and green turtle survival. From 1969 through 1976, up to 10,000 green turtles were exported annually. Already depleted by Cayman Island turtlers on the Miskito Bank feeding grounds and by Costa Ricans on the nesting beach at Tortuguero, the largest remaining green turtle population in the Caribbean was being subjected to massive year-round exploitation. Each year their numbers were fewer and the pressure greater. And at the same time the Miskito, the best traditional turtlemen in the world, could not get enough turtle meat to eat or to give or to sell. The Miskito had entered an economic and ecological cul-de-sac. Their major subsistence resource had become valuable and scarce, and the declining chelonian population could not provide enough income to close the gap between subsistence shortfall and purchased needs. Whether the resource was green turtles, hawksbill shell, shrimp, lobster, spotted cats, caimans, crocodiles or river otters, the situation was the same: faunal resources were diminishing, while economic reliance on them was increasing. The Miskito became steadily dependent on the sale of local resources to secure money for the purchase of imported foods and goods. And each year the price for imported materials went up and the number of marketable animals went down. By 1975 most households in Tasbapauni, for example, were spending 80 percent of their income for tinned and sacked foods. People were not eating more; they were eating less but paying more for it. Despite their isolated locale, the Miskito were becoming citizens of the world and sharing the global problem of making ends meet. And whereas subsistence was once the means to an end, the market now threatened to end the means and the green turtles and several other species.

The collective impact of articles and books and a film led to changes in the Miskito–green turtle situation. Archie Carr's writings on the demise of Caribbean turtle populations had been widely read, and my material and a 16mm film by Brian Weiss, *The Turtle People*, provided information on the human and cultural repercussions in eastern Nicaragua. Apparently, these influenced people to provide sufficient pressure to push the Nicaraguan government into doing something about the problem. In June 1975, at the invitation of General Anastasio Somoza Debayle, the President of Nicaragua, I went to Managua to explain what was happening on the distant coast. I spoke about turtles and people, about ecology and economics, about history and change. I told President Somoza about the West-Caribbean Connection. He promised to do something about the problem, perhaps a quota on the number of turtles exported, perhaps a ban on taking females, perhaps . . . . I suggested he close the companies—which now numbered three and in which it was said he had investments. It took a while, but something was done about the Nicaraguan link in the West-Caribbean Connection.

7. The West-Caribbean Connection

A Most Successful Way of Life

I really don't know why so many people in the world are interested in sea turtles. Certainly turtles don't have the grace and beauty of the big cats—the jaguars, pumas and leopards; nor do they have the fine lines and swiftness of such birds of prey as eagles and hawks; nor do they possess the intelligence and playfulness of dolphins and porpoises. What sea turtles do project is a sense of permanence, stability and massive magnificence. But this is anthropomorphizing. I suppose everyone has his own animal totems. Why so many are curious about sea turtles is a mystery to me; maybe it's because turtles are such a remarkable enigma.

> After perhaps 50 million years of land life, a number of reptiles entered the sea about 170 million years ago, in the Triassic period. They were huge and formidable creatures. Some had oarlike limbs by which they rowed through the water; some were web-footed, with long serpentine necks. These grotesque monsters disappeared millions of years ago, but we remember them when we come upon a large sea turtle swimming many miles at sea, its barnacle-encrusted shell eloquent of its marine life.
>
> Rachel Carson, *The Sea Around Us*

Sea turtles are large; they have a unique protective body armor, their shell; and they are one of the few survivors of the Age of Reptiles, 90 million years ago. They have a long evolutionary history. The early reptiles evolved on land, but millions of years ago some turned to the marine environment, adapted physically and behaviorally and became sea-dwelling. With the exception of sea turtles and the saltwater crocodile, all of these marine reptiles are now extinct. Over the ensuing millions of years, marine conditions were much more stable than those on land, so the sea turtles were able to remain relatively unchanged, and they spread their populations throughout the world's seas and oceans, where they found suitable environments. There are a few other reptiles that live in the sea—marine iguanas, sea snakes and one species of crocodile—but sea turtles are the only other modern reptiles to adapt successfully to a saltwater environment.

> The sea turtles we know today provide a direct link with the Age of Reptiles. Not only have they remained virtually unchanged, but, were it not for man, would still abound in large numbers in all suitable tropical and subtropical seas. Clearly, theirs is a most successful way of life.
>
> <div align="right">Robert Bustard, <i>Sea Turtles: Their Natural History and Conservation</i></div>

When they adapted to the marine environment, these large creatures retained particular reptilian characteristics that later became important when humans began to exploit them and, more recently, to study them scientifically. The body temperature of sea turtles, as of other reptiles, is regulated by their environment; thus, water temperature is a primary limiting factor in their distribution. An exception is the leatherback turtle (*Dermochelys coriacea*), which is not strictly ectothermic and is much more pelagic than the other sea turtles. The four other genera of sea turtles (*Chelonia*, the green; *Caretta*, loggerhead; *Eretmochelys*, hawksbill; and *Lepidochelys*, ridley) are found in tropical and the warmer subtropical seas of the world. More specifically, they are found in these warm waters along the shallow margins of continents and islands where favorable habitat and food exist. Sea turtles must return to land to lay their eggs. As this is the only time most sea turtles emerge from the water, nesting beaches are important focal points for their exploitation and study. Even though these turtles live in the sea, they have lungs and breathe air, as do all reptiles. Therefore, they must surface occasionally for air, which also makes them vulnerable to human predation. Whereas all five genera of sea turtles are to some degree migratory, the herbivorous green turtle may be the only one that makes periodic migrations across long stretches of open water between highly specific feeding and breeding places.

> The fundamental aspect on sea-turtle ecology is that they live in the ocean and nest on land. Little is known about the relation between foraging territory and nesting locality in four of the five kinds of sea turtles. In one kind, however, the herbivorous green turtle, there seems to be a worldwide pattern of commuting between feeding territory and nesting beach. The two phases of the habitat rarely occur close together. Turtle grass grows in expansive stands only in protected water, while good nesting beach forms only where waves come in unhindered and break against the shore. This duality of habitat imposes on the green turtle the need to travel. In many cases

the travel covers distances of hundreds of miles in the open sea, but the animals have adapted themselves to this situation to such a degree that they can hold a course through long periods of open-water cruising, and can home to a short section of breeding beach after a thousand-mile cruise in the ocean.

Archie Carr, *The Reptiles*

Exactly how green turtles are able to navigate over wide reaches of trackless sea, apparently holding a definite course for an extended period, to return to a familiar tiny beach is not yet fully understood. Archie Carr believes that their travel may be guided in part by a highly discriminatory sense of smell; that is, they are able to find a far off nesting beach by swimming into an increasingly stronger olfactory gradient, much as salmon are believed to do. They may also navigate by sun and stars. Much of their behavior and ecology, as well as that of other sea turtles, remain on the twilight edge of what is known and what can be imagined.

Sea turtles have an exceedingly old and successful way of life. One of the few marine reptiles, they become a subsistence and economic mainstay of peoples throughout the seaside tropics because of their prodigious numbers and unique behavioral patterns. Yet their life cycle, natural history and incredible migration and navigation are only faintly understood by science. Extraordinarily successful survivors of the past, they have a seemingly dim future.

Turtle Reef

Night. Dark sea. Long smooth swells retain the momentum given by the day's now-ebbed trade winds and roll on westward toward the main. Below, a reef. Dark coral waterscape. A small oasis of life sustained by sunlight and current-borne organisms. A Nassau grouper patrols the edge of a coral head. Big-eyed squirrel fish, hidden during the day, now spread out and feed. A large shadow rises from the reef, trailing thin streams of phosphorescence that leave a phantom outline of its streamlined bulk. It ascends. Overhead, the moonlit silver surface silhouettes the receding form—a sea turtle. Just as it breaks the surface, its fin touches something, but a quick sidethrust moves the skittish turtle away. Head up, the sea washing over its water-glassed shell, it expels long-held air with a strange puff-sigh blowing sound. It breathes and floats. An air-breathing marine reptile, it must leave the sanctuary of its reef ledge and surface periodically. Now ready to return to the reef below, the sea turtle takes a last breath and slips beneath the surface. Again it touches something. Reacting instantly, it turns with powerful sweeps of its long fins, pulling against the drag now felt high up a front fin near the shoulder. Huge muscles strain. The turtle twists, dives, turns; but the drag force is ungiving, and every explosive attempt at escape further hinders it. Now caught around the neck and both front fins, it continues to try to flee with diminishing strength. Still beating against the force that anchors it over the reef, the turtle tires. Occasionally a fin slaps the surface as the exhausted turtle floats at the end of its tether. Each sea swell pushes against the turtle, then parts around its body, re-forms, and drifts on relentlessly toward the mainland.

First daylight. Splashing on the surface. The reef's indigo waters turn gray. A black line angles upward from the jumbled coral topography pointing ruler-straight toward the feeble splashing; at its end the turtle's profile is focused edge-sharp by the rising sun. Another dark outline approaches—long, narrow and bluntly tapered. It stops next to the turtle. Hands without bodies penetrate from another realm and grasp. The line pulls spring-taut. The turtle disappears through the roof of its water world. Slack now and still anchored to the reef, the line bends in a gentle bow to the surface, suspended by a drift net. The commotion above has long since driven the rest of the turtles from their sleeping holes on the reef. Silently slipping by other hanging black lines, they have left the reef to feed.

Morning. Three turtles from thirty nets set the day before. The last turtle must have fought the net all night long. It hardly struggles when pulled from the water. A big she turtle, too. Maybe 350 pounds. Rare to see that size anymore. Two turtlemen strain to ease the big turtle to the bottom of the canoe, its long fins slapping wide arcs through the air but finding no purchase. "This is the second time this turtle's been caught," one of the men says as he struggles to pierce the fins and tie them together. "Look at the little pin on its fin." The turtlemen cut the tag from the turtle, scrape off a thin crust built up from long immersion in salt water, and examine the small metal object. Yes, it is similar to the other ones found from time to time by other turtlemen. Stamped into the metal are the words PREMIO REWARD REMITE SEND. Someone else is interested in this particular turtle. The turtleman shoves the tag deep into his pocket. The sea wind begins to stiffen. Patched cotton sails are raised, and the canoe sweeps westward with the sea swells, heading to the mainland, going home with turtle and carrying a small metal tag to talk about and wonder over that night.

This turtle was important to me because it was the first of many turtles I would see there in the Miskito village where it was taken. As I watched the Miskito butcher the big turtle and distribute the meat to their kin and friends, I began to learn about the extraordinary significance that sea turtles had for the Miskito. To me that turtle has always represented more than just another turtle caught by the Miskito. It symbolizes this species' remarkable biological, cultural, economic and scientific history. This catch occurred in 1968, but with the exception of the metal turtle tag, the same event had been repeated innumerable times before.

The behavioral patterns of sea turtles and the cultural and economic ways of humans have long been closely meshed in the western Caribbean. The pathways of turtles, the Miskito, and visitors had crossed many times before. Turtle Reef was used by the distant ancestors of the big green turtle with the metal tag. Countless generations migrated to far nesting beaches, and still found such tiny spots as Turtle Reef upon their return to home waters. When the first indigenous peoples came, they found turtles on Turtle Reef. When the first Spanish, English, French, and Dutch ships began exploring the western Caribbean and eastern Central America, there were Miskito Indians and turtles at Turtle Reef. By then, the Miskito had evolved into the most skilled and highly adapted turtle fishing culture in the world. Sea turtles were a major reason that later English, Jamaican and Caymanian seafarers and traders had such an inordinate interest in and influence on the mainland coast. Read James Parsons's book *The Green Turtle and Man*, Archie Carr's *The Windward Road* and *So Excellent a Fishe*, and Peter Matthiessen's *Far Tortuga*, and you'll come away profoundly amazed that so much history in the seaside tropics is linked to sea turtles in a chain of biological and cultural circumstances that have made the green turtle the world's most valuable, and now one of the most endangered, reptiles.

The Last Turtle Line

If you were to search the entire pantropical range of the green turtle and sift through its long economic history looking for the geographical nucleus of the green turtle story, you could not find a more ideal spot than the western Caribbean. Take out a map of this area and see for yourself. Place one end of a straightedge at Tortuguero in northeastern Costa Rica, just south of the mouth of the Río San Juan, and then slide it across the map until the edge crosses the Miskito Cays. Now follow the straightedge beyond the Cays, and you'll see it cross the Cayman Islands. Go still farther until it reaches the Straits of Florida and the Gulf Stream. The history and much of the future of the green turtle as a species and as a resource lie along this edge. These four geographical locations represent the most significant interrelated elements in the saga of *Chelonia mydas*. Each location contains part of the picture.

When you take away the straightedge, a line will still be there even if you can't see it. I call this line the West-Caribbean Connection. It runs from the tropics to the mid-latitudes, crossing international boundaries, sea turtle life cycles, different cultures, and years of history. Not so long ago, if you could have traced a green turtle far enough and long enough along this line, from birth on the black sand beach at Tortuguero, through maturation on the marine pastures and turtle reefs of the Miskito Bank, to probable capture for food or for shipment via the Cayman Islands to markets in the United States and Europe, not only would you be able to solve many of the great mysteries that surround this remarkable animal's natural history, but you'd learn a great deal about the Caribbean, about human behavior and about economics.

The green turtle–human geography along the line is a wondrous thing. Some segments in the line are older than others. The green turtle migration route from the Nicaraguan feeding grounds to the Tortuguero breeding beach is old, very old, and its patterns only faintly understood. The Miskito link in the line has been there for several hundred years and has made them the most turtle-dependent people in the world. The Caymanian tie lasted about 130 years, during which time their schooners, captains and voyages became Caribbean legends. Joined by particular environmental, ecological and economic conditions, these diverse peoples and places formed the West-Caribbean Connection: Costa Rica gave birth to the turtles; Nicaragua fed and raised them; the Miskito were sustained by them; Cayman Islanders marketed them; and the English and Americans dined on them.

The West-Caribbean Connection held strong for many years. Now there are weak links and even gaps, and the line is no longer straight, but parts are still intact. The Caymanians have been replaced by local turtle processing and exporting plants; the American market has been closed, while those of a few other countries have expanded; the Miskito have begun to sell what was their most important dietary resource and a major unifying element in their social and economic system; and the Caribbean's last large green turtle colony has become imperiled.

In tracking that fictitious turtle from Tortuguero to Turtle Reef, from one among thousands of nesting turtles to one with a specific number, and from the Miskito to the processing plants, I learned more about the capriciousness of humans than about the natural history and ecology of sea turtles. I saw irresponsible and shortsighted exploitation of this species, but I saw many good things, too, such as the vestiges of an indigenous conservation ethic and the beginnings of new conservation programs.

Tortuguero

Along the remote northeastern shore of Costa Rica, isolated by rain forest, rivers and rough, open sea, there is a very special beach. Between the Tortuguero Estuary—where the Tortuguero, Suerte and Sierpe Rivers empty into the Caribbean—and the Parismina River stretches a twenty-two-mile-long ribbon of dark, deep, friable sand. Tortuguero. Scalloped by storm surge waves, laced with sea purslane, railroad vine and rush grass, and backed by trade wind–sheared cocoplum and sea grape, this special beach has all the environmental requirements for the highly discriminating green turtle: it is wide, deep and secluded.

The persistence of an important nesting beach and large breeding colony during the tumultuous centuries of European settlement, population expansion and resource plundering represents a remarkable survival in the American tropics. Almost all the other big rookeries are gone—the Bermudas, the Dry Tortugas, Cayman Islands, Alta Vela and Trinidad—exploited to feed colonists and slaves, ships' crews and overseas gourmets. Here and there small nesting aggregations remain, such as Isla Contoy, Isla Blanca, Isla Cancún and Cozumel off the Yucatan Peninsula, and Cayo Lobos off southern Quintana Roo; but these are small, secondary sites, and they are also fading fast. What is left of importance in the natural history of green turtles is Tortuguero, the last stronghold for *Chelonia* in the western Caribbean; and Isla Aves, a tiny, low, uninhabited island 100 miles southwest of Montserrat, the remnant nesting site in the eastern Caribbean. The breeding colonies at Tortuguero and Isla Aves have survived because these places were virtually inaccessible—far removed from the major sailing routes and from large concentrations of people.

Tortuguero is both refuge and remnant. To this secluded beach green turtles journey from distant feeding grounds to reproduce more of their kind. Although located within one country's national territory, Tortuguero is really an international beach in that the returning turtles come from Venezuela, Colombia, Panama, Nicaragua, Honduras, Mexico, Cuba and elsewhere.

The nesting colony is the best-known sea turtle population anywhere in the world, based on almost twenty-five years of research by Professor Archie Carr and his students. To study the migration patterns and nesting beach ecology of green turtles, Professor Carr initiated a tagging program in 1955 that has to date marked almost 13,000 adult females and yielded tag recoveries from all over the Caribbean. Carr's research has shown that green turtles are international long-distance migrants and that they possess a fantastic navigational sense which enables them to return to the same small beach after a several-hundred-mile journey and a long absence.

Of the 1,110 tags recovered by July 1977, an astounding 82.6 percent were from Nicaraguan waters, while 4.1 percent were from Colombia, 2.5 percent from Panama, and 2.3 percent each from Mexico and Venezuela. The significance of this is plain: green turtles of the western Caribbean are born in Costa Rica, and the vast majority of them grow to maturity in Nicaragua.

Green turtles are one of the few migratory species whose breeding periods occur at intervals longer than one year. Any one female does not migrate and nest every year, but every two, three or four years, the average being three. This remigratory pattern is staggered and flexible so that in a particular home foraging ground, such as Miskito Bank, only a portion of the mature males and females depart in May and June for Costa Rica; the rest stay behind until the next and following years. Although a three-year nesting cycle is predominant, individual turtles may change from longer to shorter reproductive cycles and *vice versa*, possibly in response to ecologic influences. Thus, there is an oscillating year-to-year rhythm in the number of migrating and nesting turtles.

The main breeding season at Tortuguero is from July through September. After arriving at the nesting beach, the turtles rest and float and copulate in the water beyond the surf break. Males spend their entire post-hatchling lives at sea. Only females emerge on the ancestral beach and then only at night. During the nesting period, each female may lay eggs one to seven times, with intervals of approximately twelve days between visits to the beach.

I was at Tortuguero in August 1967. August is a high nesting peak, and every night many turtles, perhaps two or three hundred, came in to nest. After dinner Carr and his students broke up into small groups, some going down the beach, others walking the beach from the research camp to the mouth of the Río Tortuguero, just to the north. There's a lot to learn about green turtles during their short visit to land. They can be weighed and measured; a numbered marking tag can be placed on them for future renesting identification or migration analysis. You can investigate their ability to return to similar portions of the beach after an absence of several years, their capability of finding their way back to water on a moonless, rainy night, and other similar things that zoologists care about. There is much to study, and the time available is too short. You'd

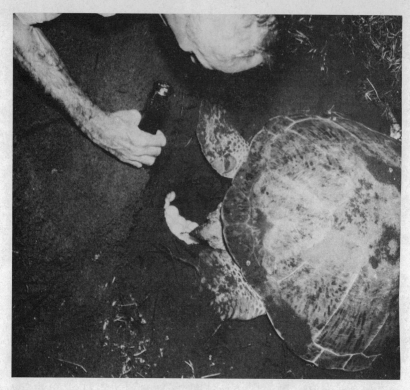

Zoologist Archie Carr watches a nesting green turtle lay approximately 100 eggs, each about the size of a Ping-Pong ball.

like to learn as much as possible, but without interfering with the turtle's main objective for being there, her nesting.

Turtles are terribly timid when they are getting ready to leave the sea. They wait cautiously in the shallows until they decide the beach is safe. If they see a movement or a light from someone striking a match or turning on a flashlight, they'll turn around and return to the sea. But if you wait quietly and let the turtle find the spot she wants and begin to dig a body pit, you can come close and watch her meticulously but unseeingly excavate a flask-shaped nest with her rear fins and then lay about 100 eggs. After she has finished and has concealed the nest site with violent sweeps of her front fins, she can be tagged, measured and released to the sea.

After an incubation period of about fifty-eight days, the eggs hatch and the young work their way through the packed sand, always emerging at night. Instinctively and with unerring accuracy, they head directly toward the sea even though the nest site may be as much as seventy yards from the water. Not all make it; in fact, very few survive beyond the surf line.

A green turtle returns to the sea after having nested and having been tagged at Tortuguero, Costa Rica. When she returns in two or three years or if she is captured, the tag supplies data important for life-cycle study and conservation programs.

During the period when hatchlings are leaving the thousands of nests, numerous land and sea animals gather to catch them. Birds, crabs, raccoons, coatis, ocelots, dogs and even pigs make heavy inroads on the scurrying hatchlings. Once they are in the water, barracuda, sharks, jack and snook further reduce the survivors. It has been estimated that perhaps only five out of one hundred survive the beach and only three or four out of one thousand survive to adulthood.

From a turtle's perspective, nesting would appear to be a hopeless task; for after she has come so many miles at sea, has laboriously crawled across the beach, has selected just the right spot to lay 100 eggs, and has nested one or more times, the chances are great that no young will survive. Of course, a turtle doesn't know this; and even if she did, I'm sure instinct would prevail over human probability estimates. After all, her kind has been around for millions of years, which is more than slide rule pushers can say. But this is beside the point. The fact is that each 100-egg nest contains a small chance of a survivor; several nests spread out temporally and spatially on the beach have even more of a chance; and each female nests every two to four years for many, many years.

The turtle's solution for surviving despite heavy predation and environmental resistance is one hundred eggs times multiple nestings each season. As Carr says, "any fewer, and the resistance prevails and the race wanes. Any more, and the eggs are too heavy to carry in the turtle's belly, or too costly to fill with the right amount of yolk." This survival strategy evolved during thousands of generations of turtles, but the ability to cope with predation pressure by humans was beyond the turtle's evolutionary capacity. For years, tracts of the Tortuguero Beach had been leased to concessionaires who hired *veladores* ("stayers-awake") to turn all nesting turtles. Picked up by a launch, the turtles were taken to Limón, Colón and Bluefields for market sale. So many adult turtles have been removed from the rookery and resident feeding colonies that the estimated reproductive life-span is no longer forty-five to sixty years, but more like fifteen or sixteen. After years of being exploited at both the nesting beach and the feeding grounds, green turtles have joined the ranks of the fading species.

At Tortuguero I saw much that was interesting and much that was disturbing. I saw a turtle nest within a few yards of where she had nested and been tagged three years before. That's pretty amazing when you consider that she may have spent the intervening years in the waters off Venezuela, Colombia, Nicaragua, or some other far turtle place, and then found her way back to the exact spot on a virtually featureless beach in a distant corner of the Caribbean. I saw hatchlings emerge from their nests and immediately head toward the sea even though their view was blocked by sand ridges and beach debris. Born on an almost exclusive sea turtle beach used by greens and occasionally by hawksbills and leatherbacks, these hatchlings confronted a suddenly hostile, predator-filled shore and began their first years as prey. This was a natural tragedy, and not a tragedy at all if you looked at it from the perspective of the crabs, birds, barracudas, sharks and others who were simply feeding. I saw other tragedies, however, that weren't a natural part of green turtle survival. Offshore, three miles out from the final green turtle breeding refuge in the western Caribbean, fishermen from Puerto Limón were catching turtles. Egg-carrying females and accompanying males that had migrated oftentimes several hundred miles and were part of one of nature's most spectacular phenomenon were being captured for a soup and meat factory. Also, when walking the beach early in the morning, sometimes I'd see a big green turtle, dead, awash in the rising tide, its belly shell slit by a calipee poacher the night before. Killed for a few pounds of gelatine-like material that would be made into soup in a foreign country. The offshore fishermen, the turtle company in Limón, and the turtle poacher were not evil types bent on destroying the green turtle population. They were just trying to make a living in a part of the world where there were few other economic opportunities. I tried to look at it from their perspective as well; that is, they were only making money to buy food, just as the birds, crabs and sharks were only feeding on a food source, the hatchlings. After all, you can't like sharks more than people, can you?

Through all of this, the one thing I remember most vividly is sitting on the beach and wondering, Who will kill the last turtle? I sat there for a long time thinking about this, with a dead calipeed turtle a few feet away, the fishermen's boats small specks on the gray sea offshore, the miniature night tracks of hatchlings still visible in the damp sand, the cries of sea birds overhead, and an occasional dorsal fin or shark body showing in the thinning wave forms. It wasn't whether or not I liked sharks more than people at all. The situation was that there simply were not enough turtles to accommodate all the predators, animal as well as human. And because I was getting to like turtles more and more as I learned about them, I was leaning toward their perspective, too. Of course, all these perspectives were really mine. I didn't know much then about turtles or sharks, and I hadn't even talked to the fishermen. All I could see was that there were a lot of bodies dependent on eating or selling turtles, and I knew that Archie Carr and others had solid proof that the Caribbean's sea turtle population was declining every year. It seemed pretty clear that it didn't make much sense, in terms of either evolution or economics, to become dependent on a declining species. Certainly the sharks, barracudas, crabs, birds and forest mammals that ate the hatchlings also ate other things as well, and they would survive even if there were fewer turtles. But I didn't know if the fishermen, poachers, workers in the turtle company, makers of green turtle soup, and eaters of green turtle soup would survive if there were no more green turtles. Yet it seemed to me that humans were much more adaptable than other animals and that they would endure one way or the other. That left the green turtles, which were caught in a cross fire on the beach and in the water. Besides, I knew that those that weren't caught on or off this beach would be heavily hunted in their home waters. They were just too valuable and had too much meat to overlook. It seemed pretty certain that the turtles were the ones that wouldn't survive. And that would be a tragedy, for they were just too magnificent an animal to lose.

I sat there a little longer and thought of the herds of green turtles out there, just off the beach or swimming to Tortuguero from hundreds of miles away. This beach was the focal point for one of the most astounding migrations in the animal world. The instinct to migrate and the ability to navigate had evolved over millions of years and tied this last tiny beach to remnant turtle colonies and feeding grounds scattered over the western Caribbean.

During that year, 1967, perhaps 10,000 would nest and lay some 3-4,000,000 eggs. Now that's a lot of eggs, but from what I'd seen so far, it wouldn't be enough. It wouldn't be enough because from beach to feeding ground, from birth to adulthood, from Costa Rica to Nicaragua, Mexico, Venezuela, Colombia and Panama, green turtles would be hunted almost every day and every night of the year, year after year. And each year there would be fewer turtles, and the pressures would be greater. If you carry on with this kind of reasoning, you end up thinking about who will kill the last turtle. Would it be a shark off the beach? a fisherman from Limón? a Miskito Indian for food? or a turtle company for meat and soup? Who would eat the last bowl of turtle soup? the last turtle steak? or wear the last pair of turtle skin shoes? Of course, you could never be sure it was the last turtle, and even if it was, there would be nothing much you could do about it.

The stiff trade wind carried spindrift from crashing waves, misting the last turtle beach in atomized dampness that defied the clear-sky tropical sun. Spent surf advanced over scalloped beach, pushing a thin line of cinnamon-brown sea spume that cloaked yesterday's flotsam. The tide rose and covered the dead turtle on the beach, and the last turtle image was gone. The sea had recovered one of its own. And beyond the high-tide margin, turtle eggs incubated in thousands of nests in the warm Tortuguero sand—tomorrow's progeny from an ancient way of life and from new human efforts to preserve.

Miskito Sea Grass

North from Tortuguero along the line that makes up the West-Caribbean Connection is Miskito Bank, historical center of the world's most famous sea turtle grounds and turtle people, and now their last stronghold.

Four of the world's five genera of sea turtles, all of them endangered, are found off the east coast of Nicaragua. Of these, the leatherback or trunkback *(Dermochelys coriacea)*, a huge, long-distance pelagic wanderer, is the least common; and the loggerhead *(Caretta caretta)*, a widely scattered, varied-habitat resident, although still fairly common, except for its eggs, is rarely used by turtlemen. The remaining two sea turtles—the solitary, reef-dwelling hawksbill *(Eretmochelys imbricata)* and the mass-grazing green turtle *(Chelonia mydas)*—have been the key factors in much of the colonization and commerce that tied the east coast to European, Jamaican and, later, Caymanian and North American markets and cultural influences. The hawksbill supplied extremely valuable and greatly prized tortoise shell, which soon became one of the leading exports to Europe from the Caribbean coast. The green turtle became world renowned as a source of meat and soup, and it was generally acknowledged throughout the Caribbean and Europe that the best-quality green turtles were procured from the western Caribbean, especially Miskito Bank.

Beyond the thin sand strip that marks the end of land is a continuation of the continental land mass, a relatively flat, gently dipping underwater shelf that ends abruptly at the continental slope. There the dark blue of the deep sea meets the vibrant blue-green of shallow waters and leaves a color-contact trace line that starts 110 miles eastward from Cape Gracias a Dios and angles southwestward toward San Juan del Norte, where the dropoff is but fifteen miles from shore. The configuration of the continental shelf is similar to a huge inverted triangle, with its 110-mile base to the north and its apex lying 280 miles to the south near San Juan del Norte. Covering the 15,500-square-mile shelf are clear, warm, shallow marine waters of a quality rarely seen in such extent. Gin-transparent and floored by sand, coral and grass, these waters receive relatively constant daily and seasonal amounts of sunlight and have a stable marine climate.

The biotic response to abundant light, warmth and environmental stability has been copious, resulting in a prolific, species-rich, diverse marine zone that in every way rivals any other tropical littoral in the world. The tens of thousands of coral reefs and numerous and extensive coastal lagoons and estuaries are major food-producing, breeding and refuge areas for resident marine organisms. But the most spectacular environmental feature of all is the prodigious beds of sea grasses that cover enormous tracts of the sea floor. Composed primarily of species of *Thalassia* and *Syringodium*, these marine angiosperms make up the largest sea grass zone anywhere in the world. Herein lies the environmental secret of the shelf's once abundant *Chelonia* aggregations.

The key to understanding why green turtles were so numerous off coastal Nicaragua and why this region became such a famous turtling area, producing the most esteemed and delicious turtles anywhere, rests with the simple biological fact that a species with no competitors and few predators will increase its population to the carrying capacity of its food source. And here the herbivorous green turtle's food source was in almost unlimited supply.

> The abundance of Chelonia expressed a straightforward ecology, a simple way of life. It ate one kind of plant that spread continuously over great areas and that recognized no seasons in the underwater climate. This was an utterly practicable way to live, the classic way to live, and the only sure way to be abundant; and as the grown-up greens were too big and hard for most predators and too fast and wary for the rest, the schools grew to limits set only by the area of the feeding space.
>
> There were other kinds of turtles in the sea, but the rest you found only here and there—only one-one-one, as they say in Grand Cayman. All the others gummed up their energy cycles by eating animals, which of course had their own complex problems and uncertainties. The carnivorous turtles had to keep moving to forage, and they wound up solitary and scattered. You couldn't even depend on their tasting good. The green turtle, on the other hand, stayed in one place and grazed all day, unhurried and untroubled in the rich pastures, only one link down the feeding chain from the sun itself. It grew fat and numerous and succulent, and in every way a blessing. It was . . . too great a blessing to last.
>
> Archie Carr, *The Windward Road*

Even in these prolific waters, there were natural limits to the numbers of turtles that could be harvested. Regardless of benign environment or altruistic economic intent, to exceed that limit would signal the demise of the species. Today these animals are everywhere sought after and nowhere plentiful. The ultimate tragedy is that in some of the richest tropical waters of the world, sea turtles, as well as other such economically valuable marine fauna as shrimp and lobster, are disappearing due to years of insatiable harvesting by people from many nations who little understood the basic biology of the species upon which they based their livelihood.

Through the years the pursuit of turtles has given both fame and names to Nicaragua's Caribbean littoral. Most of the offshore submarine environment is invisible because of either depth or distance from the mainland. Yet a hydrographic chart of the area reveals a dense mosaic of named reefs, shoals, sea grass banks and small cays. In addition, huge expanses of reefs and sea grass pastures which don't appear on maps or charts are known and named by coastal peoples, principally the Miskito. The discovery and the naming of these places were intimately tied to turtle fishing. Inherited from the past are Miskito, English, Jamaican and Caymanian names that designate both marine and historical terrain.

Centered around the Miskito Cays is the extensive reef and shoal area known as the Miskito Bank. Outlining this area, important turtle fishing sites are found at Outer Mahagen, Waham Reef, Dead Man Bar, Sukra, Diamond Spot, London Reef, The Whitties, Limarka, Nasa Cays, Miskitnaka, Waham Cay and Morrison Dennis Cays. This is the largest and most productive turtling area of the Caribbean, and the Miskito villages of Cape Gracias a Dios (Old Cape), Big Sandy Bay, Dakura and Auastara have long utilized Miskito Bank.

The second important turtling area is found to the south, between Man O' War Cays and the Set Net Cays (Pearl Cays); it is the offshore zone from Río Grande Bar to Pearl Lagoon Bar. Within this region are numerous sea grass pastures, reefs, shoals and small coral cays. The villages of Little Sandy Bay and Río Grande make use of the Man O' War area, including Halfway Shoal, Wangkloa Bank, North and South Schooner Shoals, Tyara Cay. In the middle of the southern turtling tract, from Crawl Cay and King's Cay to Asking Cay, is the 600-square-mile sea territory fished by the Miskito of Tasbapauni. At the southern edge of this zone, the Set Net Miskito focus their turtling activities on the Set Net Cays, Long Reef and adjacent banks and shoals.

Other turtling areas are found south of El Bluff around Pigeon and Frenchman's Cays, where Creole people from Bluefields and Rama Indians from Rama Cay catch hawksbill and green turtles. Farther south, few green turtles are found because of the lack of adequate forage on the narrowing and deepening shelf. The omnivorous hawksbill, on the other hand, exists in numbers off San Juan del Norte on a group of rocky shoals called the Greytown Banks. The beach at El Cocal, twenty-five miles north of San Juan del Norte, is the only important sea turtle nesting beach in eastern Nicaragua; it is used mainly by hawksbill. Throughout the rest of the offshore and mainland beaches, hawksbill and loggerhead turtles nest in a scattered pattern.

The two densest areas of Miskito Indian settlement, the Old Cape and Big Sandy Bay communities, and the villages between Little Sandy Bay and Set Net are situated adjacent to the two most important turtling areas. In ancient times and at present, the Miskito have followed the turtle.

Their Principal Occupation Is the Turtle-Fishery

Beyond the Miskito Cays, 375 miles farther on the same compass heading, are three islands—Grand Cayman, Cayman Brac and Little Cayman. Small islands, but large in their historical role in the West-Caribbean Connection.

The schooners, captains and crews that sailed from Grand Cayman to the Miskito Cays were a magnificent rarity. The old captains knew more about turtle and those shoal waters than just about anyone else. You can't simply teach someone about the ways and idiosyncrasies of turtles or about reef channels and bad sea weather. These things must be felt in the body, not just known in the mind. You grew up with it if you grew up in the Cayman Islands. Turtles and the sea were a way of life. Teamed up with the Miskito Indians—their only equals when it came to turtle knowledge—they transformed mere commercial turtle fishing into a life-style with a particular flair and flavor, complete with heroes, folklore and sea tragedies. The Caymanian turtle schooners no longer follow the line to the Miskito Cays, but their mark is, nonetheless, indelibly traced into the sea history of the Caribbean. Their passing may have eased the plight of the green turtle a bit, but more was lost than just a few captains and ships; what is now missing from the Caribbean is a little of its spirit.

Turtling built the Cayman Islands. Settled by a collection of retired pirates, soldiers from Cromwell's army that was disbanded after successfully capturing Jamaica in 1655, shipwrecked sailors, and a potpourri of British subjects from Jamaica, these tiny islands gained their livelihood from the sea. In *The History of Jamaica* (1774) Edward Long wrote:

> Their principal occupation is the turtle-fishery; in which article they carry on a traffic with Port Royal, and supply some to such of the homeward-bound merchant-ships as touch here on their way to the Gulph. The Bermuda sloops have a pretty regular intercourse with them; their crews are attentive to two points, turtling and plundering of wrecks. . . . The chief advantages drawn from the inhabitants of

Cayman are, that they . . . furnish a very wholesome article of food, chiefly for the Jamaica markets; and the shells of the Hawksbill species form a commodity for export to Great-Britain.

After some 150 years of intensive exploitation of the Caymanian nesting beaches and feeding grounds to provision passing ships, swelling Caribbean populations and European gourmets, the green turtle population had declined drastically; so in 1790 the turtlemen turned to the waters off the coast of southern Cuba. Through overfishing, this source, too, began to be seriously depleted by 1830, and to preserve their livelihood the men of Grand Cayman began making long voyages to the Central American mainland coast, especially to the Miskito Bank. For the next 130 years or so, Caymanian turtle schooners made semiannual visits—from January to March or April and from July to September—to the distant turtle grounds. In a good year, up to twenty schooners would bring back 5,000 green turtles for the Caribbean and European markets. Later an export market was opened in the United States, and the turtles were taken to Key West, Florida.

When I first went to Nicaragua in 1968, the Caymanian voyages were just ending. After years of problems collecting taxes on turtles caught by the Cayman Islanders, the Nicaraguan government rescinded their fishing privileges. It was the end of an era. The last schooner got its load of turtle; the crew said good-bye to the Miskito turtlemen who had brought live turtle and hawksbill shell to sell; then they pulled anchor and disappeared to the north, making the final leg along the line that had once joined Tortuguero, the Miskito Cays and Grand Cayman.

And so the Caymanian fleet passed from Miskito sea grass waters, as have the big turtle herds they once sought. Though one hastened the waning of the other, it's too bad that the sea lost both.

> When our turtles had been crawled, we paid a visit to the Adams. The Alice M. Adams—to give her full name—is a much larger vessel than the Wilson, being well over a hundred feet in length, but the two are very similar in their lines. . . . Captain Chesley was a heavy man with a patient voice that seemed simultaneously courteous and implacable. His boat was the queen of the remnant turtle fleet, and she had had a successful voyage, four hundred turtles stowed already in her hold and a few yet to come. Standing at the hatch of the Adams, I peered down at the creatures. The turtles lay in vertical tiers, rack upon rack of broad, pale bellies extending aft into the gloom. Over the hold was rigged a canvas chute that caught the wind and funneled it down for the refreshment of the cargo. "See dot?" Leewell spoke quietly at my shoulder. "Dey already lost dem pretty sea colors."
>
> Peter Matthiessen, "To the Miskito Bank"

The Caymanian presence is still there, however, in the lore of the coast. And once in a while a vessel will slip southward to Miskito Bank to pirate some turtles. Occasionally, a captain is caught by the Nicaraguan coast guard and fined. In January 1975, when I went to the Cayman Islands, only two or three ships were still used to fish turtle. With so few ships and a watchful coast guard, illegal visits to the Miskito Bank are rare. Even though these forays are a territorial infringement, the old captains are but following their heritage. The days of Caymanian pirates and turtlers are gone, but every so often a newspaper clipping from Bluefields or Managua announcing the chase or capture of an old schooner revives the memories of times past when Edward Long wrote of these islands, "they became much frequented by rovers of different nations . . . for the sake of turtle."

Over the years that I stayed with the Miskito, they told me many stories of the Cayman Islanders—of the captains and of the schooners that used to come, such as the *Adams*, the *Wilson* and the *Lydia E. Wilson*. But my favorite story concerns a small Caymanian catboat, now called the *Surprise*. Each of the turtle schooners carried a number of catboats, which were used to set the nets and bring in the turtle. Often a vessel would bring a couple of extra catboats to loan to Miskito or Creole turtlemen—called rangers—so that they could fish the turtle grounds to the south of Miskito Bank. At the end of the turtling season, the Caymanian crews would empty the crawls, load their catch on board, and sail to Man O' War Cays, King's Cay, Asking Cay and the Set Net Cays to pick up and pay for the turtles caught by the Nicaraguan rangers and to get back their catboats. The date of their expected arrival was set weeks in advance, and everyone was to have the season's catch ready for loading. One time, however, when a turtle schooner stopped at King's Cay, the Caymanians could not locate one Corn Island turtleman, a man reputed to be the best on the coast and therefore expected to have many green turtles. They looked in the camp—no turtleman. They looked in the "clar," the coral-walled holding pen—no turtles. They looked in the harbor and around the adjacent waters—no catboat. They waited. They waited until the crew became impatient to return home. And so they put up sail and left for Georgetown, Grand Cayman. A few days later the turtleman returned to the cay from Corn Island with the catboat. He looked around. He saw the Caymanians' footprints where they had gone to his camp and to the turtle crawl and to the landing where the catboat was usually kept. "Surprise, surprise, surprise," he drawled innocently. "It looks like they are gone, and the catboat is here." That catboat is still there. The stern was cut off, a transom built on, and a small gasoline engine installed. This happened years ago, but

Part of a 300-turtle shipment butchered and processed at one of the turtle companies in eastern Nicaragua. 1972.

it's still a pretty little craft, all painted up and with a nice cut to the sails. I've been on it. You might see it someday running from Corn Island to the cays or to Bluefields. You'd know it right away; just look for the name *Surprise* painted on the transom. Every time I see it, I can't help but smile. Someone pirated the pirates.

If you're interested in sea turtles or in the history of the western Caribbean, one day you'll end up in the Cayman Islands. You can't help but go. The magnetic attraction is undiminished. Though the schooners rarely run, the tradition of the sea and turtles is still there.

To Purchase or Protect

The green turtle: Survivor of ages, once existing in prodigious numbers over extensive areas, source of subsistence to the original residents and those that followed, and an article of commerce that opened up the far reaches of emerging worlds. Judging from both historical records and contemporary research, it is evident that the green turtle has long been an integral part in the developing seaside Caribbean. One would be hard pressed to find another wild species that has done so much for so long in furthering human endeavors along tropical shores. Eradicated or seriously depleted over much of its former range, it has, nonetheless, tenaciously persisted in sequestered corners of the Caribbean despite tremendous exploitation.

The economic and natural history of sea turtles along the western edge of the Caribbean has been one of the most significant in the annals of tropical marine resource use. At first, the relationships were simple: a small group of highly specialized sea-oriented Indians supplied themselves with meat from the abundant chelonian herds that grazed on the rich tropical sea grass pastures. What was a low-drain subsistence tap on the green turtle's life cycle became a major provisioning pipeline with the opening up of the Caribbean and the subsequent waves of European explorers, colonizers and settlers. It was the Miskito who taught the English the art of turtling, and it was the English, and later the Cayman Islanders, who organized the commercial West-Caribbean turtle fishery. For years, the rookeries and reefs supplied turtles to growing populations on the big islands and to the luxury markets in Europe. After some 330 years of operation, the supply line had drained the herds from coastal waters and beaches; and the reduced but continuing protein flow to the north threatened to annihilate both the residual sea turtles and the Miskito's subsistence base. With Costa Rican–supported protection of some of the nesting beach and Nicaragua's expulsion of the Cayman Island turtle schooners in the 1960s, there was some hope that the green turtle might be saved, both as a species and as a potential local food resource. It was a short-lived reprieve. In 1969 Nicaragua failed to ratify an agreement with Costa Rica and Panama to ban commercial turtling for three years; and immediately two turtle companies in Nicaragua began purchasing and exporting three and four times the number of turtles once taken by the Cayman Islanders. The supply line was back in operation. Only this time it was siphoning the last of the Nicaraguan herds and the core of Miskito subsistence and society.

The investment philosophy of many foreign-owned companies such as the turtle processing ones is quick return on low investment and overhead and prompt reinvestment elsewhere when the market or resource fails. The turtle companies had full knowledge that the chelonian population would be decimated through intensive commercial exploitation. No matter; a healthy return would be realized on their investment, and the resultant ecological "costs" would be borne by others.

Turtling changed from a culturally and seasonally regulated means of subsistence to a year-round business. The resulting massive increase in exploitation of the already endangered species drastically reduced the remaining chelonian population. In 1968 when the Miskito still fished turtles primarily for subsistence, it took an average of four hours for two turtlemen to get one turtle. By

1971 commercial fishing had depleted the herds to the point that eight hours were needed. And by 1975 turtlemen were spending twenty-four hours to catch one turtle, or 500 percent more time than it had taken in 1968. To maintain intensive fishing necessitated further intensification. Even though turtling was less efficient, more turtles were taken every year because more Miskito were fishing, and they were doing so daily rather than seasonally. The return of turtle tags from eastern Nicaragua also reflected the heavy fishing pressure. From 1969 through 1976 there was a huge increase in the number of tags recovered from the Miskito Bank and central coast turtle grounds, indicating large-scale expansion of exploitation levels over the precompany period.

Between 1969 and 1976 some 15,000 or more mature green turtles were taken annually from the total West Caribbean population which is made up of an estimated 62,500 sexually mature individuals: up to 10,000 were taken in Nicaragua, 4,000 from Costa Rica, and another 1,000 or more for local consumption by coastal peoples from Colombia to Mexico.

The case of the green turtle aptly illustrates the complicated problems inherent in attempts to protect sea turtles. Because they yield flavorful and abundant meat and valuable by-products and are economically valuable, they have been pursued relentlessly throughout most phases of their life history and migratory reproductive travels that take them across international boundaries. Their wide-ranging behavioral patterns and present endangered survival status clearly point to the need for strong national and international conservation planning and cooperation if this species is to be saved from extinction as a result of continued commercial exploitation for foreign markets.

At present, the green turtle can no longer support export markets from its meager populations in the western Caribbean. To continue to mine this depleted resource commercially for short-term economic gains will result in (1) the extermination of the Caribbean's last large green turtle herds; (2) the loss of the primary subsistence resource of the coastal Miskito Indians and other local peoples; (3) the further drain of animal protein from tropical areas of scarcity to mid-latitude areas of relative abundance; (4) the loss of the *only* large, edible, potentially prolific animal that feeds on the extensive sea grass pastures (besides the low-reproducing manatee and dugong, *Chelonia* is the only animal with these qualities that grazes on the earth's underwater "grasslands"); and (5) the passing of an almost irretrievable chance to conserve and manage this valuable resource effectively and intelligently.

With the help of an advisory group of scientists and strong and enforced international and national legislation, the once large populations of sea turtles in Nicaraguan waters and in the western Caribbean could be reestablished. The green turtle and other sea turtles could be saved, and important future protein sources for resident human populations could be guaranteed. The necessary marine habitat is there; sufficient sea turtle stock exists to regenerate the herds to their once vast numbers; and now, for the first time, meaningful legislation and protection are at hand.

> In the long run, marine turtles, like the seas themselves, will be saved only by wholehearted international cooperation at the governmental level. That is almost legendary substance. While waiting for it to materialize, the critical tactical needs seem to me to be three in number: more sanctuaries, more research, and a concerted effort by all impractical, visionary, starry-eyed, and anti-progressive organizations, all little old ladies in tennis shoes, and all persons able to see beyond the ends of their noses, to control the international commerce in sea turtle products.
>
> Archie Carr, "Great Reptiles, Great Enigmas"

Recent national and international legislation has improved the survival outlook for the West Caribbean turtle population. The 1973 Convention on International Trade in Endangered Species placed controls on imports and exports and cut back commercial markets in many countries. In October 1975 the Tortuguero nesting beach was designated a national park by the Costa Rican government, and in January 1976 the government placed an indefinite ban on turtling for international commerce, thus effectively closing the two processing plants operating in Limón. And in early 1977 President Somoza banned commercial export turtling and closed the three companies in eastern Nicaragua. With the protection of the major nesting beach and breeding colony and the severing of Costa Rican and Nicaraguan conduits to international markets has come the first real chance that this species might yet be saved and replenished.

But what of the Miskito who are also part of this zero-sum problem, where for every winner there is a loser? Protecting the green turtle meant erasing the primary source of income from coastal Miskito communities. That the turtle colony would certainly have declined in a few years to the point where commercial turtling was no longer a viable source of livelihood did not weaken the sudden economic impact of the turtle decision on Miskito households. Representatives from Miskito communities went to Bluefields to speak to the *jefe político* (the equivalent of a state governor in the United States). "Does the government want us to dead?" they asked. "Can't live if can't sell turtle." Despite their protests the decision stood.

It was no secret in Miskito communities that Mr. Barney had played a part in "humbugging the turtle business." The person I felt closest to out of all the Miskito wrote, "This is my word to you. The Government put the turtle on control. It was one thing that you the one that do it. All your friends give you Hell. You get lots of cursing. Was sad." My visits to their villages, their help in gathering information, and their patience in training me in Miskito skills had ended up directly affecting their lives. This drift coconut had turned out to be the Bloodman after all. Helping a species meant hurting a group of people who had become part of my life.

That the Nicaraguan green turtle population may be restored does little to assuage my grief over the Miskito's plight. They still hunt turtles for subsistence, and they still continue to sail out to the far turtle grounds and shoals following their heritage and the fat turtles. But money is scarce and purchased goods are expensive, and those economic pressures make it hard to understand a visitor's concern for what was being lost.

Distant decisions, economic inflation of market goods, new information and aspirations, and foreign visitors have over-whelmed culturally insulating factors of distance and isolation. The Miskito once inhabited a strandline island, separated culturally from inland Hispanic and Mestizo ways and physically cut off by miles of rain forest and open Caribbean waters. Now economic dependency and commercialized exchanges have transformed isolation into proximity. All things are near and dear. The Miskito no longer inhabit a cultural refuge. As Edna St. Vincent Millay once lamented, "There *are* no islands anymore."

The visiting academic sees an abstract culture, and the elderly of the society see a memory culture; we both interpret the present in terms of the past. But the younger Miskito must cope with the everyday problems that are the residue of economic waves generated from far-off shores.

Perhaps the Miskito will turn again to the sea and forest for sustenance and to their own society for material well-being. They have weathered other boom-and-bust squalls and calms—bananas, lumber, gold. For the time being at least, there is hope that the green turtles will persist. In our hypercoherent world the Miskito and the turtles represent an anachronism that just might continue to survive.

Daybreak past, early morning sea clearing at Turtle Reef. Smoky blue water sparkles with sun flecks of coral sand stirred from below by yesterday's storm, now settling on fringing sea grass carpets. Surface wave forms break morning light into patch patterns below.

Pieces of yellow sponge fall from a feeding hawksbill and drift away. Smooth, fresh and fast—young green turtles dart through liquid reef tunnels and arches. New to the reef, they stay close to eat and sleep.

Three miles away, due north, big turtles on the banks. Feeding, then floating on the surface, "wind and water" as the Miskito say, with the sea beneath and the trade winds above, halfway between their world and the past. Turtle backs rise and fall with the sea swells. Ancient heads lift for air. From a small sea crest, wary turtle eyes catch brief views of vacant open water.

8. A Silver-Looking Tag

"What are you doing with that turtle, Mister?"

"Putting a tag on it so we'll know where it goes."

"Why do you want to know where it goes?"

"Because no one knows where they go or how they get there. If someone finds this turtle and sends us the tag, we'll learn something about turtles."

"If they can't catch that turtle again, then it's the turtle that learned."

> Conversation with a Miskito boy. Little Sandy Bay,
> August 3, 1972

Conversations like this are one of the rewards of studying sea turtles. Research with sea turtles always seems to produce delightful, unanticipated encounters with seaside peoples. In the Caribbean, surviving sea turtle populations are largely confined to isolated tracts far from the hustle and bustle of heavily settled coastal areas and busy modern ports. In these out-of-the-way places live people whose cultures and philosophies are often as unknown to the outside world as are the sea turtles upon which many of them subsist. If you're studying sea turtles and you have the good fortune to visit one of these secluded communities, you'll most likely come away feeling you've learned a lot more from the subject of turtles than about them. When people find out that your interest is sea turtles, they usually volunteer a great deal of information gained from years of practical experience. And in their telling, you learn as much about these people as about the animal they're describing. To study these unique animals is to meet some very unique people. Their native knowledge, insights and philosophies are as refreshing as the trade wind that cools their shores.

I didn't know which was eroding faster, the rain-splattered map I had scratched on the beach sand, or my audience. I was trying to find out what the Miskito knew about green turtle migration. They

A hawksbill surfacing for air. Off the Man O' War Cays, 1972.

hadn't heard the details of Archie Carr's study at Tortuguero, so I wanted to learn their theories gained from generations of turtlers and years of experience. There were four of us left on the beach in front of the village; all of the younger men and children had abandoned the discussion when the rain started and had taken shelter in a nearby canoe shed. The ones I wanted to talk with had stayed, however: three of the best turtlemen in Tasbapauni, apparently oblivious to the light rain that was soaking their patched work shirts. Either they were used to getting wet, or they felt I needed help so badly that they ignored the rain. That was all right with me; I didn't want to have to draw the huge sand map of the western Caribbean again. And so we stayed in the rain, talking and pointing at various places on the map, while the sea became rain-smoothed calm and the wet-feathered coconut palms dripped impressionist patterns.

Each listened closely to my questions and then smiled. If it was turtle I wanted to talk about, they knew turtle better than most. Among them, they had almost a century of experience. Cleveland Blandford was seventy, a solid, deep-chested man who still had the power and the eye to paddle twenty miles out to sea and strike a turtle for the noon meal. He'd been fishing turtle for fifty years.

Flannery Knight in his canoe.

Flannery Knight had been at it for twenty years; he was one of the village's best strikermen and had worked several seasons with the Caymanians, so he knew net setting, too. His purple-sailed canoe was usually the first to return with turtle any time the men went out. The last man was Percival Hebberd, who was said to be their luckiest turtleman because he always got three or four, the maximum a small canoe could hold. He said his luck came from skill, but most of the men believed he had a secret turtle charm.

I'd told them that not much was known about the life cycle of turtles and their movements at sea and asked them to explain what they knew.

"Turtle navigate, you know, Mr. Barney. They go direct to the Bogue; go direct to the feeding banks; go direct to their rocks. They travel just like they have a road to follow," Cleveland Blandford said. He added that everyone knew that, and he wondered why such an obvious thing wasn't known in the States.

"That seems to be true, Mr. Cleveland, but how do they find their way?" I asked.

"No matter where they are, turtles are never lost at sea. That's born into them. They don't carry chart, don't have compass, but they use turtle sense, and that's the best there is," Cleveland said, finishing with an emphasis that left no doubt that he considered turtles to be something special.

"You remember the time we carried those turtle to Corn Island on the *Surprise?*" Flannery asked the other two. "That southeast squall burst the crawl and let those turtle escape two days after we returned to the cays. The next morning after they get out, Weddy Ebanks caught one of them at the same rock as before. Now that's forty miles that turtle made in one night. They know the way, and they know where they belong."

"How did that turtle find that exact rock? And how do they find their shoals and rocks when they come back from feeding all day?"

"Well, Mr. Barney," Flannery said and smiled, "that's a question that only the turtle can answer. They figure that out every day. Maybe high science should learn from the turtle. Last year I went to Managua and was walking past a movie show when all the people came out. There were plenty of people, but quick time each one of them headed for their own place. I studied that. That's the next question. How did they all find those homes, mixed up and scattered all about that big city? If people can do that, turtle can too."

"And turtle don't ask if they can't find," Percival added. "Those Managua people get lost, and they just have to ask a taxi driver. That's not as good as turtle."

"Maybe we can talk about the map again," I said, trying to change the subject a bit; I was finding it increasingly difficult to handle a

Flannery Knight and the author visit Weddy Ebanks at his camp on King's Cay to ask for his assistance and advice on catching and tagging hawksbill turtles for our migration study. Photo by Judith Nietschmann.

viewpoint of the world that was based on a dominant turtle metaphor.

"Just like we showed you here on your map, the turtle leave off from Miskito Cays and from all these other places in May and June and head south to Turtle Bogue." Cleveland drew some more lines in the sand, all pointing to Tortuguero. "They travel far. The Caymansman say they come from all about. Do the turtle in your place go to the Bogue, too, Mr. Barney?"

I started to tell them that there weren't any turtle where I lived in Michigan, but they began to shake their heads and look doubtful. No one could live without turtle.

"You see, Michigan is several hundred miles from the sea . . . "

"Oh, well, that's why you don't have turtle, then," Percival injected. "There are no turtle in the bush."

By bush, Percival was referring to dense woods like the rain forest to the west of Tasbapauni. If I didn't live by the sea, the only other place possible was the forest.

"No, I don't live in the bush, either. Where I live is more like Managua."

Flannery laughed. "Mr. Barney, if you live in a place all packed up like Managua, then you already know how to find the way like turtle, so why are you asking us?"

We laughed long and hard at that. By then the rain was falling in heavy drenching sheets that hissed across the water, pounded us, and moved on like some giant rain-bird sprinkling system. Our clothes were soaked, water ran down our faces, the sand map was obliterated; but we kept on laughing. The young men in the canoe shed must have thought we were out of our minds. And I guess the whole thing was pretty crazy. I didn't learn much about how turtles find their way, but I'll tell you something: I still think of turtles whenever I leave a movie.

When you stick a tag on a turtle, you're hoping it will help clear up some of the mysteries that surround these animals' natural history. If and when the tag is found by some fisherman, oftentimes in a remote part of the Caribbean, and sent to the address stamped on the tag, you have a piece of solid evidence about turtle behavior; but you often end up learning a whole lot more about people and the Caribbean. Two turtle tags stick in my mind. One was from a green turtle, the other from a hawksbill; both were from the summer of '72.

For two years with the help of my wife and son, I'd been keeping records of the numbers and kinds of animals the Miskito caught by hunting and fishing. The records showed that the hawksbill was being caught in large numbers because of the high market price for its shell. But most Miskito wouldn't eat hawksbill because they

Miskito Indian removing the valuable shell plates (tortoise shell) from a hawksbill carapace. Little Sandy Bay, 1972.

believed the meat would weaken a *kangbaiya*, a special personal bodyguard obtained with the aid of a bush medicine practitioner and retained by following particular taboos. Neither did many Miskito have much idea what the shell was used for once they had sold it. While cleaning some barnacles from pieces of hawksbill shell, one inquisitive and perceptive Miskito asked me, "What do they make from the hawksbill shell?"

"Oh, combs, bracelets, earrings—things like that," I answered.

The turtleman shook his head in a melancholy comprehension and replied, "So that's why the hawksbill is in trouble. Because of these things, he have to be careful."

Primarily due to the luxury-market tortoise-shell trade, the hawksbill was disappearing from Nicaraguan waters, and from everywhere throughout its range. As with other vanishing species, it was becoming increasingly rare before much had been learned about its ecology and natural history. When we decided to begin a study of this animal, the National Geographic Society was good enough to sponsor it. The low numbers and diffuse geographical and temporal distribution of remaining hawksbill presented a serious problem: How were we going to find any to study? We couldn't just wait on a nesting beach for them to come to us, as there were simply too few left and they nested over a period of several months. So we decided to go after them, living aboard a small boat at sea. We wrote to Brian Weiss, who was living in a Miskito village on the coast, and asked him to scout around for the most seaworthy boat and crew he could find. We ended up on Bugs Sinclair's boat, the *Glendora*, out of Río Grande Bar.

We had already been at sea for one out of the four months we'd allotted for the research project on hawksbill turtles. One of the turtlemen who had come along to help set nets for hawksbill wore a green turtle tag on a piece of nylon cord around his neck. I'd been watching that tag for thirty days, but he still wouldn't even show me the number; he said it was his lucky number, and he didn't want to lose his luck fishing turtle. When we had left Río Grande Bar, I had explained to our turtling crew that we wanted to catch as many hawksbill as possible and weigh, measure, tag and release them, and that recovery of the tags would tell us something about hawksbill behavior. That's when I first saw the green turtle tag hanging from Rudy's neck. I referred to the tag in my explanation and described how and why it had been put on a nesting green turtle at Tortuguero; I told them that we were going to do something similar with the hawksbill.

Later I asked Rudy if he wanted the complete address where he could send the tag. No, he didn't. Nor did he want me to send it along with some others I'd picked up in Río Grande. I explained that a great deal of effort went into putting one of those tags on a turtle, and it would be a waste if one was found and not returned. He said he wasn't going to sell or send back his good luck piece. Ever since he'd caught the turtle with the tag, his fishing luck had improved. I said I hoped his luck was good on this trip and he was able to catch plenty of hawksbills, and that if he ever wanted to claim the tag reward, I'd give him the five dollars, or thirty-five *córdobas*.

After some four weeks of fishing for hawksbill off the Miskito Cays, our water ran low and we needed to replenish some food supplies. We headed for the mainland and Big Sandy Bay some forty miles away. Once through the bar and across the lagoon, we dropped anchor and prepared to go ashore.

"Mr. Barney, we have been at sea a long time," Rudy said, pulling at an invisible thread on his good shirt, "and I been thinking about how Mr. Carr would like to get back the tag after all the trouble he went to."

"What about your luck, Rudy? You've been a real help in catching those hawksbill."

"Well, I was hoping to turn that tag into some other good luck if I could get the reward from you. I'm thinking of taking a *pasear* tonight, and some money will help catch something easier than the tag will."

Now, the verb *pasear* means "to walk around" in Spanish, but I think Rudy had more in mind than that. However, that was his business. I was happy to be able to get the tag to send on to Carr in Florida. All the turtlemen on the coast knew that the tag reward was five dollars and that it was paid without any questions. I wasn't going to ask any questions either, but I did think it interesting that turtle tags had become a medium of exchange. You could learn something not only about the movements of turtles from the tags, but also about people.

I ended up with tag #6810; Big Sandy Bay got the thirty-five *córdobas;* and I never asked Rudy what he got. I did write to Carr about what happened to #6810. I also suggested that he change his tag recovery procedure a bit because the tags were being sent back too soon. The full story potentially contained in each tag would never be told if it was sent straight to Florida fresh off the turtle. Oftentimes, as I was to find out later, the most interesting journey of all was just starting.

One of the first tags we put on a hawksbill that summer turned out to be the most significant. We were setting nets to the north of the Miskito Cays with the help of two groups of turtlemen from Big Sandy Bay. They knew the reefs and shoals and suggested that we try a spot called Hawksbill Rock. That reef wasn't too far from where we were based in a small house the turtlemen had rebuilt after the '71 hurricane at Sukra, a hard sand shoal forty miles from the mainland. So we went out in their catboats early in the morning and set a dozen nets. Later that day we caught our first hawksbill from the Miskito Cays area at the Hawksbill Rock set. It was a big female,

146 pounds. Tagged and released, she was numbered only as the first, one of the many that we eventually caught and tagged there.

After the four months were up and we had returned to Michigan, we were pleased that we had been able to catch as many hawksbill as we did, sixty in all. That really isn't very many in terms of a tagging program, but the hawksbill's low population numbers and dispersed distribution make it a very difficult animal to capture in large numbers. We hoped that the return of some of the tags would tell us more about local patterns of hawksbill movements, because they were not believed to be long-distance migrants.

In late November of that same year, 1972, I received a letter from a man in Jamaica who had caught one of the hawksbills we had tagged in Nicaragua. After checking our records, we found it to be that first one from the Miskito Cays. This was a significant tag return, the longest distance ever recorded for a hawksbill, and it turned out to be even more interesting in other ways.

Weighing hawksbill number N-002 prior to release, Miskito Cays, 1972. This turtle was eventually captured by a Jamaican turtleman, Earl Smikle, at the Pedro Cays, 390 miles from the release site. From left to right: Flannery Knight, the author, hawksbill N-002, our son Barney, his Tasbapauni friend Walter Blandford, and some of the crew from the Glendora, *including Rudy of the green turtle tag #6810 fame. Photo by Judith Nietschmann.*

Premio-Remite
Dept. Geog. U-M
Ann Arbor MI U.S.A.

Dear Sir:

I am a Jamaican fisherman and fish the Pedro Cays about 60 miles from Jamaica. On the night of November 14, 1972, I caught a turtle with a silver-looking tag on her front fin bearing the serial no. N-002, the other side PREMIO-REMITE, DEPT. GEOG. U-M ANN ARBOR, MI U.S.A. I don't know if it has anything to do with you. I am looking forward to getting some reply from you.

> I remain yours truly,
> Earl Smikle

I answered Mr. Smikle straightaway, assuring him that this certainly did concern us and that he had a reward coming, and asking him would he please write back and explain more of the details about finding the tag. In a couple of weeks I received another letter and a small package.

Dear Sir,

I have received your letter and a check for $5.00. I was glad to hear from you about the turtle I caught. She came up on the cays about 7:45 P.M. and I turned it on its back until the next morning. She weighed 155 lbs. and had about 3½ lbs. of shell, 115 fully matured eggs and about 200 young eggs. The meat is sold in Jamaica for 40¢ per pound, the shell at $5.00. But I don't sell the shells, I make earrings and bangles with them. I get from 30¢ to $1.00 per pair. I send a sample of them to you as a souvenir for any of those beautiful girls in your studio who have pierced ears. Nice to be in touch with you and hoping to hear from you again.

> Yours sincerely,
> Earl Smikle

It was very nice of Mr. Smikle to write back and provide the additional information, which was very useful, and to send a gift. But there were two things about his letter that bothered me, and still do. The first was that the hawksbill that provided the longest distance tag recovery on record (390 miles) gave that information with her life and ended up with parts of her made into jewelry. I realized that she would have been caught and killed with a tag or not, and that without a tag we would never have learned about her amazing journey to the Pedro Cays. Yet it distressed me that each tag recovery signaled the demise of another turtle. The tags certainly weren't causing their deaths; in fact, some of the information would eventually aid in achieving protection for the species. Nevertheless, it was sad to think that this hawksbill should be killed—after being caught once, not killed but released, and then making such a long trip to lay eggs to produce more of her kind and carrying a piece of metal to prove her feat. Too bad there isn't some retirement reef for turtles, for those that made good, did their thing for the species or science or whatever; they could retire from the game and breed other winners, as successful fighting bulls or racehorses do.

The other thing that bothered me about Mr Smikle's letter was that I really didn't have a studio filled with beautiful girls with pierced ears.

There is one small turtle reef that has a retired turtle on it. Hawksbill N-039 deserves special mention because its saga is one of the few that produced some valuable tag information on homing behavior without the demise of the turtle. After being caught at a coral shoal several miles east of a Miskito Indian village, this hawksbill was brought to the village for measurement, weighing and tagging before it was released. The next morning it was caught again at the same coral head at the same shoal. The turtleman received a five-dollar recovery reward, and the hawksbill was again released from the beach in front of the village, only to be caught once more the next morning at exactly the same place as before. Another reward was paid. The cycle of reef-village-reward-reef was repeated with several variations on release sites. Every morning it would reappear in the same turtleman's net at the same coral head on that small reef. This one hawksbill threatened to break our National Geographic Society research fund, while at the same time making one turtleman very wealthy, as he was certainly not going to kill the turtle that carried the golden tag. If there is such a thing as waving a white handkerchief for a sea turtle, instead of for a brave fighting bull, we tried to do it by buying a lifetime no-more-setting-turtle-nets-at-that-reef guarantee for that hawksbill. Thinking hopefully of number N-039 still swimming around that coral head helped get me through long Michigan winters.

To place a tag on a migratory marine animal that comes ashore only on very isolated beaches for just an hour or so at night requires extreme patience, perseverance and logistical effort. Similarly, when a tagged turtle is recovered, it often takes as much work and persistence to send the tag in and receive the reward as it did to put the tag on the turtle in the first place.

In the western Caribbean, along the coast of eastern Central America, most of the turtling peoples live in very remote locales, far from towns, cities and post offices. When a person catches a turtle carrying a tag, it may entail considerable trouble to communicate this information to the outside. A tag's journey after it is taken off the turtle is almost as instructive as what can be learned by putting it on the turtle. For example, some of the tags we put on hawksbill were recovered by turtlemen from Little Sandy Bay. Boats are infrequent in that area, and to return a tag to us sometimes necessitates walking twenty-five miles on the beach to Tasbapauni, finding someone going to Bluefields by boat, and giving that person a letter about the tag recovery and two or three *córdobas* for carrying and mailing it. The letter then has to survive the rigors of a night in Bluefields bars, the vagaries of postal services in Nicaragua, and the crytographic powers of U.S. postal employees to decipher addresses containing words such as "Dear Remite," or "Dear Send." If the letter arrives, it's a pretty special piece of mail. Archie Carr knows about these problems. I had to learn.

Carr's tagging project at Tortuguero has been going on since 1955, and enough tag-carrying green turtles have been caught off eastern Nicaragua by Miskito turtlemen that the checks and tags have long been considered as another form of local currency. Tags are often bartered, sold, and exchanged for money or credit from merchants in the Miskito villages, although not for the full value, hence the efforts to send them out personally. At first the checks were sent in envelopes with little cellophane windows showing the name and address of the intended recipient and a portion of the check. We gradually learned that some of the checks never made it to the right person, having been "lost" somewhere in the maze of so many miles and hands from Managua to the villages. The envelopes were easily identified, and their contents could be cashed anywhere on a no-questions-asked basis. The tags, too, frequently "disappeared," or entered the local turtle currency exchange, where they could circulate for months without being sent on to Carr in Florida.

The tag letters and subsequent five-dollar reward checks that are lost or rerouted somewhere between the turtlemen and the U.S. are a worrisome grievance from the researcher's point of view, because either the information or the turtleman's confidence—or both—is lost. I wrote to Carr and told him that local delivery and mailing abuses were complicating or nullifying the retrieval of turtle migration information—a problem of no small consequence, for at least 80 percent of all tag recoveries are from eastern Nicaragua.

May 7, 1969

Dear Barney,

Thanks for the letter. I can't figure what has caused the reverse in my Nicaraguan correspondence. There always is a delay in answering tag return letters, because they are paid out of a grant, and the check is issued in the business office here or in Tallahassee. This always takes about a month, sometimes longer. On the other hand, we are really very careful about getting the rewards back, inasmuch as my whole migratory study is based on tag returns, and each tag that comes back is looked on as a gem and its returner as a hero.

So as regards your local folk's folk belief that we don't really pay afterwards, tell them that is nonsense. I hope you'll do me the favor of explaining to the people there that we do make a consistent effort to get the rewards out and that the inherent delay is at least four weeks.

Sincerely yours,
Archie Carr

June 13, 1969

Dear Barney,

I'm afraid I still don't understand the alleged six-month delay in rewards to people there. The odd slip-up, yes, but a delay of six months, no. I wonder if the long holdup could have occurred down there?

Many thanks for your continued interest and liaison work.

Sincerely yours,
Archie Carr

November 5, 1971

Dear Barney,

I had been getting hints here and there that our tag-return correspondence with Tasbapauni and Set Net fishermen might be miscarrying. A young man from Pearl Lagoon worked for us on a tagging team this summer. He was one of the best turtlemen we ever had on the project. Before the season was over, however, we began to suspect that he was jerking the tags off of turtles, with the aim of taking them back to Nicaragua to send in later as international returns. A very nice guy he was, a grandson of Old Chief Sambola at the Carib settlement of Orinoco, whom I wrote about in *High Jungles and Low*. So his chicanery grieved us; and now you have not assuaged the grief. But many thanks for your warning. We will change envelopes at once, and perhaps have letters sent from some other address—maybe Bermuda, or Tegucigalpa, or other such red-herring-like locality.

Sincerely,
Archie Carr

Once a tag or check goes astray, it is difficult to track down. A follow-up letter from the turtleman helps if he has kept a record of the tag number. A missing check, however, is an altogether different problem. The waiting turtleman often simply gives up and doesn't write again or send any more tags, feeling that his effort has been ignored. It's a rare thing to find a missing check under any circumstances, but when one rises like a Phoenix from the ashes, it deserves elaboration and a place in the Tag Recovery Hall of Fame.

In late March or early April 1969, Sulanus Lauriano caught a green turtle at Waiwin Shoal off Little Sandy Bay; it carried tag #4515 (which had been put on it August 11, 1967, by Archie Carr's tagging team at Tortuguero). Mr. Lauriano walked to Tasbapauni to see if he could get·someone to help him mail the tag to the inscribed address. A missionary wrote the letter for him and mailed it April 20. Mr. Lauriano waited, but never received the reward check. He asked me about it in 1972 when we passed through his village; I suggested that he write again, but he never did.

When we were in Tasbapauni, in June of 1975, a woman asked me if I would send some tags for her husband. As I was copying the numbers, dates and places of recovery, she asked if I would like to see something strange. She went to a small wooden suitcase, unlocked it, and brought me an envelope, charred and singed around the edges but unopened. It was a reward check from Archie Carr, drawn on an account at the University of Florida, made out to Sulanus Lauriano, and dated August 8, 1969, almost six years before. She had been troubled about the check for several years, but felt she could do nothing about it because of the circumstances. Some years back—she couldn't recall exactly when—a little boy had been burning some trash on the beach for the missionary. He saw the check and rescued it just as it was about to go up in flames. Somehow it had mistakenly found its way to the "out" rather than the "in" basket and had been thrown away instead of delivered to Mr. Lauriano. The boy brought the check to the woman, who realized the double bind it created: she knew the man in Little Sandy Bay and should send it to him, but if she did, the missionary might discover that the boy had found it in his trash and taken it. She didn't know the reason it had been discarded, and felt she couldn't inquire. Therefore, she had saved the check, guarding it and worrying over it for years.

The check had expired, but I told her how it might yet be delivered. She gave me the check, and I sent it to Carr in Florida with a note explaining the unusual circumstances and asking if he would issue another one. He did, and Sulanus Lauriano got his reward and the woman a note thanking her for tending the check that had risen from the ashes.

Most people are gratified to hear that their tag has helped provide information on the behavior of sea turtles, and when they learn about a tagging project and get a check to validate their contribution, they often feel a little less isolated from the outside world and a little more in touch with their own. Nevertheless, one might have expected Mr. Sulanus Lauriano to have been upset and irritated over the six-year delay in obtaining his check, but he wasn't. I later heard from him: "I receive the check and glad to hear that the pin received Florida side. The premio come at a hard money time . . . help plenty. I hope the pin give help to the man what pinned it and all the turtle them."

I wish I could have been there when he finally got his Phoenix check.

It should be pretty evident by now how important it is for a turtleman to know a dependable person in one of the villages or coastal towns who will mail the tag and deliver the check. This is not as simple as it may appear, for this person must have paper and envelopes—often scarce in the villages—pay for stamps, and accept some of the responsibility for the safe delivery of both tag and check. American missionaries and occasional visitors will sometimes do this, but they move around a lot and may not be there when a turtleman shows up bearing a tag. A local person is best, and one who will do it, who is dependable and attentive to details as well, is a real help in alleviating postal problems for turtleman and turtle researcher alike. A person who'll provide the connective link in the tag recovery system is an important part of the entire research project and a contributor to science in his own right. That's why I felt so bad about inadvertently messing up Rev. John Hooker's efforts and causing him much anxiety and trouble.

I first became aware of what I'd done when Archie Carr forwarded a copy of Rev. Hooker's letter to me:

Moravian Church
Prinzapolka,
Nicaragua, C, A,
June; 25, 1975

#; Dr; Arcchie Carr;

Dear Friend;

This is another horied letter to you, to make you know what is taking place.

As I am lives in Prinzapolka, that is Betwin Bluefields ands, Puerto cabezas; down the south it is abouth 35 milles there is a Little Indian Settlement name by little Sandy bay (SHARON, there where I am belongs to so my people day working on the sea, fishing tourtle, now, this tatgs day sented to mi, are the number of tag, day don't guive mi the real tag, as day are varry difficults to sented, many where last on the way; so no, after I raceived the Checks, far the two tags; this last time, I sented the checks to the oner. in SHARON: and nat tu long tuday I raceived, a letter, that, day sold to one man that came from the Stats, name by MR, BARNY now there is a problems, by he awaything so long, so he solded, so what can be dont to this, now?

As The oner of this, tag say that he alraday loos, two tags, you se, this man he is nat a fisher man, but he usualy buying this tags, from the fisher man, I reely dont know what day payed farit; so he loos two tags so he is woried, as he solded to the anather man, I am making my way cleir it is nat my fault, so I shal be awaything your Riply, Please answerd mi varry quickly, Sinserely yours;

Attee;
Rev. John Hooker;

P.S. it is a urgentes Letter.

I had never met Rev. Hooker, but I had heard of him from his brother, Baltizar Hooker, a storeowner in Little Sandy Bay, the same man he was vexed at. It took a bit of deciphering and remembering to get at the problem Rev. Hooker had described, but when I did, I realized why he was so disturbed.

Whenever I go to eastern Nicaragua, I always look around for turtle tags. Most of the tags I obtain from the turtlemen are among those Carr and his students have put on green turtles at Tortuguero; sometimes, though, I find one from a hawksbill we tagged. During our stay in Tasbapauni in 1975, I collected five tags from the turtlemen there, wrote down the necessary data for Carr on when and where they were taken, and gave them the five-dollar reward in *córdobas*. Soon word spread that tag rewards were available, and another sixteen tags were given to me by turtlemen from neighboring villages, including two from Baltizar Hooker in Little Sandy Bay. Now Baltizar isn't a turtleman himself, either having given up the sea or never taken to it, but as a storeowner he was in a position to obtain tags from turtlemen in exchange for goods or in payment of debts. At the time I came on the scene and got the tags from Baltizar, he'd already given the numbers to his brother, who had sent the information to Archie Carr and was waiting for the arrival of the reward checks. Since Baltizar had "sold" the tags to me and taken the cash reward, Rev. Hooker was caught in the middle, as he couldn't accept checks from Carr for tags his brother no longer had. It looked as if Baltizar Hooker would receive double rewards for his tags, and Rev. Hooker would feel poorly about his inability to vouch for the tags and his unintentional role in his brother's financial windfall.

Now there's an honest man, I thought to myself after sorting this out, and certainly deserving of better treatment than he had received. For many years Rev. Hooker had relayed tags to Carr and checks to the turtlemen, and I didn't want my intervention to change any of that. I wrote a letter to him describing what had happened and hoped it would all work out.

I never did learn what finally happened between the two brothers, but the next letter from Rev. Hooker showed that he was still willing to help return tags. He apparently bore no ill feelings toward me and in fact had gone so far as to recover one of our hawksbill tags. Carr sent a copy of his letter so I could forward the reward.

> Moravian Church
> Nicaragua, C, A,
> November 4, 1975

Dr. Archie Carr;
University of Florida

Dear Eteamed Friend;

This is anather letter that comes to you. from your good friend whoos always willing to cooaperet with you all;

Here is 3, more tags, so I am sending the Nombers them as usual; 10768 this tourtle cauth in month of sept. at mawarkeygs; 7321 this tourtle cauth in month of october at manawar keygs. N-62 this Tag was in of the Axbils, in spanish word say CAREY; this cauth in month of octobar to; at manawar keygs; so I am sending this nomnbres so you will know that #### I have Interest to help you all out at any time, that you may need services; Regards to you, and to your friend whoom you laybord there;

Fraternaly yours;
Rev, J, Hooker;

That's some idea of the kinds of things that can be learned from turtle tags besides facts about turtles. If you're at all intrigued by the human stories involved with turtle tag returns, I encourage you to read the chapter called "Señor Reward Premio" in Archie Carr's book *So Excellent a Fishe*, in which he wrote:

When the turtles tagged at Tortuguero leave the nesting ground, most of them go away to some pretty remote, back-country places. The reason for this is simply that green turtle colonies have been wiped out in the regions easily accessible to man. When tagged turtles are caught, the letters that tell of the captures, besides providing data for the migration study, bring nostalgic glimpses of the diverse, sequestered people of hidden Caribbean shores and islands. . . . I have been to most of the places the letters came from. I went looking for turtles, but almost everywhere the people became an essential part of my reconnaissance, partly because they know a great deal about sea turtles, partly because they themselves are so beguiling.

9. Letters from Nicaragua

To receive a letter from an isolated place backed up against miles of rain forest and fronting the open Caribbean is a rare and important event. Whatever the contents, its delivery and reading are often sufficient to make one sit back for the rest of the day and contemplate the communication that has managed to thread its way to "the outside."

Most of the letters mailed to us from Nicaragua are sent to my office at the university, and I've asked the secretaries always to place them on the bottom of the day's correspondence because I like to save the best for last—and also because I frequently don't do much work after reading one. Each letter brings back memories of humid forest trails, the reassuring feel of trade winds stiffening in the new day, clear reef waters, the new tempo, pressures and problems of village life, and the individuals who have become part of our lives and have a strong emotional grip on us.

One night at home I was rummaging through a box on my desk labeled "Letters from Nicaragua," looking for a particular piece of correspondence from Tasbapauni. In flipping from one letter to the next, I caught brief glimpses of names and places and of fragments of things that had happened over the years. The searching slowed down and then stopped as I became engrossed in the letters. I had found something else quite unanticipated, a story far larger than described in individual letters. Taken together, they were a raw but powerful chronicle of changing human and ecological conditions among a people once secluded on remote tropical shores.

I picked up the pile of letters and read through them, beginning with the first and turning from one to another with consuming interest and building emotion. Most of the letters were from Miskito villagers, but some were from "outsiders," foreigners who were living with or who had visited the Miskito. Villager and visitor often gave different perspectives on similar events and each other, thus providing reflections from both sides of the double-faced mirror that separates one culture from the other.

Although isolated from the capital and the government, the east coast and the Miskito receive campaign posters and broken promises.

The Miskito's letters are rough in prose, yet eloquently express their reactions to the coming of modern times, the changing of old patterns, the struggle to participate in the new cash-based economy with its attendant increasing prices, the passing of sea turtles and a way of life, the confrontations with new visitors and new experiences, and the deaths and sicknesses of relatives and friends. The letters also reflect the nature and development of personal relationships established during our trips to their coast and the way we became enmeshed in one another's lives. There are requests for help and for advice and to be remembered. And there is concern over the progress of our research, as well as unsolicited contributions of information believed important to it.

We went to Nicaragua looking for answers to economic and ecological questions involving an indigenous society, its resource base, and sea turtles, but we found that our research became inexorably mixed with the things we had come to study. People who were once "informants," "sampled families," or "case study subjects" became friends; and the nature of our research and our personal philosophies changed as we were increasingly immersed in their lives, joys and heartbreaks. The roles of spectator and actor continually merged and reversed. For better or worse, our trips to eastern Nicaragua reciprocally modified our lives and the lives of people to whom we grew close.

Whether close or far, we rejoiced and mourned for people and things past, some coming, and a few that never really existed at all. Sometimes I was half-convinced that my work and my presence on the Miskito Coast were constructive, and sometimes I wondered if they were destructive. But it is the academic's penchant to infuse everything with significance. And it is the Miskito who defuse exogenous tension and influence, and who endure.

Some of the people and events referred to previously in other chapters appear in these letters. Bits and pieces of the correspondence add both unity and ambiguity to my descriptions. They are as they are, not as they ought to be.

The letters are organized chronologically, just as they came. There are gaps in time and continuity, resulting from letters lost en route to or from Nicaragua. The Miskito letters are reproduced with moderate literal translation to facilitate understanding yet retain poignancy.

Their content has no beginning and no end. They are a series of images and vignettes that hint of the past but provide few clues for the future. The letters are also testimony to the tensile strength of the human spirit and a moving account of a people and a species caught up in the incoming tide of modern times and visitors to the edge of the Caribbean.

                                        Bluefields, Nic.
                                        10-25-69

Mr. and Mrs. Nietschmann,

   Well I am writing this few line to you all in hope that it may find you all well at present. Well Mr. and Mrs. Nietschmann and little Barney, when you all left from the Bluff with the "Cubahama" I was so sad to see you all leave me and going away. I watched the Cubahama from the Aduana House and looked at it till it went right out of sight. And from the 28 of September I didn't want to go to school and I felt like my Mother did die and my Father and one of my brothers. Mr. Barney please tell little Barney that I miss him very much in every thing. Now I don't go to the movie much like when he was here.

Well Mr. Barney I am studying very hard because this is the last month in school. Next month will be final exams. So I am trying very hard to pass my grade.

Mama and Papa are right here. Mama is taking some more vitamin from the doctor so she is here. They will go up to Tasbapauni about the 25 of this month.

Also, Papa said that he receive your letter and was glad to hear from you. He said that he will send your work or papers—you know is what—he will send it next week around the 24 of this month.

Please give my good regard to Mrs. Judi and little Barney. This is all I have to say.

From sincerely yours,
Eliterio Sando Garth

Tasbapauni
Dec. 6/69

Dear Mr. Barney,

Your letter Oct. 6/69 I receive. Glad to hear you get home safe.

Sando give me all the news of his trip to see you off at the Bluff. Kuka is making trouble as I am writing you. My wife is still in care of the doctor in Bluefields.

I told all the Tasbapauni friend your hello and about the plane that was circling around the village.

I hope to hear about how you meet your professors and your report on your trip to Nicaragua and how they receive it.

Remember me to Miss Judi and Barney and other friends.

Sincerely,
Baldwin Garth

23 Dec. 1969
Bluefields

Dear Barney and Judi,

When one reaches a certain age—my age, for instance—one arrives at certain universal truths which had eluded one in the younger years when we stumbled magically through webs of mystification and were therefore bereft of "true sight" and other saintly characteristics. Now that I have attained, and become a particularly astute soul, able to differentiate without much work all the complexities of my earlier and now past youth, I have arrived at my universal truth. The truth is that there are two types of peoples in the world. This I am sure of. One type are those who have been in Bluefields, and the other type are those who haven't. Therefore, how does it feel to be the only ones on your block who have?

The cultural **synthesis** of Bluefields, with its two divergent lines of development, fantasy and hard-core realism, has jaded, to some extent, my development. Of course you may not be interested in this, but I mention it anyway. I always enjoy making others aware of my delicate woes. Regretably, the paths of other less-blessing oriented culprits, usually in the guise of anthropologists or hedonists, often cross my path. I have devised a booklet of subtle tortures aimed at "liberating" their souls, to be edited by a Miskito Indian. Of course even with the possible publication of this profound booklet, I fear many more anthropologists will visit this vicinity, bringing with them their clever concepts, their boxed social theories, their youthful enlightenment, their abstracted wisdom, their dissected noble savage, and their six-month supply of Aralen. There is no way out. Several have appeared so far and have only left appalled, because no savage here desires to take up arms in protest of his government, sit next to a white guy, or have equal housing. All they want to do is fish, a thing, it appears, which has little to do with the up-coming cultural revolution.

Your house is inhabited by strange people who look at us in fear. They firstly tore down the kitchen, cut down all that lovely yard growth, belligerently rebuilt the fence stronger, and have the *Guardia* over for dinner. I don't know. . . .

Occasionally people ask about you here. We tell them stories. You might have lots of explaining to do when you return.

Sando left yesterday after receiving his "notas" to pass. He was most happy to return home, talking about it incessantly.

Daniel Boone is somewhere up the Turswani or Kukra or someplace and no one has seen him. Heironymos is here, however. He almost died once. But he didn't.

I visited Tasbapauni and Mr. Baldwin. He is well, and everyone else. No one you knew got killed or anything, I don't think.

Anyway, hope to hear from you soon. I'm writing another novel and also doing paintings of native women.

Yours,
Robert Wilson

Tasbapauni, Nicaragua
Jan. 20, 1970

Dear Barney Nietschmann,

I am dropping you this few line hoping to find you enjoying life.

Why I never write your letter just because Mr. Baldwin Garth taken the note of things and I went Setnet Point in the month of September. They had 200 hundred head of turtle between 8 dories. In October month there was 135 head of turtle in town. In November month 70 head of turtle. December month 53 head of turtle. Three fishing boat went aground Longreef Shoal.

Mr. Robert Wilson come to Tasbapauni. I never see him because I went Setnet Point and he went on up to Little Sandy Bay. Some say he writing book also. So he the next one for around these places.

We are well and all the children are well and my wife is well. My wife say to Miss Judi hello and her best regard.

Nothing more to say.

Hello to all.

I am your truly friend,
Flannery Knight

MISIONES EPISCOPALES
(Costa Media del Mar Caribe)

Río Grande Bar
February 8, 1970

Hola,

You should be exposed to a little Spanglish now and then—lest you forget. Greetings from your favorite vacation spot, the "Bar." It's hardly a suitable one, even if wet, but if it makes them happy to call it a bar, so be it. Situation normal—same as when we were up here together—rainy, wet and windy. And it looks the same only more so. Weather has been hellish (really quite violent winds for the last four days). A house here and one in Karawala collapsed in the process, and on Friday night there was much excitement in Tasba-pauni. A "fishnin" boat blew ashore, all the way into the wash. The whole village, including yo mismo, stood near the now missing beach offering free advice and we were quite sure we could float it. There is nothing like the sublime assurance of a Tasbapaunian. We all but swamped twice getting out to Jackson's boat Saturday and since we leave for the return trip at 3:00 A.M. tomorrow in the probably vain hope that the wind will be less, I look forward to the whole thing with unbridled joy. I don't envy your 20° weather. In fact, I've vowed I'll do most anything to avoid having to return to it; but you do have certain compensations: you can die of exposure rather than drowning.

Many thanks for the slides. They are excellent. Did my best by the Coleman's late light to view them. Am going to take them to Managua next week and see them with a projector. Especially enjoyed the dancing scenes from Orinoco. What a fantastic day that was. Ass that I am, I opened my big mouth (I should know better by now, seems I do not) and I now am the dubious manager of eighteen Carib Rockettes. They are going to Bluefields on the 20th to "put on" the Walagayo, yet. If you hear of a riot and a mass arrest for drunk and disorderly conduct, you will know why. The awful part is that some church people from Managua were here, expressed interest and now my little sylphs think they are going from Bluefields to Managua to dance at "The British Embassy for the Queen." And I quote. Surely campus life can't be any more idiotic.

Probably Baldwin has written you of their trials and tribulations. Mrs. G. broke down with a touch of T.B., but she is completely negative now thanks to INH & PAS, and actually looks far better then I have ever known her to look. They are I think in reasonable shape. Sando starts back to the Colon tomorrow—and Junior as well—so if I don't grow completely broke and the well run dry, the Garths at least should have some educated progeny and better health.

The "fire burn" (you mustn't lose all your Creole) was more than grim, but, to my surprise, the whole country pitched in to help and there is actually a great deal of necessities and food for the "damnificados" in reserve right now, if some local "leaders" don't try to "sell" it as they were attempting about ten days ago. If the merchants (you've got to hand it to Willie Woo; he was open for business one week later in a little rented building) get some long-term help and present ideas are retained, downtown Bluefields could look and be far better, healthier and safer in a couple of years.

I'm off to fight the Obeah and Elements. Some things just won't change. Again, muchas gracias, hope you can get to your writing and all the rest.

David McCallum

Tasbapauni
Feb. 10/70

Mr. Barney Nietschmann.

My few line to you. The last set of chart I am sending care of Mr. Robert Wilson. Every day the sun rise and go down your name is mentioned in the home. Through the loving parrots make us remember good friend. All is well at present. My wife feel much better. Well all of Bluefields had a very bad burndown. Sad to look at. Tasbapauni news. A white man from the U.S.A. come to work timber for lumber. So the work start in Sumie. Two Army man from U.S.A. want to fish on the cays. Nothing is down as yet about fishing.

My work shoes tore off my feet. I cry that day for they were a recuerdo. Goodbye. Please remember me to Miss Judi and little Barney. Hoping to hear from you soon.

Your friend,
Baldwin Garth

Tasbapauni
May 6/70

Mr. B. Nietschmann and family,

News, turtle is in swing. The company is here to buy turtle. Turtle, the new company buy all at 60.00 cordobas a head, big or small. "Hawali W." got shore in front of Tasbapauni. "Rosemar" got shore below Tasbapauni. Heavy weather. A US man start mahogany work in Sumi. The work put him in the hole so he stop work and went home back US. Father Mac is going on furlough 25 this month. Shrimps catching is going on very good. Kuka is very rude, like to bite. Sando and

Baldwin Jr. down in Bluefields to school at the Colon. Both getting on good. All the family is well, thank God. Leopold Cayasso built a new boat—only upper work left and caulking then launch. Mr. Cromwell built a movie show house—about to work soon.

Remember me to little Barney, Miss Judi. My best wishes for your family and the work you are doing.

Yours,
Baldwin Garth

Tasbapauni
Jan. 10, 1972

Hello Barney and Judi,

We glad to hear that you receive our letter and we receive your Christmas cards New Year Day in church. We spent our Christmas and New Year fine. Had plenty to eat. The year begin with plenty weather. True that I get two turtle for the New Year and for the Old Year in December month I did get five head of turtle. I harvested my rice.

The time is not so good as yet. I don't know later on how it will be. Everything going by pound.

The white people are here right now to buy coconut and copra. Right now they are building coconut house to store the coconut. I hope later on will be better.

I want to get in the business but I don't have any money as yet. Mr. Barney and Miss Judi we are asking you if you will please like to be my baby's godparents. You must let me know. The baby is not baptized yet. Her name is Jean Darlin.

Mr. Cleveland and Miss Agatha spent Christmas at the Bluff.

The children send their best regards to you all.

I don't get any answer from Islestone Reed from the time I write with you. Maybe he forget me down so far this side.

Pungi Perez

Bluefields
February 28, 1972

Hello Mrs. Judi N.

Now Mrs. Judi there is nothing new here nor in Tasbapauni. The only thing strange was in Tasbapauni around the 10th of January. Mr. Granville Garth and Mr. Wyman Martínez did kill a swordfish that was the biggest I ever see. It had about 15 feet long or more. They kill it right on the beach in front of Miss Angela Cayasso's house. A next thing is the copra business. Some white people come to teach copra.

Please tell Mr. Barney and L.B. that Walter Blandford's mother is sick in the hospital San Pablo. Mr. Kitty's wife.

E. Sando Garth.

Tasbapauni
Mar. 1, 1972

Miss Judi,

We receive the baby card and very thankful for it and the chain. I did write to you in February month. I don't know if you get it because you don't mention to me nothing about it. All the family is well.

In last month I went out to the cays and the north wind keep me on King's Cay. We were out there for one week. I never struck. In the same month the turtle were running very good for one week. Plenty turtle pack up on Prata Bank. All the turtlemen happy for that. After that the weather came.

The copra work soon start. They want plenty coconuts to start. That will be plenty help for the town. They are building the drying house. The white people are building another house. I don't know what kind of house is that round house. We don't see that kind of house down this side. And the women are taking girls to give to them to do clothes.

And Kitty Blandford's wife is sick. She get operate but she is not so well. She is in the hospital. And my brother Amsted's wife is very sick. I don't know if she will recover her sickness. Miss Glades daughter die and Agosta die the 5 of February. Plenty of deaths, most children.

Mr. Barney this year my plan is to try for a little home. I am trying for that hard.

Cleveland is still at the Bluff. He was sick but he is feeling better now.

The children are sending plenty of love for little Barney.

Pungi and Ena Perez

Tasbapauni
29 Feb. 1972

Dear Mr. Barney,

It's good indeed to be back in Tasbapauni. There are many

changes, some not so good, I fear. There are three Peace Corps people here, working on "development." Let me tell you, Mr. Barney, a classic story. Mr. Tim, he's here with FUNDE (Fundación Nicaragüense de Desarrollo) money to develop co-ops. Well, he's starting with copra. He chartered a boat, went to Corn Island, looked at their copra dryer and now is building one here. Meanwhile, he is buying coconuts from any and everyone at C$ 0.20 each—double the old price. He now has a stockpile of 18,000 nuts, and reportedly wants 50,000! Now, all that's fine, except . . .

Except that it's had some interesting side effects. For one, the small storekeepers have gotten messed up, since they used to exchange two coconuts for 25¢ of stuff—their "currency" was, as it were, revalued. Second, and much more revealing, is what people think is going on. The FUNDE people in Managua told me that "community leaders" were "very enthusiastic" over the program. Hmmm, thought I, very interesting. Sure enough, several "community leaders" understand pretty well what goes; however, a lot of people have very different thoughts. Flan says that Tim is an Oklahoman who came here for a *pasear* and decided to do some copra. "Well," says I to Flan, "why should he pay twice as much as the right price for coconut?" "Well, Mr. Brian, he's tourist and the tourists them they always pay too much." One old man (Hayman) yesterday pointed out that a disease has struck many of the coconuts, blackening and ruining the nuts. His analysis: "Every time some stuff is money, it comes a disaster." So that's how the co-op looks to some. Flan says the price of coconut will go right back when this man leaves off.

Meanwhile, P. Corps #2, Dan, is building himself a *round* house, in good Lower Amazon stylistic tradition. Consensus is it will blow away when bad weather time comes, because it's very high, and right on the beach.

Tasbapauni apparently lucked out during last September's hurricane that hit Monkey Point. There was some damage to the fields, but hardly anything in town. Everyone crossed over to the other side of the lagoon. Salvarita and Joseph Dixon tied the box of stuff I left with them last June to a house post, so it wouldn't get washed away!!

Brian Weiss

Tasbapauni
14 March 72

Dear Barney,

Things are moving on after many hassles. I finally got my motor here. The canoe—now named KUKU AWRA (drift coconut)—is almost done. I fiberglassed this morning and all the paint blistered, so I'll have to remedy that. Between us, we've made a bad name for fiberglass here.

There is almost no coconut oil to be had, and what is around has gone up 50% in price! Another side effect of the copra co-op: all the people who used to buy or be given coconuts from relatives who had large cocals now have to pay the inflated price and no longer receive coconuts as gifts. Turns out the Co-op and dryer will be a good deal for the 6–8 people who have large cocals, but the little folks take gas. That's development?

You think I have troubles with the monkeys Asman gave me as a gift? Guess what you've got coming? Raccoons, two of them, to be exact. Seems you mentioned that raccoons were interesting animals to someone last year, a Julias maybe? Anyway, he wanted to know when you'd be here, because he's got your two raccoons. Hurry on down.

Kuku Waikna,
Brian Weiss

Bluefields
March 23, 1972

Hello Mr. and Mrs. Nietschmann,

I did receive the letter.

Well now about the Co-op's people. I hear they said that they would buy coconut at C$20.00 cordoba a hundred right to their bodega and with that coconut they already buy they will transfer them to Managua to the owner of the copra company. But to my opinion this is not so good because they want to see if they can get 25,000 coconut every month and I don't think they will get that amount every month. And likewise their houses are out of papta stick. They are really cheap. They said they want to help the people but I don't think in that way. Their house that I'm refering to is round. It seems to me that the Co-op's and Peace Corps are working together. Soon as I come from Tasbapauni I will let you all know the latest. Also, one of the white boy named Daniel get married with Miss

Valda Garcia whom we know as Mother Possum. She is a girl
from Tasbapauni. I think you know her.

Regards to little Barney and Sabi.

Sando Garth

P.S. Also I'm letting you all know that the owner of the
"Rompe Cabeza" and the "Ciudad Rama" [boats that run from
Bluefields to Rama] the owner of those boats die last month.
Antonio Machado got his death by gun [pistol] in Managua. I
think that you all know him.

Author's note:

Two months before we were to leave for Nicaragua to do a
National Geographic Society–sponsored research project on the
ecology and migration of hawksbill turtles, we began writing to
people in Tasbapauni to let them know we were coming. Brian
Weiss was in Little Sandy Bay, a Miskito community twenty-five
miles north of Tasbapauni, doing fieldwork for his Ph.D.
dissertation, and we wrote to him to see if he knew of a boat and
crew that might be available for our four-month study.

Little Sandy Bay
25 March 72

Barney, Judi, and Barney:

Medical problems abound and we seem to be the only ones
for miles with any medicine. We've been treating 6–8 people a
day, everything from bad belly to toothache. This morning we
escalated a bit, to a case of what looks like appendicitis.
Nonoperative treatment should rarely be attempted, counsels
the Merck Manual. They don't live in Little Sandy Bay. It's just
been incredible; it seems like a constant stream of people
through here, "begging a pill" for all matter of complaints. We
also do first aid, and make house calls. I cannot complain, as it
has given us an entree to an awful lot of people, and has raised
our stock considerably in the village.

Ah, but there is a payment system. Reciprocity is still alive
and well in Little Sandy Bay, and our ministerings have been
rewarded in water coconuts, chicken eggs, fish, pineapples
and plantain. It's the old country doctor system, and it works
nicely for all involved. We've had to start redistributing water
coconuts, due to a surfeit.

I would happily receive any and all medicine you might find
space for. Would a call to Dr. Anderson at the Health Service
produce any quantity of free samples, do you think? I mostly

need broad spectrum antibiotics, antibiotic goop for cuts and such, Darvon for pain and anything for diarrhea. You might bring me a couple of large boxes of telfa-covered pads, to put over machete cuts, sawed-off limbs, and other minor traumas. Ah, the things they didn't teach us in graduate school. I may get an M.D., not a Ph.D., out of this.

More soon. Hope that spring smiles upon you shortly, and that you're soon again on Miskito Shores.

Kuku awra,
Brian Weiss

Tasbapauni
7 of April, 1972

To Mrs. Judi,

Now Miss Judi, I was glad when I heard that you all are coming again to Nicaragua. We will be glad to have you all with us in this year again. Also, I did ask you to bring something for my boys when you all are coming. I don't know if you forgot about it, I hope you don't forget about it, because you did say that I was to remind you about it whenever writing, so here I am reminding you. I hope you know what I'm speaking about is about the wrist watch. Please see if you can bring one. Nothing more to say and till I hear from you or see you soon.

From your sincerely (Cook)
Alodia Garth

P.S. It is me that write this letter for Mama and Papa—Sando.

9 April 72
Little Sandy Bay

Estimado Bernardo, Judits, y Bernardo Sirpi,

Yea, verily happily did we yesterday receive yours of 20 March. I'm delighted to hear that you're headed this way. I'll do everything I can to get some things in motion. If you are looking for a boat to use on the NGS hawksbill tagging project may I suggest a possibility? Lindbergh (Bugs) Sinclair operates a really nice machine out of Río Grande Bar, mostly running turtle from this neck of the woods. With the turtle season closed, he might be open to a charter at a good rate. It's a very good boat, capable of the run to the Miskito Cays. Bugs is one of those demi-legends around here, known to and by everyone. His grandfather is British, I'm not sure about his father, and his mother Indian. He's trilingual, of course, aren't we all.

Would you please bring me 3 of those small, rubberized, blow up pillows. I brought one, and it may prove to save my ass, literally. Having studied the problem carefully, I find that girls are built different than boys, particularly as regards the derriere, or posterior region. I suffer all the pains of hell sitting in a dori for more than 15 minutes, having been provided with almost zero fat to cover the bones which protrude from my butt when I sit down. Have a heart, save a butt.

You'll be happy to know that stories about my walking are again making the rounds, assuming ever-more-daring proportions. I added to it yesterday by setting a new land-speed record, Río Grande Bar to Little Sandy Bay in 45 minutes, carrying a 25 pound load. There are rumors that I'm unreal. That's untrue, I'm for real. I think.

> Aisabe,
> Brian Weiss

> Little Sandy Bay
> 19 April 72

Dear 'awksbill:

Here's an interesting turtle statistic for you: 40 head were taken in this village last week—33 sold to the turtle company and only 7 butchered. How to kill more and eat less.

I got a letter from Archie Carr the other day; he's agreed to advance me a lump sum to use to pay the rewards for recovery of turtle tags. I've gotten 15 since arriving, with leads on a half dozen more . . . and next month is the big turtle month! I'll need a ship to get the tags to the post office in Bluefields.

> Brian Weiss, Kuku Awra

> Little Sandy Bay
> 2 Sept. 72

Dear Barney,

I've been computing the number of "man-nights" it takes to catch one head of turtle each week. The figures have been 4.5, 3.9, 5.6, 3.3, and 11.0 (there were only 15 head taken this week, but 55 men went out for 3 nights). The body count for the year is now 514 (that is, April through September . . . excluding the closed season), 358 of 415 turtle have been sold—86% are going to market, only 57 turtle have been butchered here in 6 months, or about 10 per month!!! Meager, man. Actually 38 more were butchered which came in from the shrimp boats. The shrimp boats have contributed almost as much as the turtlemen to protein intake in the village.

The Jamaicans have landed. They have a permit from the Nicaraguan government to fish and boy, are they fishing: 150 pots, each 4 × 9 feet, with materials to construct 200 more! I think their operation may headquarter at King's Cay, though they may work the entire area from Man O' War to the Set Net Cays. They have two big boats, shrimp boat size, and several motorized skiffs. No chickenshit operation this. They have 5 more boats fishing Miskito Cays. Apparently they are in trouble with the turtlemen, first up there, and now here. The men claim the "scent" from the fish pots drives the turtle off, as will the presence of the pots on the shoals where the turtles would normally sleep. Also, they are afraid for their nets with all the pots and lines in the water and the skiffs running around. To give you an idea, the first day they set a line of pots which stretched from Man O' War Cay to Tyara Cay! At least one ship runs to Jamaica every three weeks with about 50,000 lbs. of fish fillets aboard. So we have a wonderful new industry here, based on pillaging the local resource base, shipping the fish to Jamaica, paying some taxes to the government in Managua, none of which will ever be spent on the coast or on the Miskito. Funny, you know I was just about to suggest fish as one of the protein alternatives for the Miskito once they fish out the turtle. But you'll need a search warrant to get a fish around here if those guys stay 10 years, which is the duration of their permit.

Paz,
Brian Weiss

Tasbapauni
October 6/72

Dear Mr. Barney,

Just these few lines to you trusting that they may reach you safely. Also hoping that you and family are well. All in my family are well, thank the Lord, but in town Mr. Negdo is very sick. Turtle is getting scarce, Mr. Barney. You said it would happen in five or ten years, but it is happening now. We are getting a few but from the shrimp boats.

Nobody found any of the pins that you pinned. A pin was found by Mr. Jerome Yullit. This is the number: H-195. Reward Premio Remite-Send Dept. Biol. UF Gainesville Fla USA. Please give me your advice about it. Pin mentioned was found on hawksbill and some others were found on turtles.

Give our greeting to your wife and son. With best wishes to all.

Yours truly,
Flannery Knight

Little Sandy Bay
15 Oct 1972

Estimado profesor mío,

As for me, I'm poorly, thank you. Malaria is a prima, grade-A drag, and I've got it good. I've got fever almost every day, amazing headaches, etc. I'm going to escalate to Primaquine, if I can find some, since Aralen even in "curative" doses didn't cure. Meanwhile, it is cutting into my work, which irritates the hell out of me, making me even more miserable and obnoxious than usual.

Hey, you're right, malaria is a big problem again. Tell your class I appreciate their conclusion, but resent having helped them reach it! I'm working on getting the Primaquine. SNEM [Servicio Nacional de la Erradicación de Malaria] is almost out of business, due to withdrawal of funding by the WHO . . . "reordering of priorities." They came here after you left and took blood samples of the school kids . . . the results never came.

Paz,
Brian Weiss

Author's note:

On December 23, 1972, the capital of Nicaragua was destroyed by an earthquake that measured 6.5 on the Richter Scale. Approximately 10,000 people were killed, 20,000 injured, and 280,000 of Managua's 400,000 inhabitants were left homeless. Nicaragua's economy and communications were disrupted, and every part of the country felt the effects of the crippling earthquake.

Little Sandy Bay
28 Dec. 72

Dear Barney,

According to the Miskito, Managua has been punished because they don't respect God. If this is truth, I am in for big trouble.

Managua is a total loss; the pilot on the mission plane that came into Karawala yesterday said that the stink from the rotting bodies is so bad that you can't stand to be there more than half an hour. Only a few buildings are left standing. Even in the midst of disaster, there are always a few genuine shits—the Little Sandy Bay sindico received a telegram, probably originating from the jefe politico or somebody else looking for a couple of cordobas, saying to take up a collection in Little Sandy Bay for the people in Managua. I'm sure that the 50 cordobas LSB could get up will alleviate the problem. Of course, if the request is legit, it's worse. Imagine the audacity of Managua officialdom appealing to the east coast for financial help after bleeding them all these years.

No word, of course, on any of our friends in Managua. I can only hope that everybody got out ok.

The company price on turtles has gone up to 80 cordobas, and there has been a corresponding drop in the availability of meat in the village; get this: since the price has gone up from 70 to 80, the percentage of turtles sold to the company has gone from an amazing 85 to an incredible 90! I think the only reason it isn't 100% is because turtles die on the cays and can't be sold, or get butchered because there's no boat that week. You've a better chance of seeing a piece of turtle meat in Ann Arbor! I have been back almost two weeks, and have eaten turtle exactly once, and then it was only a side dish to something else. These are the turtle people?

Guess that's about all from Miskitoland.

Aisabe,
Brian Weiss

Tasbapauni
March 25, 1973

Dear Mr. and Mrs. Nietschmann,

Well Brian is down here from Little Sandy Bay so its a chance for me to write to the family. I wrote two letters when you were in the Pacifica and receive no answer. I'm sure you will get this one. Well all is well with us at present. My wife feel much better. Miss Hega Blandford dead. Father Mac is not helping me with Sando in the school anymore, so if you and Miss Judi can help I would thank you very much for things is not so good with us. From all the hawksbill you pin, Rose in Set Net get one. We are taking care of Kuka the best we can. All the family say hello to little Barney. Tell him that Waltito's mother dead. Also I made to understand that Mr. Florentine Sambola die Orinoco side. Sad to hear. He treat us real nice when I take you to know the Carib people.

We have a lot of Jamaicans in Tasbapauni getting married so later on there will be alot of Jamaican children here. Maybe a whole nation.

Our best wishes for the family.

From the Garth family

Tasbapauni, Nicaragua
March 28, 1973

Mr. Barney Nietschmann
Dept. of Geography
U.S.A.

Dear Friend,

Just these few lines to you trusting that they may find you and family well, just as we are at present by the Lord's help.

I don't know if you received any pins from the hawksbill from down here or further north. Things are as usual. Nothing strange right now. Work is very scarce in the country. Turtles are very scarce. Not plentiful like first time. Things going down, turtles going down. I went to Bluefields and I spoke to the lady at the Atlantic in the month of October and she is willing to let me have a little motor but since that there was an earthquake in Managua and everything went bad. But I was lucky that I didn't come under any agreement. Don't know what we are going to do here now. If don't catch turtle, no money. And no help from the interior.

And the family joins in sending greetings to you and to all in the family.

Your Friend,
Flannery Knight

Tasbapauni, Nicaragua
July 20, 1973

Dear Mr. Bernard,

Just these lines to you trusting that you and family are well, just as we are.

Everything is just as usual. What is getting really scarce in the village these days are meat and provisions. Plenty of fish but only the Jamaicans on the cays. Too far. Right now things are very slow on account of the earthquake that we had in Managua in December last year. The price for beef is 2 cordobas, turtle 75¢, beans 1.50, rice 1.20. The price of things are going. Later in the future I will let you know how things are going on.

Miss Mary Lam and Alvin Bendless died in the early part of this year. All your friends send regard and myself and family.

Sincerely yours,
Flannery Knight

Tasbapauni
Sept. 23/73

Dear Mr. Barney and family,

I receive your letter you sent me c/o Moravian Bookstore and was glad to hear from you, Miss Judi, little Barney. Thanks for the money you sent for us. It like a sweet odor. It was just in time to fill a hole for the boys in Bluefields. I think 1974 will be the last year for both of them in school and my way is dark to get them ready but I trust some way may open for me to end their study.

Mr. Barney, Johan dead, Sostero dead, Naldo we find dead on the beach three Sundays ago. Alvin who help us build the dori for the Cape trip dead. Sad. All Tasbapauni people sad. My family is well. My wife is a little better, thank God. One of my wife's brothers dead.

Mr. Barney the cost of living is high in Nicaragua. Flour is 1.50#, rice 1.30#, beans 1.50#. Things are very high. Not only these three articles I mention but everything raise up.

Our best regard for you, Miss Judi and little Barney.

Baldwin Garth and family

Bluefields
October 8, 1973

Dear Mr. B. Nietschmann,

I'm well here in Bluefields along with my brother Baldwin Jr. All are well in Tasbapauni in the Garth family. My father receive your letter that you wrote him in the month of August. Did he answer your letter? Why I'm asking is that I know he takes a lot of time to answer someone who he receive a letter from.

Likewise Mr. Barney this is my third letter to you and I don't receive an answer. I don't know why if you receive them or not but I hope you'll receive this one.

We all in Nicaragua are living a different life than before. Why it is different is that foodstuff are very expensive. Here flour is C$1.50 a pound and in Tasbapauni C$1.75, rice C$1.50 a pound, all down to chiclets is expensive here. Things would be better but the government is very hard. A plane from Costa Rica (APSA) come to Bluefields twice a week. Some trip they bring flour, rice, beans, and sell very cheap right at the airport. But is seems that they soon stop bringing food because the government them are charging them a high tax for these things. Before I close this is what Tasbapauni is getting. They bought a light plant [generator] from Bonanza in good condition and now they are getting a bigger one from "Pescanica" free of charge. The alcalde of Bluefields plans to give it to them because the President send a new one to "Pescanica" at Schooner Cay. The clinic is finished. Nothing more to say. Hope to hear from you quickly. Regards to L.B. and Mrs. Judi N. Please answer quick because I want to hear from my old friends.

Sincerely yours,
E. Sando Garth

Author's note:

In June 1973 Ned Kelly, head of the Natural History Unit at BBC, wrote to say that they were planning to make a film of the Miskito–green turtle story and asked for some information on weather and transportation conditions, boats, and the names of people they might contact to help them during their two-week visit in September. In my reply I told him that the weather would be variable, possibly nasty; gave him the names of some turtlemen; and suggested that he try to charter Bugs Sinclair's *Glendora*, the boat that had served us so well the year before.

Tasbapauni
October 14, 1973

Hello Barney and Judi,

We received your card from Mexico and glad for it. All the family well.

In September month something strange happen here in Tasbapauni. Mr. Ned the Englishman and a next one, Hugh, come to town to make a filming of the turtle and we turtlemen. He have my name on a paper and when he meet me he was glad to check my name off. He look Flan and then he take Naham Duncan (Renales Duncan's son) and Sudland. He come on Bugs boat the "Glendora" with Lindolfo, Rudy and a man from Walpa on board. But the motor running poorly and give us plenty of trouble on the trip to Clar Cay. One dori pass us on the way. Mr. Ned ask Rudy about the motor but Rudy don't know about diesel. Mr. Ned say that if they going to charter have to do better than that for business. Ask if Rudy sure that this is the boat that Mr. Barney use. Rudy tell him it work fine when you all take it. Out on the cays Mr. Ned want that me and Flan paddle him around with the camera. Naham and Sudland tell to strike the turtle when they come to float. Mr. Barney I want to cry, turtle floating all about and Naham can't strike one, fall overboard one time. I tell Mr. Ned to make Flan and me have a next try but he say no. He want we to do paddling. Those boys don't know turtle like we. I feel shame for them. How he going to make filming with those kinda turtlemen. Next thing is that we pass some bad weather on the cays. Everything get wet up. Mr. Ned take it good and treat us good too.

The children send plenty howdy to little Barney.

Pungi Perez

Some next man here have it when the next rocket go to the moon it will bring plenty more trouble for people in Nicaragua.

BBC
BRITISH BROADCASTING CORPORATION
Broadcasting House Whiteladies Road Bristol BS8 2LR

6th November, 1973

Dear Bernard Nietschmann,

I have delayed writing to you as I hoped I might have a fuller report to give you on our complete operation in Central America, but, as yet, I still await the outcome of our filming at Nancite in Costa Rica where, hopefully, David Hughes has obtained coverage of a Ridley arribada.

Our Nicaraguan trip went well, thanks to all your most helpful advice and a most co-operative British Embassy. I think I should say, however, that Bugs Sinclair's boat turned out to be one of the slowest machines on the Seven Seas. It was Lindolphous who ferried us around and he explained that something was wrong with the engine—it took us 14 hours to Tasbapauni through the lagoon and on our way to the Cays we were overtaken by a two-man 'dori'—paddling! However, we survived the experience and had a most interesting time, finding most people very friendly and helpful. Everyone we came into contact with asked after you, your wife, and "little Barney" and sent their best wishes. You'll see there's a letter from Baldwin Garth, and Flannery Knight asked especially to be remembered to you. One great moment from Flannery was when I asked him why hawksbill shell was so expensive and he said that it was because the Queen of England used it to roof her palace! And I thought that the Duke was a great conservationist!

After a great deal of discussion, we ended up basing ourselves on Clar Cay, but unfortunately there weren't many turtles about, so we spent a great deal of time on the open sea before we "struck" our first turtle. We were also caught in a tremendous squall on the Cay which threatened to carry everything away—it had to happen at 3 A.M. of course. Our tent, having a sewn-in ground sheet, gradually filled with water, so we balanced boxes of film and cameras on our heads to keep things out of the wet—a sight frequently illuminated by impressive and close flashes of lightning.

In Bluefields we found people not at all keen on the idea of our filming at the processing plant, but they made the mistake of turning us away on the grounds that "there aren't any turtles this week." At that moment a boat pulled in with forty-eight on board, so there was little anyone could do to prevent us filming—apart from saying no. Luckily, no one felt that way. I heard that the first week after the closed season finished there were five hundred or more turtles taken to Bluefields.

By the way, do you happen to know what the "take" must have been when the Caymanians were turtling off the Cays? One defence I heard for the operation was that the Cayman fleet used to take far more turtles away when they had permission to fish that area.

I am shortly off to Antarctica for Christmas and then to Australia for more turtles in the New Year—I'll let you know how that goes.

Meanwhile, my deepest thanks once again for all your help and advice.

Best wishes,
Ned Kelly

Tasbapauni, Nicaragua
December 15, 1973

Dear Mr. Nietschmann,

Just these lines to you trusting that you and your family are well. We are still here and all in the family are well by God's help. I received your last letter just before Mr. Ned Kelly arrived.

Mr. Ned spent one day here in Tasbapauni. I was to take Mr. Ned to Asking Cay and King's Cay also to Man of War Cay but we couldn't go to any of these cays because the boat motor was not working right. But we got to Clar Cay, the one by Man of War. It took us a whole day to get to the cay. Mr. Ned asked me if that's the boat you use to go around. I told him yes. I was sorry that the boat was so slow. All the film he took came out all right. He also treated us very nice. But the tent that he had was not so good. The rain blew right in. I inquired all around for hawksbill pins but none. Lots of pins but all turtle.

At Miskito Cay they caught up to one hundred hawksbill per month. Things are very hard around here Mr. Barney. I cannot go where I would like to with the boat because it has no engine. I went to the Atlantic but they want the premium of 5800.00 cordobas for a 15 horsepower. I just can't afford that. But I am holding on some more but if I don't get the motor I plan to sell the boat. The prices of things are very high. Flour is up to 1.75 pound, rice 1.30, beans 1.60, and for clothes its worse than all.

Things are the same old way. The family join in sending regards to your family. We also wishing you a Merry Christmas and a Happy New Year.

Yours truly,
Flannery Knight

Jan 24/1974
Tasbapauni, Nic.

Mr. Barney Nietschmann,

My dear friend, I did receive your two letters and one Christmas card. I was very glad to hear from you. I am right here. I did receive the book and it was pretty to see. Things change a lot. In your letter you mention about the hawksbill pin. That pin was found from Swirry Cay, seven miles south east from Prata Bank. Things is very slow around here. No work. One hundred and fifty turtle butcher for one year. The turtle are getting scarce around here. Only the Miskito Cay have plenty. I can't send my letters often to you. It is hard to get it post. The turtle company is now closing down in March for turtle and lobster crimes. So now everybody farming now for food. Everybody receive their Christmas card from you and they were glad. They always talk good about you and Judi. I am sending my greeting from me, Tina and all children.

Nothing more to say.

Your truly friend,
Flannery Knight

Tasbapauni, Nicaragua
The 7 of February, 1974

Hello Barney and Judi,

I hope this letter will find you all well and all my family is well only my wife is feeling sick because she lost her father the 8 of December, Mr. Theo. Waggam. My wife say if you have any picture of her father if you would please do her the favor to send one for her because her father die in Managua and she didn't get to see him.

This year, I went bad with the rice. I really trying to make a home. We were to start it last year but we went bad with the rice so we don't start it as yet.

Well my daughter pass her grade again to second year. But this year I don't know what to do with her because the main thing is the turtle that help us and now the turtle going to close down so through that I can't send my daughter to school. But that is the world that come to pass.

I have one pin for myself and the boys them here have six so in all are seven. I went to Cromwell and he say that he didn't have money to pay the premio.

All the children them send hello for little Barney. Nothing more to say.

Pungi Perez

Tasbapauni
February 8, 1974

Dear Mr. and Mrs. Nietschmann,

Now we are in the New Year, the year 1974, I hope that it can be a better year than the year that past away.

The reason for my letter is to let you all know how situation is around here in the east coast of Nicaragua so that you all can know about our condition here. Sickness is terrible here in Tasbapauni. In last month and the beginning of this month we had five death in the town, three babies and two old persons, Miss Emirosa Leban and Mr. Simons Johnathan. Also my grandfather Mr. Espinoza nearly die. He was on the last and the last thing they use on him to bring him back was a suero, the drinking one. So now he is feeling much better. He can walk around the house. He ask me if you still remember things he taught you about sickness and yumu.

Things are really expensive here in Nicaragua right down to kerosene. For your pass from here to Bluefields cost C$12.00 and C$15.00. For the diesel oil is expensive. Food stuff are expensive too. Everything is getting on more prices. It is really bad for we school boys. The cheapest food bill is C$150.00 month. So things are really bad here.

Regards to L. Barney. Tell him that I receive his mail and was glad to know that he can write now and tell me about his animals.

From sincerely your friend,
E. Sando Garth

Tasbapauni
Feb. 14, 1974

Mr. Barney and Judi,

I am writing you this much. I get the Christmas card. I hope you are all well. By God's help I am. I did have another little new born but she die when she had six months old. She die January 2 last year. We went bad with the rice. The cow eat it up. This year the things are very high. Flour is two cordobas pound and beans are two cordobas. Everything from the shop is very dear. Ena is sick. All the children are well. And hello to little Barney from the children. I want to hear about Sabi. Time is very hard with us and I am trying to get a house but I can't get it as yet. No help. Ena say hello Judi.

I send my best regards for you all.

Pungi and Ena Perez

Tasbapauni
March 14, 1974

Dear Mr. Barney and family from Baldwin Garth and family,

We is so far from one another that it takes too long to talk to each other in letters. I am waiting for the book you promise me. Kuka lay on 12 March so I am hoping for young parrots soon.

Sad news. Naldo was sick in front of the Episcopal Church, 26 August, Sunday morning. Adelina, 18 December, Emirosa Leban, 6 January, Symon 18 January, Cacho Prudo 9 March, all dead. Mr. McKey Tinkam get in collision with a fish boat. He lost his boat. Mash to pieces and 6 life dead. He was in gale and have to pay twenty thousand cordoba. He was wrong for no light on his boat.

The government gave a light plant to Tasbapauni and a school hall is building right now.

I hope to hear from you soon. Our best wishes for your family.

Baldwin Garth

Bluefields
March 30/74

Dear Mr. and Mrs. Nietschmann,

Hope that these few line may find you all enjoying the best of health out there.

Now Mr. Barney and Mrs. Judi I'm right here in Bluefields back in class to see if I can finish my last year and be done with my studies. In Tasbapauni there are a lot of Jamaicans that are living out at King's Cay. Some are planing to get married right there in Tasbapauni. They get money from fishing with pot and selling to fish boat from Jamaica. They buy all kinds of pretty things for the girls them and drink out some of the money too. Plenty of the Tasbapauni men mad but what can they do? They don't have any money.

Last week I saw a man pass with a tigercat on the street. Oh it looked like Sabi when he was small because this is a baby one too.

Nothing more to say.

From truly yours,
E. Sando Garth

Tasbapauni
June 3, 1974

Dear Barney and Judi, hello,

I receive the letter and was glad to hear from you all. Now the coconut Co-op is closed, went bad and the white boys them leave off. The turtle is closed from April on till August. When they were buying hawksbill shell they was paying C$50.00 cordobas a pound and the dried calipee C$4.00 a pound. Now the time is hard. I am not doing anything. I get answer from Islestone, he was glad to know that I have a friend in Michigan. The children are sending hello for little Barney.

Pungi and Ena Perez

Tasbapauni, Nicaragua
July 12/74

Dear Mr. Barney,

Just these lines to you trusting that they may find you and the family feeling fine, just as we are at present.

I wrote you two letters but I didn't get an answer. On the 7th of July I received a copy of the Natural History magazine. I was very glad to receive it, also thankful. A lot of people ask me to show it to them. Some see their picture and ask me why you take pictures to send to the States. I tell them about your study and they overhaul the magazine.

Things around here are the same but the catch for turtle was small. They butchered around 50 head. Turtle tight. I always remember what you told me about meat here in the future and it seems to me that its beginning right now.

Tell little Barney that I always remember him when I am cooking. He said never to scald the meat. I was waiting to see if you were coming in this year. Mr. Ned wrote me and said that his film got wet. So they weren't so good. Maybe next time when he comes back.

The family joins in sending greetings to you and your family.

Sincerely,
Flannery Knight

Tasbapauni
February 22, 1975

Dear Mr. and Mrs. Nietschmann,

This is my second letter to you in this year 1975. I don't know if you receive the first one I wrote. We are out of class now but I'm right here in Tasbapauni, Junior too. We are not on any job as yet. I myself am feeling a little sick from last month. I am taking some treatment. Things are really hard around here in Tasbapauni. We are having lots of death in town. Miss Etelina Brown die (Leonda Duncan's grandmother) also Edmundo Garth die in Siuna, Mr. Jerimiah Garth's son. He was killed while eating by one of the Sandinistas. And my Papa's nephew die in Prinsapolka last week. Likewise Joel Garth got shot yesterday in Kuringwas while hunting. They took him down last night to Bluefields. So lots of people are dying now, children and adults. I don't know if Joel will live. He got shot over the his heart with a bridgeloader gun No. 12. So that is all the latest for news.

My plan for this year 1975 is to go to Managua in the first week of April to look for a job. There is nothing here on the coast. I guess Junior will go too. Our delay is because we had expenses at the ending part of 1974 at school. We just have to pay our bill. I want to get out on a ship. Nachito Yullit is out on a tourist ship. I can't do anything here in Tasbapauni.

Until a next time.

Yours,
Sando

Author's Note:

For many years there have been plans to create an inland water route to connect Bluefields with the Río Grande and eventually as far north as Puerto Cabezas. Heavy sea and rough weather conditions throughout much of the year severely limit offshore traffic. To alleviate this problem and to provide far up-river pioneer agriculturalists a means to market their surplus, the Nicaraguan government planned to dredge a deep-water channel through the lagoons and creeks and across the narrow "haulovers." In 1974 the work began. When the "canal" is finished, it will make once isolated communities accessible, and every Miskito along the way will be a little closer to the world beyond the edge of his experience.

Tasbapauni
Oct. 18, 1975

Mr. Bernard Nietschmann,

My dear friend, just these few lines hoping it will find you well by God's help. All my family is here by the help of God. Everything is the same old way because the life of living is costable here. Rice is C$2.00 pound, sugar 2 cordobas, flour 2 cordobas, banana 2 for 25¢, beef meat C$3.00 pound. Turtle meat is the same price 75¢. Things are going up every day. Coconut is 25¢ for every one.

The Caymans boat that they capture to Miskito Cay did just come and set their nets and then they capture them and bring them back to Puerto Cabezas and multa them C$3,000 cordobas. But the captain said that they don't have that amount of money so they charge them C$2,000 cordobas and they take away what turtle they did have and release them. Some white people are dredging canal from Bluefields to Pearl Lagoon. They soon get to Pearl Lagoon. Now they are in front of the haulover.

Tina send hello to you Miss Judi and little Barney. I am sending my best regard and all friend and family too.

Nothing more to say.

Yours truly friend
Flannery Knight

And please give Brian my best regard and till next time.

Tasbapauni
November 3/75

c/o Kindness Doctor Greg

Dear B. Nietschmann,

Hello to Michigan. Its a long time since I wrote to you last. We never heard from you since you leave to know if you arrive safe or not. How things with the family? My family things are not so good but I hope for better some day. Sad to say my sister Rosy dead, Mr. Kelly and Maggie Sucker son, the cripple

Lamsy, these three dead since you leave Nicaragua in June.

The crop of rice is very nice this year, thank God. A doctor from Ohio is here with us. He doing a very good job with the bad belly. Some old and a few children die from the sickness. What about little Barney and his animals and his study in school? We remember you all very often and hope to see each other before we die. I am taking my family to the doctor today before he leaves for Karawala.

Hoping to hear from you all very soon. Hope you return back to Nicaragua to go with me in the woods to hunt.

My best regards to you all.

Sincerely,
Baldwin Garth

Tasbapauni
Dec. 13/75

Mr. Bernard Nietschmann,

Dear Barney, just these few lines hoping it will find you well by God's help. Now I did receive your letter on the 3 of December. I did get the picture in it. Nothing strange now. No work in the country as yet. The dredge is from Bluefields to Pearl Lagoon dock. They are going to continue dredging as far as Puerto Cabezas on the inside. So after anyone can make the trip that you and Mr. Baldwin made. The Caymans boat that they catch to Miskito Cay the government charge them C$2500 cordobas and the captain said that they only have 2000 so they release them. Turtle is scarce. Plenty dori come from the cays empty, some don't catch, some only sell. About 60 head of turtle butchered here this year. Now the food is very high. Flour is 2.00, sugar 1.80, beans 2.25, rice 1.75, fish 1.00, wari meat 1.75 pound, turtle meat 75¢, coconut 35¢, beef 3.00, banana 9.00 each bunch. Clothes prices going, food prices going up. Everyone feeling poor.

Give little Barney my best regard and Miss Judi and yourself and I wish you a Merry Christmas and a Happy New Year.

Flannery Knight

My dear godmother I wish you a Merry Christmas and a Happy New Year. An old man pass here and said he will pass there.

Daisy Knight

1/17/76
Tasbapauni,
Nic.

Barney, Judi, and Barney
The University of Michigan
U.S.A.

Hello friend,

It is a great joy and happiness for me to write you this few lines hoping it will find you well. The first letter I get I wasn't home, I was out until December I get home, that's why I get late in answering your letter, but still I write you in December as I come home but I don't know if you get it. So I am writing you again. The prices of the things is the same bad thing and not even turtle left to sell the company. Hard to catch even one. Meat scarce in town.

We get the Christmas card, we thank you very much for the help. Everybody send hello for everybody and the children send their best regard for little Barney and all. I get the picture and I get answer from Islestone. We spend the Christmas and the New Year good. Thank God everybody is good.

From your friend,
Pungi Perez

Tasbapauni
April 16, 1976

Mr. Barney Nietschmann,

Dear Mr. Barney. Just these few lines hoping it will find you well by God's help. I did receive your letter and was glad to hear from you. Things is the same way. A dori came from Big Sandy Bay on April 15 and went to Set Net Point but they never bring any turtle pin along with them. So I told the boys them if any hawksbill pin is up there they must try and bring them down. Well now the turtle is closed. Them closed the turtle and all the animal in the bush, manatee likewise. So the people went down to Bluefields and talk with the jefe and ask if it so then how the people will live on the coast. No answer as yet from the jefe and no work to do. Control on lobster too. Only little help the people have down here is the coconut. But just imagine the upper coast, they have no coconut. The planting of coconut was by an English man named Hendry Bacon. He told the lower coast people to plant. Suppose he didn't give them that plan, how people going to make it now?

I went to Rio Grande and Mr. Bugs told me that he receive a letter from you to give all his friend your best regards. All of us is good by God's help. I am working on my house. It broke down and I'm building a bigger one. I am sending my best regard and same from all the family.

I can't send the letters with any one because they open it and read and tear it up and throw it away. I have to go myself and mail it. Daisy receive her 5 dollars and buy a dress and pay her school fees.

Flannery Knight

Tasbapauni
May 27, 1976

Mr. Barney and Miss Judi,

Hello. How are you today? I do hope that you are well and working. I receive your letter and was glad to hear from you. We are well by the help of the good Lord.

The company is not buying turtle in this year. I hear that the company is going to buy but not until next year. I don't know how true. I will let you know when they going to buy.

Yes the government did have a meeting in the town about hunting to stop the people. The people against it. They ask the government if want we town people to dead because when turtle close that was the only help for the town to get a piece of meat to eat. So they are against it. Some of the people say that these things happening through you. One of these time when you come to Nicaragua, you will hear who the person give us this word.

I glad to hear about little Barney, how he is so big.

And my baby name is Burton Perez.

Pungi Perez

Tasbapauni
March 6, 1977

Hello my dear friends Barney, Judi and Barney,

How are you? I do hope that you are all well by the help of the Lord and I hope that this letter will find you all well. By God's help we are well. I lost one of my little boys, the last one, Burton. He died 19 of Dec. so I never spend a happy Christmas. And I get the Christmas card.

From the New Year the weather is bad. We can't go out and start turtle on account of the weather. We are almost to close the turtle right now.

The company that is digging the canal almost reach Tasbapauni. But no men working as yet from here. I don't know if they will take men from here. It is a beautiful work that they do. The canal is big and wide and deep water.

Well, Mister Barney, the old man Cleveland Blandford dead the 2 of March.

Pungi Perez

Tasbapauni
Sept. 3/77

Dear Doctor Bernard Nietschmann,

Hello to your family. I long time since I never write you, but not too late now.

I would like to hear from you about your trip to Australia, the other side of the world, what the people eat, what they do to make life happy. Are the people kind or not, friendly or not? Tell me some of your story.

This is my word to you. The Government put the turtle on control. It was one thing that you the one that do it. All your friends give you Hell. You get lots of cursing. Was sad.

Pertaining to my family. All is well. Only my wife very sick. I have to take her to doctor. She move around some day. Some day she is down. I am trying to finish my house. But through taking her to the doctor things are dark with me.

Cleveland dead. Zepora Matilda, Adam Suho dead. Marlin and Cranley was shot. The canal is almost through to Rio Grande.

I write you a letter and get no answer so I stop writing. Please remember me to your wife and to little Barney.

My best wishes for you and family.

Baldwin Garth

San Juan, Puerto Rico
Sept. 19, 1977

Dear Mr. and Mrs. Nietschmann,

Thanks very much for answering my letter. I have a job on the "Sun Viking" cruise ship. Work is hard but I am trying my best. I was on vacation for two months and went to Nicaragua to see my Mother and Father.

There is nothing much to say about home only that a few persons that I used to go around with departed from this world. Adam Suho die right in Tasbapauni. Also Marlin Dixon got shot and die. Next is Cranley Garcia. He also die by gun, a Spanish guy shot him in Managua. Tasbapauni is very strange to me now. The younger generation is very different from the older generation. Bluefields and Managua are the same way as before. They are building up Managua little by little.

I feel bad and I want to go back home (I have home sick). I will be ok in a few days. Please answer my letter. I want to hear how you all are getting on in life. Please give my best regards to little Barney and tell him I'm still alive and wishing to see him.

From sincerely yours,
E. Sando Garth

Author's Note:

The last three letters refer to Nicaragua's "bad state" and "the war," alluding to the violent demonstrations against the government of General Anastasio Somoza Debayle and the military reprisals that have ravaged the western portion of the country. News of these conflicts reached Miskito villages by radio. Physically remote from what they call the "Spanish interior," the Miskito are nevertheless increasingly affected by major events on the other edge of their world. The 1971 volcanic eruption of Cerro Negro, the 1972 Managua earthquake, and the 1974 floods all cut off or sharply reduced the flow of store goods and mail which link the Miskito with "the outside." Sending a letter or a turtle tag to the United States is always a special matter; when outside circumstances intervene, it becomes a worrisome thing.

Tasbapauni
March 18/78

Dear Doctor Nietschmann,

I was glad to hear from you. I write you several letters and get no answer. I take very long to answer you back because I am sick with my eyes. For very long I can't read or write—just getting round with my eyes now. My wife is still going round, thank God.

My country is in a bad, bad state. Thing is not good but hope is good.

Elias and Ruth was here with us. All friend say hello to you. Remember me to Brian and other friend. Ruth said that Brian was her teacher and Elias said that you was his teacher. Good to meet friend.

My household say hello to you, Judi, and litle Barney and good luck. Hope to hear from you soon. My eyes are bad but I'm feeling my way to answer your letter.

Best wishes,
Baldwin Garth

July 17, 1978
Tasbapauni, Nic.
C.A.

Mr. Barney N.

Dear Barney. Just these few lines, hoping they will find you in good health. I did write a letter and did not get an answer from you if you receive it or not. I did answer your letter the same week back and sent it but the only thing I'm sorry if you don't get it so if you get it you must write and let me know because I did not carry it to Bluefields myself. I sent it with one of Mr. Meliano's sons.

They don't catch turtle now. Most they work on lobster. The canal is through the inside now from Bluefields to Rio Grande Bar.

I am sending you two pins. N-061 was found three miles to the east of Man O' War Cay. H-348 was found 7 miles north from Man O'War Cay. They find it in November. Why they could not send the pins is because of the war. They ask me to send it for them. If you receive this letter you must answer me and I can send more things in the same way as before.

Nothing strange. I am sending my best regard to you Miss Judi and Little Barney. I know we is in the same world living but I know you is busy all time.

Tina and all her children send her best regard. Daisy said to tell her godmother hello, hello. She is getting big.

Flannery Knight

Jan. 4, 1979
Tasbapauni, Nic., C.A.

Mr. Barney Nietschmann,

Dear Barney. Just these few word to you hoping it will find you by God help. I receive your two letter and was glad to hear

LETTERS FROM NICARAGUA   269

from you. I receive the money for the turtle pin. But the two other pins I send I don't get nothing as yet. They are for Mr. Baltizar.

It seems like thing is getting worse now. It is from no work. I don't know if you still have the story about how the old Miskito people used to work. Well now the younger race condemn that plan. The hardness of meat and provisions and the hardness of money come because we have no work to help the situation. What we have is plenty of war. The Indian say the coast is very rich from history. But I feel like it is the poorest place out of the five Republics.

By God's help now we spend a Happy Christmas and a good New Year. Well I don't know if you will come back around here again. Give little Barney and Miss Judi my best regard from my family. If you meet Brian you must give him my best regard.

Flannery Knight

In March 1978 we received a telephone call from the radio room of the *Sun Viking*, a passenger ship on its way from Miami to Kingston, Jamaica. The ship-to-shore call was from Sando Garth, Baldwin and Alodia's son, who had lived with us in Bluefields and who had finished high school and gone on to find work on the ship. He called to let us know that he was well and to pass on the latest information about Tasbapauni and about his travels. He'd already made several voyages around the Caribbean, and he told us about the places he'd seen—where Columbus had gone, the old pirate bases, the early European settlements, the good reefs and turtle grounds. He was seeing things that he had heard his father and me talk about, the events and places that were part of the cultural history of his people, and he had called to say these were worth knowing about. The work on board was hard, but the pay was good; he had run into other Miskito here and there in his travels, and that made being away from home more tolerable. He said he had a vacation coming up when the ship got back to Miami, and we asked him to come and visit us in Berkeley. Many thanks, he replied, but he was feeling homesick, and his family needed his help, so he was planning to take the first LANICA flight out of Miami to go home to Nicaragua.

Index